PACIFIC MARITIME HISTORY SERIES

Number 3

Published by the
ASSOCIATES OF THE NATIONAL MARITIME
MUSEUM LIBRARY

and

THE GLENCANNON PRESS

With the generous support of
Mystic Seaport Museum

CLIPPER SHIP CAPTAIN

Clipper Ship Captain

Daniel McLaughlin
and the
Glory of the Seas

by
Michael Jay Mjelde

Associates of the National Maritime Museum Library
Pacific Maritime History Series

1997

Pacific Maritime History Series
Number Three

Copyright © 1997 by Michael Jay Mjelde
Published by the Glencannon Press
P.O. Box 341, Palo Alto, CA 94302

First edition, second printing.

Library of Congress Catalog Card Number: 94-12045

ISBN 1-889901-05-9

In Remembrance

Michael John Mjelde
"Mikey"

firstborn son of
Wylla R. and Michael Jay Mjelde
June 18, 1964 - December 19, 1995

He will destroy death forever.
Isaiah 25

Never in these United States
has the brain of man conceived,
or the hand of man fashioned,
so perfect a thing as the clipper ship.
In her, the long-suppressed artistic impulse
of a practical, hard-worked race burst into flower . . .
for a brief moment of time
they flashed their splendor around the world,
then disappeared . . .

Samuel Eliot Morison

CONTENTS

List of Illustrations

Foreword

This book is a sequel to my earlier work *Glory of the Seas*, published jointly in 1970 by Mystic Seaport Museum (then the Marine Historical Association, Inc.) and Wesleyan University Press as the first volume of their prestigious series, "The American Maritime Library." It deals with a specific period in the history of the ship *Glory of the Seas*, 1876-1884, but also is a concise biography of Captain Daniel McLaughlin, her master during this period.

The medium clipper ship *Glory of the Seas* was a remarkable vessel, not only because she had the distinction of being the last "clipper" built by Donald McKay, builder of *Flying Cloud, Stag Hound*, and others, but because she lasted so long in heavy trade at a time when sail was dying. Her name caught the attention of the maritime public through the years, and in 1897, the year after Daniel McLaughlin died, a Victoria, B.C., newspaper writer wrote a feature article on the *Glory of the Seas* which well sums up the fame of this vessel. It began as follows:

> Full of years and honors, as the saying goes, the Am[erican] ship
> *Glory of the Seas* . . . is a vessel whose name is familiar to most shipping
> men the world over, and whose history if told in detail would fill a
> book of many chapters.

The *Glory of the Seas* was not the fastest, the biggest, or the most successful sailing vessel of her time, but she was an outstanding example of the medium clipper ships operating under the American flag in the Cape Horn trade after the American Civil

War when a marked decline in the United States merchant marine was already having its effects, especially in the New England states. The almost eight-year period during which Captain McLaughlin commanded her was fraught with mishaps, lay-up periods, and economic uncertainty, though she did achieve financial success.

The latter years, 1911-1923, of the *Glory of the Seas* were presented several years ago in a series of articles appearing in four separate issues of the quarterly publication of the Puget Sound Maritime Historical Society, *The Sea Chest*, of which the author is editorial chairman. At a future date more of the history of the *Glory of the Seas* and of the people who managed and sailed her, and whose lives were touched by this clipper ship will be published in book form.

Many people have been helpful in providing the nucleus of material in this book as well as being valuable critics in the early drafts.

My special thanks to Captain Adrian F. Raynaud, master mariner and former second mate on the bark *Edward Sewall* as well as last master of the West Coast schooner *C.A. Thayer*. Captain Raynaud carefully read the text and assisted in minimizing technical errors. He also helped in the preparation of the illustration captions. My thanks also to the late Charles S. Morgan, one of the members of the original editorial board of Peabody Essex Museum's *American Neptune*, who acted in the same capacity.

Joseph Gribbins, director of Publications at Mystic Seaport Museum, provided invaluable support by being a co-sponsor in the publication of this work.

Without the assistance of various public and maritime library staff members, it would have been difficult to verify much of the reference material as to its authenticity. Paul O'Pecko, reference librarian at Mystic Seaport; Irene Stachura and William Kooiman, reference librarians at the National Maritime Museum at San Francisco; volunteers at the Penobscot Marine Museum in Searsport, Maine; and staff members of the following libraries: the John F. Kennedy Museum at Vallejo, California; Library of Congress; Merseyside Marine Museum at Liverpool; National Maritime

Museum library at Greenwich, England; and Malden Public Library at Malden, Massachusetts — all provided important support.

On a local level, Millie Kirk, Janet Kovacik and other staff librarians at the Kitsap Regional Library in Bremerton, Washington enabled the author to obtain much material through the national interlibrary loan system.

Also, my thanks to Elizabeth Engle, production editor of *The Sea Chest,* for her assistance in proofing, editing, and preparing the final typescript of the text.

Special effort was made to authenticate contemporary shipping information and crew data, relying on Bureau of Navigation and Custom House records on file at the National Archives and Records Administration in Washington, D.C., San Bruno, and Seattle. Over a period of years such staff members as Kenneth Hall, Teresa Matchette, Angie VanDereedt, William Sherman, Joyce Justice, and others, provided invaluable aid in extracting material from the public record and making the same available to the author.

Residents of Grand Manan and Eastport were also helpful. The late Keith Ingersoll gave the author a nucleus of McLaughlin material many years ago; and Joyce E. Kinney spent many hours extracting information from the *Eastport Sentinel* as well as Eastport city records. She authenticated much of the early McLaughlin history.

The late Robert W. Weinstein, maritime historian and specialist in historic photographs, assisted the author by providing some of the illustrations and captions in this work. Over a period of years Weinstein helped to isolate the most suitable images which would enhance McLaughlin and the *Glory*'s story.

The Associates of the National Maritime Museum Library have been a tremendous help in providing support in the way of critiquing the text of *Clipper Ship Captain.* Under the direction of David Hull, Principal Librarian of the National Maritime Museum Library at Fort Mason, volunteers from the Associates — Captain Francis E. "Biff" Bowker, Nicholas Dean, Captain Harold D. Huycke, and Andrew Nesdall — provided constructive criticism to the author in the effort to weed out technical errors. Also, Ted Miles and Stephen Canright with the U.S. Department of the Interior assisted in this capacity. Captain Walter W. Jaffee, editorial director of The Glencannon Press and Peter Evans, also members of the Associates, provided valuable assistance. Their time and effort have been much appreciated.

Since the publishing of *Glory of the Seas* in 1970, some maritime artists have used that book as a guide in painting the *Glory*. Their works are represented in *Clipper Ship Captain*. The author wishes to acknowledge and thank Carl G. Evers, Mark H. Myers, and Thomas W. Wells for their contribution to this sequel.

Lastly, my thanks to certain descendants of Captain McLaughlin who made it possible to write an accurate story of their forebear, and my special appreciation to his great-grandson, Merlyn McIntyre, who first contacted the author in 1971. Through the years he and his wife Eleanor have provided invaluable support in putting the story in print. McIntyre's sister, the late Mrs. Josephine Ball; his cousin and her husband, Frances and Clarke Savory, now both deceased, and their daughter, Mrs. Mary Ann Snedeker, all of whom preserved the "Around in the *Glory*" story; and others — all played a role in putting parts of the family legend into proper perspective, and in correcting errors that had been perpetuated or facts that had become distorted through the years. With their assistance the superior master mariner but fallible family man Daniel McLaughlin emerged. He is revealed as a sensitive but strong person who faced tragedy and heartache on many occasions, and who overcame adversity over a period of nearly a half century of following the sea.

Preface

To be asked to write the preface or the introduction of a book is an honor that is not offered every day. Therefore, when I was given the opportunity to review the manuscript of *Clipper Ship Captain: Daniel McLaughlin and the* GLORY OF THE SEAS, I undertook the task seriously, mindful of those whose lives are reflected in this history, and of those who, like the author, have researched so carefully those lives and times. The name of the *Glory of the Seas* has now passed into nautical history. Many years ago she was part of the last grand chapter when sailing vessels were paramount in carrying on the commerce of the world.

Reading and re-reading this very fine account of a period in the career of this medium clipper ship brought back to me the many instances of shipboard life which I experienced during my years at sea aboard the *Edward Sewall*: the stress and strain of setting sail and taking it in, encountering and signalling other ships on the high seas, the daily work of maintenance from morning to late at night, the never-ending changes of weather that brought about the hardships of storms, the washing of the seas along the decks, the bitter cold of the ice and snow off Cape Horn, and the drenching of the tropical storms. All that, and the sometimes scanty feeding that left an empty stomach unsatisfied, and the fresh water that was always in demand but in short supply. Nevertheless, one overlooked the hardships that were always accepted as part of the life of a deepwater sailor. It was a life of youth and adventure that attracted us, and that I experienced and survived, even unto my hundred and second year.

The author has made a very clear and concise accounting of the ships of that day, the men who sailed them, those who planned, built, owned and chartered them, and those who engaged them in long, hazardous passages. It was an era that required trust, faith, knowledge and honesty of all concerned with the ventures, and especially on the part of the masters, officers and crews who brought the vessels to their destinations.

To the author of *Clipper Ship Captain: Daniel McLaughlin and the* GLORY OF THE SEAS, and to those who assisted him with the research into the history of that time, our heartfelt thanks and appreciation for a task well done — ship shape and Bristol fashion.

Sic Transit Gloria Mundi.
Captain Adrian F. Raynaud,
Master Mariner
January 1, 1997

CHAPTER I

Sailing Day

On a mild fall day just off the eastern waterfront of San Francisco, the aristocratic *Glory of the Seas* lay at anchor with her sails furled. This Tuesday, October 24, 1876, was an extremely busy day for Captain Daniel McLaughlin, master of the stately American medium clipper ship. It was sailing day. The captain had many last-minute duties to attend to before the heavily-laden vessel could depart for the open sea.

A three-and-one-half-month, 14,000-mile voyage lay immediately ahead. The ship's ultimate destination was Liverpool in the British Isles by way of Cape Horn at the southern tip of South America. Once she put to sea and barring some major accident, the *Glory of the Seas* would rarely be in sight of land until she reached British waters. Captain McLaughlin, at five feet eight inches in height, stood taller than the average man of the 19th century. He was of slight build, and had blue eyes, a ruddy complexion, and long, curly brown hair flecked with gray.[1] On this special occasion — sailing day for the *Glory of the Seas* — the fifty-two-year-old captain, with his neatly trimmed Van Dyke beard, well-tailored suit, and black top hat, appeared as a very imposing gentleman. As many of his friends in the maritime fraternity would be seeing him off, he wanted to look his best.

Captain McLaughlin's wife Margaret, called Maggie by her husband and friends, took care of last-minute purchases and paid

1

Ship Glory of the Seas *off the Welsh Coast. Oil Painting by Samuel Walters, Liverpool artist, ca. 1876. Courtesy San Francisco Maritime NHP, Collection of Capt. Josiah N. Knowles.*

farewell calls on maritime community women who would not see her again for possibly a year or more — that is, until the return of the *Glory of the Seas* to San Francisco. Maggie was a dignified, attractive, thirty-eight-year-old woman of slim build with a heart-shaped face and expressive eyes. She wore her light brown hair up like a coronet, and, to complement her husband, was fashionably attired for sailing day.

Typical autumn weather prevailed on San Francisco Bay this day. Though the weather was mild, fog would be rolling in over Twin Peaks about three or four o'clock that afternoon. The fog normally rose just over the Peaks and blanketed the San Francisco waterfront until it stretched across the Bay to the east side. Intermittent fog signals would soon disturb the peace and quiet of the entire waterfront. However, the presence of fog did not mean that McLaughlin would postpone the departure of the *Glory of the Seas*. The captain planned to have the *Glory* towed out beyond the Golden Gate and the fog bank.

McLaughlin spent part of his time with the shipowner's new San Francisco agent, Captain Josiah Nickerson Knowles, the immediate past master of the *Glory*. The two captains took care of all the formalities accompanying the clearing of the ship at the Custom House, an old dilapidated brick building (commonly called the Federal Building or Post Office), located about three blocks from the waterfront.[2] Captain McLaughlin filed his cargo manifest with a government clerk, and Captain Knowles paid the miscellaneous fees required by Customs. McLaughlin also presented his shipping articles to a deputy shipping commissioner who, in turn, carefully compared them with a duplicate office copy. Then a clerk transcribed the names of the crew onto another government form thereby formalizing the legality of the articles.

The *Glory of the Seas*' foreign-bound clearance papers from San Francisco were also duly approved and paid for. The two captains then left the Custom House prior to the three o'clock office closing having fully complied with government red tape.

Shortly thereafter, Captain McLaughlin, Mrs. McLaughlin, Captain Knowles, and a large party of friends, including several brother shipmasters, went aboard one of the Captain Millen

Captain Daniel McLaughlin, ca. 1880. Courtesy Mary Ann Snedeker, Collection of Frances McLaughlin Savory.

Griffiths' neatly painted steam tugs, resplendent with black hull, white house, black stack and white boot top glistening in the afternoon sun. The tug transported the festive group out to the lofty sailing ship lying peacefully at anchor in the Bay. Coming alongside the imposing, wooden-hulled vessel, McLaughlin and his wife went aboard by way of an accommodation ladder rigged for officers, by tradition, on the starboard quarter.[3]

The *Glory of the Seas*, laden with grain, was not the only ship anchored in San Francisco Bay that Tuesday afternoon. Other large sailing vessels, both British and American, were preparing for the open sea, their ultimate destination being the United Kingdom.[4]

The *Glory*'s anchor was now weighed, and the large, wooden-hulled tug took the deeply-laden sailing ship in tow. The two vessels made their way down the Bay on the outgoing tide as the afternoon fog rolled in through the Golden Gate. Meanwhile, the ship's officers sent seamen aloft to loose the *Glory of the Seas*' topsails and jibs to give the steamer an assist. Once both vessels were safely outside the fog bank just off the Farallon Islands, the tug cast off her hawser. Then, with last farewells between friends echoing over the water, the tow boat captain gave three shrill blasts on his steam whistle and the two vessels slowly parted company.

As the sun gradually set the *Glory of the Seas*' forward movements were now controlled by her growing expanse of white canvas. With a competent sailor at her helm, the majestic squarerigger — nearly 300 feet long overall including bowsprit and jibboom and about 180 feet from the top of her mainmast to water line — headed out to sea. She now began her first passage under command of Captain Daniel McLaughlin, one of the vanishing breed of California gold rush shipmasters who helped make the name "clipper"[5] mean something in American maritime history.

CHAPTER II

The Master

Captain Daniel McLaughlin had the credentials to be master of a first-class American Cape Horner — even though in the year 1876 no governmental agency existed to document "official" recognition of merchant marine deck officers and masters of sailing ships. Shipmasters were recognized in shipping circles because of the efforts of insurance classification associations such as the American Shipmasters' Association, which functioned as the United States counterpart of the British Lloyd's Register of Shipping. The American Shipmasters' Association not only rated ships, it rated their masters as well. The Association, formed in 1862, issued competency certificates to shipmasters and mates who met its high experience and educational standards. McLaughlin was one of that select number. He obtained his certificate in 1863 when master of the Boston ship *Western Empire*.[1]

The captain was also a member of the Boston Marine Society. This organization, the oldest in the United States and an honored benevolent association dating back to 1742, limited membership to a superior grade of shipmaster. Captain McLaughlin became part of this elite group on July 3, 1871, when he was master of the Boston ship *Swallow*.[2]

Daniel McLaughlin was born on November 29, 1823, at Digby, Nova Scotia, situated on the south side of the Bay of Fundy. His father, also named Daniel, was a native of Londonderry, Ireland.

As a British Army cadet, Daniel the elder served with distinction in 1815 as an eighteen-year-old dispatch rider under the Duke of Wellington at the Battle of Waterloo. Following the Napoleonic Wars, the senior McLaughlin remained in the Army. Upon his discharge at Halifax, Nova Scotia, the British government gave him a grant of land in Annapolis County, Nova Scotia, as a gratuity for his war service. Young Daniel's mother, Catherine Butler, married his father at her native Halifax in 1817 when he was twenty and she was twenty-three years of age.[3]

Daniel, Jr., had a twin brother, Walter, who died in infancy. He also had an older sister and brother, Sarah and Henry. A second sister, Eleanor, was born in 1826, followed by another brother, also named Walter, in January 1829. In August, 1829, the McLaughlin family moved west about fifty miles across the Bay of Fundy to Grand Manan Island, New Brunswick, an island about twenty miles long, seven miles south of Eastport, Maine. There the senior McLaughlin built a home at the Red Cliffs near Deep Cove on the southern side of the island and worked as a herring and halibut fisherman. Eventually, he acquired an interest in several local fishing vessels and hired fishermen to work for him. In his later years he became a fishery warden enforcing the fishery regulations and laws on the island.[4]

Young Daniel received a rudimentary education from his parents but apparently had a thirst for more knowledge than they could give him. A retired English professor took a special interest in the boy and agreed to tutor him. In order to see the old scholar, who lived alone on Wood Island about a mile off the south coast of Grand Manan, Daniel regularly sailed to the island in a small sailboat owned by his parents.[5] Fortunately, being in a commercial fisherman's community gave him an early exposure to fishing and the handling of small sailboats. Thus his desire to acquire an education helped McLaughlin to become a skilled sailor at an early age, as well as developing in him a love for the sea.

By the year 1836, two more daughters had been born to Daniel and Catherine McLaughlin, increasing the family to nine. Young Daniel was now a teenager and was expected to go to work. In those days, few career options were open to a young man of modest circumstances; fishing (the major industry on Grand Manan), farming, or going to sea were the professions most often chosen. At the age of thirteen, young Daniel McLaughlin decided to follow the sea. He wanted, however, to be more than just a local fisherman. The only way a Canadian teenager could go to sea was to become a cook on a coasting vessel, or, occasionally, a cabin boy on a larger deepwater vessel. Both positions represented the very bottom of the maritime employment list.

Young Daniel's father made arrangements for the boy to join a coasting vessel out of Eastport as cook. Farewells were said to his parents, four sisters, and two brothers. Treatment was harsh — the feel of a rope's end on his shoulders, a kick, or a fist in his face to make him step lively — standard shipboard discipline for fledgling ship's boys. Nevertheless McLaughlin began learning the seafaring trade.

Daniel McLaughlin learned by making mistakes, accepting the discipline, and refraining from retaliation upon his tormentors, most of whom thought that a sound beating helped to make a boy into a man. Despite this hard initiation into shipboard life, McLaughlin, as an adult, maintained discipline without resorting to sadistic cruelty, commonly called "belaying pin soup." Shipping on coastal trade as well as fishing vessels, he advanced to ordinary seaman, then to able-bodied seaman qualified to "hand, reef, and steer,"[6] and finally achieved the status of mate.

During his early years at sea, young Daniel served on American as well as on Canadian vessels. He soon realized that he would have more opportunity for advancement if he acquired dual citizenship — a fairly common circumstance for sailors living on the Canadian/United States coastal border. On October 5, 1843, when his vessel called at Norfolk, Virginia, he and one of his shipmates listed themselves as American citizens sailing out of Eastport, Maine. Even though he continued sailing on Canadian vessels for several more years, the U.S. government officially viewed the nineteen-year-old Daniel McLaughlin as an American citizen "sailing . . . under the protection of the American flag."[7]

In the summer of 1845, McLaughlin took command of the small Canadian schooner *Olive Branch* and for several months hauled stone and other materials for the Gannet Rock Lighthouse on Grand Manan where his oldest brother Henry would become head keeper assisted by Daniel's sixteen-year-old brother Walter.[8]

In November of 1845, young Daniel McLaughlin left Grand Manan as mate of the brigantine *Wanderer*, Captain Henry Benson, and thereafter made his home in Eastport, severing his maritime ties with Canada for the next forty-seven years.[9] Eastport had a population of about 4,000 and he felt that his deep water shipping contacts necessitated his living in the larger community.

The following year he began sailing as mate on Eastport coasters managed by John W. Bass, a local shipowner. In 1848, Bass recognized McLaughlin's leadership qualities and appointed him to take command of his first American vessel, the coasting brig *Stephen G. Bass* of Eastport, temporarily relieving Captain L. Winchester, the regular master. The *Bass* had a single deck and was about seventy-two feet long with a breadth of twenty-four feet. Her full complement consisted of McLaughlin as master, two mates, a cook, and four seamen.[10] This three-year-old, wooden squarerigger was a far cry from the *Glory of the Seas*, his command still twenty-eight years in the future, but he could finally be called Captain.

Daniel McLaughlin, only twenty-four years of age, had reached the top rank of his profession. Now, thinking about his domestic future, he began courting Hannah Corbett at Eastport. Hannah was an eighteen-year-old native of Economy, Nova Scotia, who had migrated with her parents to Maine. The tall, poised young lady with long, dark hair welcomed the attentions of the young ship captain. In those years New England courtships were strictly chaperoned. Church socials, group affairs, specially-arranged house calls, and leisurely walks on the tree-lined streets of Eastport offered the only opportunities for courtship of a proper young lady of the 1840s. In spite of their limited contact, however, Daniel and Hannah became well-acquainted and eventually were engaged. They were married on Friday, August 20, 1848, at Eastport at the Central Congregational Church where much of the local maritime community worshipped.[11]

Family members from Grand Manan and Eastport, as well as business associates, attended the McLaughlin wedding, as well

Captain Daniel McLaughlin, ca. 1860. Hannah McLaughlin, ca. 1860. Courtesy
Mary Ann Snedeker, Collection of Frances McLaughlin Savory.

as many of the local maritime community, undoubtedly including Caleb S. Huston, builder of the *Stephen G. Bass*, and John W. Bass, the ship's owner.[12]

In 1849, Captain McLaughlin served as a relief master for John W. Bass' fleet, and otherwise shipped as first mate on voyages out of Eastport. Bass also managed the seventy-six-foot brig *Topaz*, which, like the *Stephen G. Bass*, operated as a coaster.[13] McLaughlin stayed in Bass' employ as deck officer with the expectation of getting his own command eventually. Despite the fact that McLaughlin was not a native Eastporter, both John Bass and Caleb Huston advanced him over local ship's officers and publicly acknowledged that McLaughlin had an important future in their employ.

Gold was discovered at Sutter's Mill in California in January 1848, but the gold hysteria didn't really start until 1849. As the eastern seaboard shipping community began to take notice, the fever for huge cargo profits spread to eastern Maine and Eastport. The California gold rush prompted the construction of Captain McLaughlin's first real command, the clipper *Gray Feather*, which would be the largest vessel built to that date in Eastport — about 140 feet long and 587 tons register.[14]

On February 24, 1850, Hannah McLaughlin bore a son. He was named John Walter.[15] At the same time, another child — the *Gray Feather* — was being carefully constructed of oak, pine, and other select woods at Caleb Huston's shipyard at Shackford's Cove on the south side of Eastport. By the end of October 1850, *Gray Feather* had been launched, rigged, and equipped for sea.

In November and December 1850, and the first part of January 1851, the *Gray Feather* took on cargo at one of the New York wharves fronting the East River. Three new vessels, the clippers *Sea Serpent*, *Eclipse*, and *Gray Feather*, were to sail on their maiden voyages during the first two weeks of January 1851. The largest clipper ship on berth, however, was the extreme clipper *Stag Hound*. This latter vessel had the distinction of having been built by Donald McKay, who in eighteen years would construct the *Glory of the Seas*. McLaughlin's *Gray Feather* was the smallest of the ships bound for California, being seventy-seven feet shorter than *Stag Hound*.

The *Gray Feather* had a large variety of cargo in her hold: including cases of tomatoes, kegs of pickles, dried apples, tobacco, whiskey and cheese; all perishable items. In addition she carried shovels, pails, brooms and other general merchandise for the mining crowd at San Francisco.[16] The *Gray Feather* also had two male passengers. With Captain McLaughlin and two mates, Hannah, and young John McLaughlin, the ship's twenty- by twenty-eight-foot after house would be very crowded during the forthcoming three-and-one-half month voyage.

The presence of captains' wives aboard sailing ships was not uncommon in this era. Accompanying their husbands on their voyages was preferable to facing loneliness ashore for a year or more. Young children also regularly accompanied their parents. Their mothers normally sheltered them from witnessing the autocratic and sometimes brutal methods used by their fathers to keep discipline among the crews. A captain's demeanor in the family cabin was usually different from his actions on deck.[17]

The *Sea Serpent* sailed first from New York on January 11, followed by *Gray Feather* on the 14th. The *Eclipse* sailed the following day. These ships had a distinct advantage over vessels traversing the Cape Horn route in years past. The masters now utilized Matthew F. Maury's "Wind and Current Chart" which enabled them to reduce the length of their forthcoming voyages by over a month.[18]

Daniel McLaughlin, who had never sailed beyond the West Indies, definitely had need for detailed charts for his passage to California. To acquire a copy of Maury's charts, plus a copy of his "Sailing Directions," he had to maintain an abstract log of his coming voyage in a government-issue form book and return it to Maury's Naval Observatory at the conclusion of the voyage.[19]

From the first day at sea, January 14, 1851, Captain McLaughlin faithfully filled out the blanks in his "Abstract Log Kept by Vessels Cooperating with Lieut. Maury in collecting Materials for his Wind and Current Charts;" this involved following specific directions: (1) determining an accurate latitude and longitude each noon; (2) checking the sea current in "knots per

Ship Gray Feather, *ca. 1851. Courtesy Hirschl & Adler Galleries, New York. Collection of Captain Daniel McLaughlin.*

hour;" (3) checking to see whether there was a compass variation as observed; (4) reading the barometer; (5) checking the temperature of air and water at nine a.m.; (6) noting the direction of the winds, "First, Middle," and "Latter" parts of each twenty-four-hour period; (7) and finally, a "remarks" column. Comments such as "Clear weather, strong breeze, latter-cloudy" were written in McLaughlin's abstract log on the very first day at sea.[20]

The *Gray Feather* took twenty-eight days in the Atlantic to reach the equator which she crossed in the doldrums (equatorial trough) at longitude 27° 55' on a day in which baffling winds, calms and baffling airs, affected her progress; thence to 50° south which took an additional thirty-one days.[21]

On day sixty, McLaughlin passed at a point eight miles west of the Falkland Islands and five days later the *Gray Feather* sailed past Cape Horn, that lonely promontory at the southern tip of South America, in squally weather. Continuing westerly against heavy swells and strong gales, the captain made steady progress until the *Gray Feather* crossed 50° south in the Pacific. It had taken fifteen days to round the Horn from 50° south to 50° south — excellent time for a first voyage by a shipmaster in those treacherous waters and testimony to both his seamanship and the effectiveness of Maury's "Wind and Current Chart" as a guide.[22]

From 50° south, the *Gray Feather* made her way to the equator in the Pacific for another thirty-four days with a number of days of light and baffling winds in the doldrums. Finally she crossed the equator on day 108 at longitude 109° 42'; thence continued northerly to San Francisco. [23]

On his final day at sea, May 29, 1851, Captain McLaughlin wrote in his abstract log book:

> Fine breeze and clear weather. Seen several whales. Strong breez and clear. At six a.m. seen mtn. Found Cape Blanco bearing NNW from eight to ten miles. Tack to the WNW. The latter part tack to the NNE and fetch in. So ends this passage.
>
> Sir. I have mailed this on your direction [to Washington, D.C.]. If a abstract of my log is of service you are welcome to it, and I will make

it a point to forward it in ensuing [voyages]. The mail leaves in one
hour. Time is short with me. I will writ you by the next mail.
    With respect your most obedient Servant
                          [signed] Daniel McLaughlin
                          Ship Gray Feather[24]

The *Sea Serpent* arrived first at San Francisco on May 17th,
1851, followed by the *Eclipse* three days later. The *Stag Hound,*
which sailed from New York on the 1st of February, arrived on May
23rd. The *Gray Feather* did not arrive at San Francisco until May
30th, making her the slowest of the fleet. Captain McLaughlin's
only consolation was that, unlike the rest of the fleet which lost
spars and was forced to put into Valparaiso for repairs, the *Gray
Feather* experienced no damage whatsoever on the voyage.

    McLaughlin's inexperience on the Cape Horn route was
no doubt a factor, but his apparent caution also contributed to the
length of the passage. His elapsed voyage time was 136 days;[25]
whereas, the *Stag Hound* took 107 sailing days. Although
McLaughlin lacked firsthand knowledge of the special conditions
facing shipmasters on the Cape Horn route, he would have ample
opportunity in his future thirty-one years as a shipmaster to become extremely competent.

    The Bay immediately east of San Francisco was a forest of
ship masts in May 1851. Hundreds of vessels lay out in the harbor.
Following their arrival many were abandoned by their crews who
were determined to find gold in the streams east of the Bay. The
Gray Feather anchored in the midst of a forgotten fleet of vessels,
some of which were now floating warehouses devoid of upper spars.

    McLaughlin and his wife were shocked to see the San
Francisco waterfront a blackened ruin for three-quarters of a mile.
The gold rush town had experienced five fires to date in the
downtown area, the latest of which occurred on May 4th. That
conflagration destroyed eighteen blocks and 2,000 buildings, and
reportedly was set by arsonists. Ultimately, four persons were
executed by a Committee of Vigilance — vigilantes — as a
community effort to restore law and order.[26]

Once wharf space became available, Capt. McLaughlin arranged to have the *Gray Feather* berthed alongside Cunningham's Wharf. During the berthing process, Capt. McLaughlin stood on the *Gray Feather*'s quarter deck overseeing the operation. As the ship was made fast, the captain glanced over the ship's side and was pleasantly surprised to see C. L. Taylor, an old schoolmate from the East Coast, standing in the forefront on the adjacent wharf. McLaughlin told the mate to take over and quickly jumped over the side onto the wharf. The two men enthusiastically hugged each other. In fact they were so enthusiastic that they lost their footing and fell off the dock into the water. Amid the laughter of the surrounding crowd, onlookers threw lines to the captain and Taylor and hauled them out. Soon, both men were safely aboard the *Gray Feather*. As their wet clothes were being dried, they brought each other up-to-date on events in their lives since their departure from Grand Manan and Eastport.[27]

Cunningham's Wharf was a short T-shaped wooden wharf situated near the foot of Vallejo Street. Here the cargoes from the *Stag Hound* and the *Sea Serpent* were already being unloaded. Horse-drawn freight wagons hauled the contents away into surviving San Francisco warehouses nearby. Each vessel had her lower yards cockbilled so they could be used as cargo booms in the unloading process. The following advertisement appeared in the *San Francisco Daily Alta California*:

> Ship *Grey* [sic] *Feather* — Consignees by this vessel are hereby notified that she will commence discharging on Monday next June 2, at Cunningham's Wharf, and are requested to call on the subscribers, pay freight, and receive orders for their goods. Goods remaining on the wharf after 5 p.m. must be stored at the expense and risk of the consignees.[28]

This notice included items specifically consigned to customers. McLaughlin's published manifest also made reference to "5,391 pkgs mdse unspecified." This is where the captain and the ship made a tremendous profit in the provision-poor and lumber-less town. Years later, the captain's youngest son Carl

View from Telegraph Hill, San Francisco, ca. 1871. Vallejo Street Wharf is the farthest wharf to the left with Cape Horners berthed alongside. Courtesy San Francisco Maritime NHP, Lawrence and Houseworth, photographer, Accession No. A20,731n.

recalled being told that his father sold "flour for fifty dollars a barrel and the lumber at a higher figure."[29]

No return cargoes to the East Coast were available for sailing ships, however, so the *Gray Feather*'s next port of call was to be Calcutta, thence return to New York by way of London. McLaughlin had stone rubble put aboard as ballast, and on June 20th, he shipped a crew for the forthcoming voyage. They consisted of twelve men, including himself, ten of whom were American citizens. The black cook, an African native, was the oldest man on board. He was only forty-five and listed his citizenship on the shipping articles as "none" and his place of residence as "The World." McLaughlin paid a shipping master a premium price of $160 advance wages per man for his crew. In addition, he agreed to pay the sailors between $40 and $100 per month for the run, except for his two mates. These agreed to a wage of $45 and $40 per month respectively. One seaman agreed to be paid $30 per month which was the going rate at San Francisco. The only thing in McLaughlin's favor was that the articles stated that his crew could be discharged at Calcutta, giving them the option of taking a drastic cut in pay or being replaced by sailors willing to accept what were considered normal wages at that port, about $15 a month for an able-bodied seaman.[30]

Shortly after shipping a crew, Capt. McLaughlin departed San Francisco bound for Calcutta, the capital of British India, located eighty miles upriver from the Bay of Bengal. Following arrival there in the Fall of 1851, the *Gray Feather* loaded cargo for London over a period of months and eventually sailed by way of the Cape of Good Hope and returned to New York thus completing his first circumnavigation of the world.

In 1852-1853 Captain McLaughlin made a second passage from New York to San Francisco in 126 days. He returned by way of Callao and the Chincha Islands where the *Gray Feather* loaded guano, following which she entered the Australian trade. Here McLaughlin first distinguished himself as a clipper captain. He made a record voyage of thirty-six days between Melbourne and Calcutta in 1854. Following his return to Boston later that year by way of the Cape of Good Hope, he again sent his abstract log to

Matthew Maury's observatory. McLaughlin's log entry on July 14, 1854, read as follows:

> 8:30 p.m. seen Fals Point bearing N by W; then shaped a course for the pilot station. At 11:45 took a pilot and proceeded up the [Hooghly] River [to Calcutta]. This ends the abstract and also the quickest passage ever made between the two ports.[31]

The elation for this record passage was dampened by the death of Daniel and Hannah McLaughlin's infant daughter on the way home. Named Helena because she was born off the island of St. Helena in the South Atlantic, the baby died at the age of one month.[32]

In 1855, John W. Bass gave McLaughlin command of his new ship the *Aetos*, another product of Caleb S. Huston. McLaughlin now had the distinction of commanding the largest sailing ship ever built at Eastport, a vessel more than twice the tonnage of the *Gray Feather*. This appointment was a definite advancement for him.[33]

Along with the captain's successful career, the McLaughlin family continued to grow, although now Hannah remained ashore at the time of the birth of the children to reduce the chances of complications. At Boston in 1856, another daughter was born to the McLaughlins. Named Helena, she was joined two years later by another sister Josephine, born at Eastport. Although Hannah McLaughlin did make some voyages in the *Aetos*, raising three children, one a toddler, the other an infant, on board a sailing ship had definite drawbacks. Dealing with the energy level of the two older children in a confined space over a period of months was a strain on Hannah's nerves. For good reason she limited her seagoing days.[34]

Capt. McLaughlin sailed the *Aetos* successfully in the far eastern West Indies and Australia trades for nearly six years. In 1857, he made a voyage to India and brought back a brass sword as a memento from the Sepoy Rebellion. McLaughlin also traded between New Orleans and Liverpool in the cotton trade until the *Aetos'* sale to Liverpool buyers on March 29, 1861.[35] This was only

Ship Aetos, *ca. 1858. Courtesy The Fine Arts Museum of San Francisco, Collection of Captain Daniel McLaughlin, Accession No. 49605.*

two weeks before Confederate Army cannon fired at Fort Sumter starting the American Civil War.

Following the sale of the *Aetos*, McLaughlin went into a ship chandlery business at London naming the firm "Ewing and McLaughlin." However, a major problem soon surfaced with the new venture. His partner was a New Orleans native and a Confederate sympathizer, while Capt. McLaughlin remained loyal to his adopted country. This caused such a division between the two partners that they dissolved the business.[36]

Daniel McLaughlin then decided to go back to sea. At this time, the family lived in London. A new baby brother, Daniel Carlton (Carl), who was born aboard the *Aetos* at Liverpool in January 1861, unexpectedly became the center of attention when tragedy struck the McLaughlins again. The nurse accidently dropped the baby Carl out of his carriage, seriously injuring his back. This, together with daughter Josephine's increasing deafness due to scarlet fever, made it a near impossibility for the McLaughlins to go to sea as a family. They returned to Boston by steamer later that year and subsequently settled at Malden, Massachusetts, a small suburb about five miles north of Boston.[37]

By 1861, Daniel McLaughlin had followed the sea for twenty-five years. He sailed around Cape Horn four times and circumnavigated the world three times. Although tragedies struck his family, he was a successful shipmaster, highly respected by his peers. And he had the loyal support of his wife Hannah and the love of his children, the oldest of whom was now eleven.

CHAPTER III

Civil War
and Post-War

Captain McLaughlin's fourth command was the Boston ship *Western Empire*, a three-decked down-Easter, in which he acquired a 1/16 interest. This vessel saw service during the latter part of 1861 and early 1862 as a transport under charter to the French government.[1]

During the first year of the American Civil War, as Union and Confederate forces fought the initial battles of a bloody war, the French Army invaded Mexico. The *Western Empire* received a charter by the French to haul a cargo of war supplies to the port city of Veracruz in the Gulf of Mexico. While she lay at anchor in the unprotected harbor, a hurricane came up suddenly with violent winds from the north. But McLaughlin's practiced eye anticipated the storm and he took precautionary measures, sending down all the *Western Empire*'s upper yards and masts and securely anchoring her fore and aft, with the bow facing seaward, enabling him to ride out the heavy seas safely. Nine other ships were not so fortunate and were blown ashore. [2]

Following her voyage to Veracruz, the *Western Empire* became a U.S. government transport under charter to the Union Army. In 1862-1863, McLaughlin provided support for Major General Nathaniel P. Banks at Port Hudson, Louisiana, on the Mississippi. In late 1863 and early 1864, the *Western Empire*'s owners chartered her as a transport supporting Major General Benjamin F. Butler of the Union Army in his defense of City Point, Virginia.[3]

Although Daniel McLaughlin wasn't exposed to direct Confederate fire, on one voyage the elements accomplished what the opposing forces failed to do. Among other things, the *Western Empire* hauled a cargo of coal, 500 tons of ammunition, 200 horses, and enough hay to feed them. During the voyage the ship was caught in a fierce storm. Half of the horses succumbed to the effects of the tempestuous winds and seas; fifty-eight of them dying from sickness and fright.[4]

In mid-summer of 1865, after four years of war, the railroad system between the northern and southern states was almost totally inoperative. Only one steamer and several sailing ships engaged in trade between Boston and New Orleans. Accepting command of the screw steamer *Cassandra*, a wooden-hulled vessel of 1,221 tons register with an auxiliary sail rig, McLaughlin hauled general cargo 1,800 miles to New Orleans and returned to Boston with cotton, tobacco, and other items. This 207-foot vessel previously saw service as a transport during the latter part of the war. Following the end of hostilities, she was considered surplus by her managing owners, J.E. Williams & Co., who sold her to a Boston syndicate for $103,000.[5] Captain McLaughlin also invested about $6,500 in her for a 1/16 interest.[6]

The *Cassandra*'s new managing owners, Wm. H. Lincoln & Co., saw a definite need for such a vessel on the New Orleans-Boston run. The question, however, arose as to which firm would become well-established first — the owners of *Cassandra* or another? A third steamer was also equipped for service between the two ports — the *Concordia*, an iron-hulled screw steamer with auxiliary bark rig. J. Henry Sears & Co. of Boston managed this 1,681-ton vessel. Eleven years in the future this same firm would give Daniel McLaughlin command of the *Glory of the Seas*. Ironically, *Concordia*'s master, Captain Elisha F. Sears, would be the first master of *Glory* under Sears' company management. Furthermore, he and Captain McLaughlin would operate competing steamers on their initial voyages in a new service.

While the *Cassandra* underwent overhaul including adding an auxiliary brigantine rig, the *Concordia* sailed on her first trip to New Orleans on August 10th. "The A-1 splendid steamship" *Cassandra* didn't sail until September 9th from the Lewis Wharf at Boston. Eleven days later she arrived at New Orleans. By the end of September, however, J. Henry Sears added another steamer to the Boston-New Orleans run, and the *Cassandra's* owners followed suit with the addition of the screw steamship *Cleopatra* which sailed on her first voyage on October 7, 1865.

Meanwhile, McLaughlin began his first return trip in the *Cassandra* to Boston arriving there on October 10 with a full cargo and ten passengers. The *Cassandra's* next scheduled departure was October 21st which gave him little family time with his wife and children.

The *Cassandra*, however, didn't effectively "leave her berth at Lewis Wharf on Saturday, October 21" on schedule. The *Boston Daily Advertiser* explained why:

> "... in getting under way on Saturday night, [the *Cassandra*] parted her hawser which got entangled in her propeller and prevented her from going to sea. She anchored in the stream near the [Charlestown] Navy Yard, and the services of a diver were called into requisition, but up to Sunday evening had not succeeded in freeing the obstructions from the propeller ... "

Captain McLaughlin didn't sail until the next day.[7]

Following his return from the *Cassandra's* second passage to New Orleans, thirteen days from the southern port, the captain had nine days with his family before departing on December 2, 1865. He ended the year at New Orleans waiting for the end of a labor strike which totally stopped all loading of vessels at that southern port.

On February 5, 1867, the *Cassandra* came to an untimely end enroute from New Orleans to New York. During thick weather she piled up on Brigantine Shoals, New Jersey. Her wooden hull was badly holed and quickly broke in two. McLaughlin saved all of his crew, and most of the *Cassandra*'s $100,000 cargo was also salvaged.[8]

Apparently the loss of the *Cassandra* did not affect Captain McLaughlin's reputation in the eyes of the Boston shipping community. Later in that month of February he succeeded to command of the wooden-hulled clipper ship *Swallow*, a Boston vessel owned by Thatcher Magoun & Co. He said farewell to Hannah and the children and joined the *Swallow* while she loaded general cargo at New York.

The 210-foot *Swallow* departed New York on March 14, 1867, bound for San Francisco, making a fast run of twenty-two days to the equator. On April 27th off the Plate River, a violent pampero[9] struck: "[the *Swallow*] lost rudder, sprung mainmast, and stove bulwarks and house . . ." Four days later he nursed his damaged ship into Montevideo, Uruguay, for repairs.[10]

McLaughlin had the *Swallow* surveyed to determine cost of repairs, then contacted the owners and informed them it would cost about $5,000 to make her seaworthy. Now, the captain received extremely bad news. Hannah McLaughlin had succumbed to pneumonia at Malden on April 12th.[11]

Daniel McLaughlin was in shock and despair. In the space of three months, he had wrecked a ship, was dealing with repairing his crippled command, had lost his beloved wife and now had the added responsibility of four children who were six thousand miles away. John, the eldest, was only sixteen years old, Helena was eleven, Josephine, still handicapped by her hearing disability, was nine, while six-year-old Daniel Carlton (nicknamed Carl), required special care due to his back injury.

Capt. McLaughlin had to make a hard decision: return home or complete his voyage in the *Swallow* to California. Fortunately, he was able to make arrangements with sympathetic relatives in Malden to care for the children so he could continue with the repairs on the *Swallow* and resume his voyage.[12]

Two and one-half weeks after his arrival at Montevideo, Daniel McLaughlin sailed once again for San Francisco, arriving there on August 11, eighty-four days from the Uruguayan port and 131 sailing days from New York. The captain contended with very light and contrary winds in the Pacific, as evidenced in his published statement: "Took in skysails only once in 50 consecutive days; had no trades . . . have been within 800 miles of this port [San Francisco] for the last 16 days."[13]

Following his return to Malden, Daniel McLaughlin began restructuring his life in the difficult position of a widower shipmaster with four young children to care for — no easy task. He made further arrangements to have relatives in the Malden area care for all four children while he went back to sea.

In the meantime, McLaughlin began courting a thirty-year-old widow from Grand Manan who had experienced violent tragedy three years before. Margaret Benson's husband, Captain Colin C. Benson, master of the Canadian brig *Zero*, was murdered at sea by one of his crew.[14]

On May 14, 1868, Daniel McLaughlin and Margaret Benson were married at Eastport, and she joined her new husband on his next voyage in the *Swallow* to California. On the return trip to the East Coast, McLaughlin made an excellent passage sailing from San Francisco on November 14th and arriving at New York ninety-eight days later. This was one of the fastest passages between the two ports that year, with McLaughlin proving once again that he could carry large amounts of sail without endangering his ship. On arrival at New York, the captain reported that he didn't take in his topgallants from the time he left San Francisco until the *Swallow* was ninety-four days out.[15]

In 1872, Thatcher Magoun & Co. sold the *Swallow* and gave McLaughlin command of their clipper ship *Herald of the Morning*, a wooden-hulled, three-skysail-yarder, 203 feet in length, with a fine reputation as a flyer in the Cape Horn trade. Subsequently, he made a passage from San Francisco to Liverpool in 119 days. Although this was not unusually fast, the *Herald* suffered no damage to sail, spars, or rigging, which insurers and owners generally considered as being more important than a fast passage.[16]

Although the official U.S. Shipping Commissioner-approved form of shipping articles for deep-water vessels like the *Herald of the Morning* stated in bold language: "NO SHEATH KNIVES OR PROFANE LANGUAGE ALLOWED ON BOARD,"[17] it was the

Margaret McLaughlin, ca. 1870. Courtesy Mary Ann Snedeker, Collection of Frances McLaughlin Savory.

exception when officers and crews adhered to this directive on ships engaging in the Cape Horn trade. The quality of both seamen and officers on deep-water sailing ships began to deteriorate seriously in the late 1870s and 1880s.[18] Brutal treatment of sailors became more common, giving rise to publications such as the *Red Record*, which documented cases of extreme brutality on American squareriggers.

Following the arrival of the infamous hell ship *Sunrise* at San Francisco on September 27th, 1873, real and conjured brutality meted out by sailing ships' officers became an almost daily topic on the front pages of San Francisco newspapers. For months, anything even hinting at mistreatment by officers was a common topic of discussion to the point of being slanderously at odds with the truth.[19]

When the American ship *St. Charles* arrived at San Francisco on October 8, 1873, 137 days from New York, boardinghouse runners went aboard her in an effort to solicit business from the crew. Several seamen told them that in the course of their long voyage they spoke the *Herald of the Morning* and were part of a boat crew that went alongside her. Supposedly, several of the *St. Charles'* sailors told them that one of McLaughlin's crew had been shot in the head and back. Moreover, another *Herald of the Morning* sailor was said to have been brutally cut down by a cutlass wielded by an angry ship's officer.[20]

In the course of the investigation, while awaiting *Herald of the Morning*'s arrival, some ten days hence, reporters from the *Daily Alta California* unofficially interviewed the *St. Charles* sailors, and two men from the boat crew provided the true story: a crew member from the *Herald of the Morning* was placed in irons, and the captain had just cause for doing so — an example of rumor gone grossly wild.[21]

In the course of the investigation, an *Alta* reporter also interviewed Captain Edwin S. Smalley, master of the *St. Charles*. He said that Captain McLaughlin was not the stereotypical hell-raising sailing ship captain conjured by unscrupulous reporters. Captain Smalley stated: "Captain McLaughlin is a humane, Christian man who would not even tolerate swearing on board his ship."

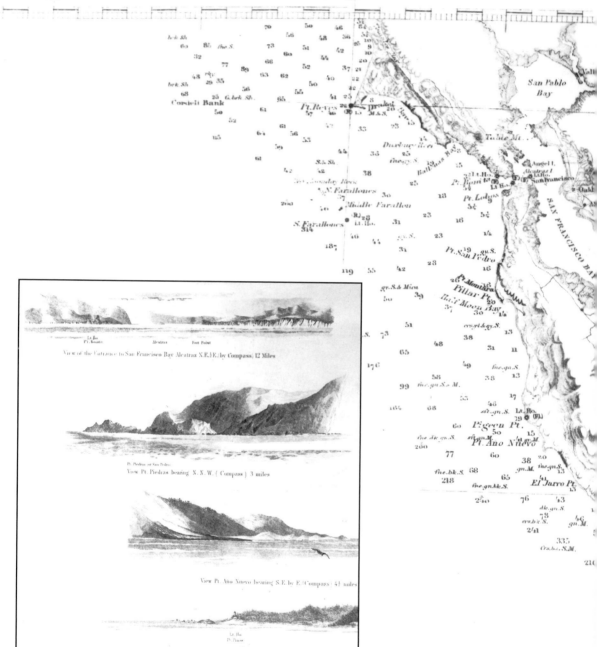

San Francisco Bay Vicinity and Approaches (inset) from a U.S. Coast Survey Chart
dated 1874. Courtesy Allen Engle, Allen Engle Collection.

This may have been a bit of an exaggeration when considering the type of men who sailed before the mast in the 1870s, but it shows how McLaughlin's peers viewed him.[22]

On October 8, 1873, the *Herald of the Morning* arrived at San Francisco, 141 days from New York. McLaughlin operated his commands without resorting to brutal methods. The charges against him proved to be entirely groundless. The *Daily Alta*, which eagerly reported the investigation into brutality charges by the *St. Charles'* sailors, remained silent on the matter other than printing the standard voyage summary or memorandum of the *Herald's* passage.[23]

Less than three weeks after McLaughlin's arrival at San Francisco, however, a sensational officer/crew incident concerning the *Herald of the Morning* appeared on the pages of four San Francisco newspapers. The trial of the officers and captain of the hell ship *Sunrise* continued as major news on the waterfront and directly under a front page article describing particulars of the ongoing *Sunrise* trial the following bold print headline appeared in the Friday, November 7, 1873, issue of the *Daily Alta California*;

THE MATE'S ASSAULT

The First and Second Mates of the *"Herald of the Morning"* Arrested for Assault on the Carpenter

The previous day, Captain McLaughlin attended to last minute shore business and cleared the *Herald of the Morning* for Liverpool at the Custom House. The ship lay at anchor in the stream just off the eastern San Francisco waterfront fully laden with 32,435 centals (1,622 short tons) of grain, as the captain had made final preparations to sail at noon on Friday.

Although the captain was not aboard ship during the day on Thursday, all the crew — a total of nineteen men, including sixteen able-bodied seamen and the two mates (with the exception of the carpenter, Thomas Peterson, a forty-three year-old Swede[23])

Ship Herald of the Morning, *ca. 1870. Courtesy of the Mariners Museum, Newport News, Virginia, Accession No. QO 734.*

— came aboard and two men immediately got into a heated argument.

The article in the *Alta* stated that the chief mate and the second mate "beat [the carpenter] badly,"[24] and that the carpenter was permitted to return ashore. This implied that Peterson was officially quitting the ship, which required his somehow justifying his action with the government shipping authorities in order to negate his having signed shipping articles for the voyage to Liverpool.

A sailor's attempt to leave a vessel after signing articles was viewed as desertion, punishable with possible imprisonment under the law.

Although the *Alta* reporter stated that Peterson was "set upon and beat[en] badly,"[25] the *Chronicle* reported the same incident but made no mention of Peterson being hurt at all. The *Chronicle* and the *Daily Evening Bulletin* gave an entirely different reason why Peterson refused to ship: "He thought if this is a hot ship in port, what will she be at sea?"[26]

Apparently, after returning ashore on Thursday afternoon, the carpenter, Thomas Peterson, had met with Colonel Jonathan D. Stevenson, the San Francisco Shipping Commissioner. Besides relating his alleged assault by Brown and Field, Peterson told Stevenson that he personally observed that "the mate knocked down two men and had placed four or five others in irons."[27] Supposedly, this occurred during the brief period when Peterson was aboard the *Herald of the Morning*. Stevenson obviously thought that he had another *Sunrise* incident in the making that had to be rooted out before the ship put out to sea. Before acting on Peterson's charges, however, Stevenson met with John Kelly, another crew member of the *Herald of the Morning*, who not only made similar charges but also stated that he was one of the mate's victims. Commissioner Stevenson felt that he had no choice but to swear out warrants for the arrest of the two mates. Both men were then placed in handcuffs and brought ashore to be transported to the city jail.

Meanwhile, all four newspapers published stories of the incident, each with a slightly different version. They were all entirely silent respecting Captain McLaughlin's involvement, with the exception of the *Bulletin* which stated: "Captain Daniel McLaughlin, master of the vessel, states that [chief mate] Brown is a kind and humane man and during the voyage out [from New York] never had trouble with the men."[28] In contrast to their castigation of Captain Clarke, master of the *Sunrise*, however, the reporters were very careful not to mention any involvement of the captain in the apparent altercation between mates and crew.

In comparing the misinformation contained in the articles of the four newspapers, some of the facts in the case began to surface. Chief Mate Brown, assisted by the second mate, George Field, struck John Kelly, but Thomas Peterson was not touched. Brown stated to a reporter that he fired Kelly for incompetence that Thursday afternoon and sent him ashore. The mate said: "I believe that I slapped the face of . . . [Kelly] with the back of my hand and his nose bled slightly. I did it to hurry him up a little . . . we found [Kelly] knew nothing of his business and we sent him back to Colonel Stevenson, refusing to take him."[29]

Shortly after his being brought ashore, Wilbur Brown told a *Chronicle* reporter why he felt Kelly and Peterson had levied charges of brutality against him and second mate Field.

> The whole trouble is made by these *Sunrise* suits. An officer of a ship in this port is completely at the mercy of the sailors. He has no protection whatever. It is almost enough to make me swear never to sail in an American ship again. We know nothing of what we are charged with, but some miserable sailor has the power to send me to jail and keep us here in ignorance. The laws of the United States are wonderfully and fearfully made.[30]

That Thursday night, the two mates "reposed quietly in cell No. 3 of the City Prison," according to the *Chronicle*. The following morning Brown and Field appeared in Police Court with counsel to answer four charges of aggravated assault and battery. Sailing of the *Herald of the Morning* was held up so that five subpoenaed sailors from the ship could be brought ashore and interrogated by the court as to the validity of the charges. Peterson, the carpenter, repeated his story to the court, and another sailor said that the mate had struck him in the face for "not addressing him as 'Mr. Brown.'"[31] However, no testimony was presented actually proving that Kelly or Peterson were brutally assaulted. Also, no adverse comments were made about Captain McLaughlin as to anything he should have done to deal with the situation.

Based on the generally accepted disciplinary standards in force on the average deep water sailing ship of this era, the local shipping community viewed a backhanded slap, kick, or punch as justifiable discipline when dealing with any kind of insubordination. It was commonly known that McLaughlin did not employ "bucko" mates who would physically beat and kick a man until he was senseless.

Mate Brown did admit to the court that he struck Kelly for "using vulgar language" at him, but George Field, a thirty-six-year-old native of Baltimore, admitted nothing. John Kelly was actually the prosecution's star witness and his testimony was essential to the city's case. Kelly, however, was strangely absent; but, in spite of the lack of evidence, the judge found Brown guilty on two counts of assault and battery, and Field on one. He released Brown on payment of $150 bail while Field had to pay $100 bail (no doubt paid by the ship). The judge continued the case but instructed Brown and Field to appear in court on Saturday morning for sentencing — that was on the faint hope that Kelly's testimony could still be obtained.[32]

Early that Friday afternoon, Mates Brown and Field, together with their five shipmates, returned to their duties on the *Herald of the Morning*. Captain McLaughlin instructed them to stay on board and stay out of trouble. The reason: the ship was to be towed out to sea early the next morning. Nothing more would be proved by their reappearing in court other than postponing the ship's departure again and the racking up of additional legal costs.

On Saturday morning a brief item appeared in the *Chronicle* showing how McLaughlin brought the conflict to a conclusion: "William [sic] Brown and George Field, first and second officers of the *Herald of the Morning*, who were ordered to appear yesterday in the police court on four [sic] charges of assault and battery, failed to respond to their names and forfeited $150 and $100 respectively. The ship has sailed."[33]

This incident is an example of the manning problems on American Cape Horners in the 1870s which were accentuated by overzealous newspaper reporters in the wake of the *Sunrise* brutality case. The prosecuting attorney for the San Francisco Police Court summed up the facts of the *Herald of the Morning* case for a reporter writing in the *Examiner* on November 8th: ". . . the principal witness Kelly could not be found . . . from the evidence adduced, he [the prosecutor] was inclined to think that the whole thing was a farce on the part of somebody."[34]

Nevertheless, incidents of extreme brutality were becoming more common and the newspaper reports and investigations helped eventually toward major revisions in U.S. maritime laws.

Following her voyage to Liverpool, the *Herald of the Morning* made the papers again, but this time it was because of a fast passage — ninety-nine days to Liverpool, the second-fastest passage that season.[35]

With the arrival of the *Herald of the Morning* at Hamburg, Germany, in July 1875, Thatcher Magoun & Co. sold her to Messrs. James B. Tibbets and Isaac Benham for £5,000 ($24,200). Because he had no financial interest in the craft, McLaughlin suddenly found himself without employment. Turning over command to a replacement shipmaster, he and Maggie booked passage as first-class passengers on the British steamship *China*, departing Liverpool on August 17, 1875.[36]

On the thirteen-day crossing to Boston, McLaughlin had time to think about his future. He recognized that he was at another crossroads in his life. Arriving home at Malden, the captain decided to retire from the sea. In October 1875 he purchased from a local merchant a fully-stocked general store located near the Faulkner Street Station, a small railroad depot within blocks of his residence.[37]

Although he had the potential to develop a good clientele, as the store was close to the main line of the Boston and Maine Railroad, the role of storekeeper didn't appeal to McLaughlin for

Captain Josiah Nickerson Knowles, master of Glory of the Seas, *1871-1876, and San Francisco agent for J. Henry Sears & Co., managing owners of the ship, ca. 1885. Courtesy San Francisco Maritime NHP. Image No. P7986.*

long. The business failed but the endeavor gave him ten consecutive, happy months with his children, three of whom were now adults.

In August 1876, the captain returned to the maritime field, this time in command of a brand new Boston-built Cape Horner, the *Paul Revere*. Unfortunately, he was a short-term master of this vessel. The following month another captain bought an interest in her and took over command.[38]

In the meantime, at San Francisco, Capt. Josiah Nickerson Knowles, master of the crack Boston medium clipper ship *Glory of the Seas* received several important communications from his employers, J. Henry Sears & Company of Boston, managing owners of the ship. Sears & Co. asked Knowles to become their resident agent at San Francisco because of the increasing number of vessels they were employing in the California grain trade to the United Kingdom. The *Glory of the Seas* was a seven-year-old, main skysail-yarder, registered at Boston, with dimensions of 240.2 x 44.1 x 28.3 feet and 2,102.57 gross tons.[39] She was the last full-rigged ship built by Donald McKay of East Boston.

Knowles' affirmative reply on September 18, 1876, dramatically affected the future of Daniel McLaughlin and his wife. Capt. Knowles, however, placed a condition on his acceptance. In his letter to Sears & Co., he stated: "Should I find the business did not realize our anticipation and I wish to join my ship [*Glory of the Seas*] in Liverpool or New York, I am to be allowed to do so on giving you timely notice of my wish to give up the business."[40] Fortunately for McLaughlin, Josiah Knowles would become an outstanding shipping and commission merchant and community leader at San Francisco.

Capt. Knowles relinquished command of one of the most popular post-Civil War ships in the California trade, a vessel in which he had broken the sailing record from San Francisco to Sydney, Australia, in 1875. Moreover, in 1873-1874, the *Glory of the Seas* made a ninety-five-day passage, joining the ranks of other Donald McKay-built ships which made the run to San Francisco from New York in less than 100 days during the 1850s. The great ships *Flying Cloud, Great Republic, Flying Fish,* and *Romance of the Seas* brought honor to their builder. The *Glory of the Seas*, was one of his crowning achievements — a vessel that would bring undying fame and honor to McKay long after his death in four short years.[41]

Capt. Daniel McLaughlin accepted the coveted offer from J. Henry Sears & Company to command the fastest and most successful ship in their sailing fleet. He quickly made arrangements for his youngest child, fifteen-year-old Carl, to stay with relatives at Malden. The captain and Maggie then traveled overland by train, arriving at San Francisco during the first week of October 1876.[42]

CHAPTER IV

Glory of the Seas
at San Francisco

The San Francisco waterfront to which Captain Daniel and Margaret McLaughlin came in October 1876 was a far cry from the gold rush city of a quarter century before when he and his first wife Hannah arrived in the clipper *Gray Feather*. That first visit was just a few weeks after a fifth fire burned out a large portion of the city, leaving a blackened, burnt-out waterfront with only a small network of wharves remaining.

The T-shaped Cunningham's Wharf, near the foot of Vallejo Street where the *Gray Feather* was berthed, had been extended and replaced by a wooden structure over 600 feet long and seventy-five feet wide. Although a few gold rush buildings were still identifiable, much of the eastern waterfront had been bulkheaded and backfilled with rock and stone rubble to reclaim the area for streets, warehouses, and commercial structures. Some of the ramshackle commercial buildings of earlier periods were also replaced with imposing structures of brick and stone, but the majority of buildings on the east waterfront were still of wood construction.

Cable car lines were well-established on the major hills, and horse-drawn street railroads traversed most of the downtown area. If one counted the multicolored fish boats, barges, small fresh produce and hay schooners, sailing and steam coasters, deep-water square-rig sailing ships, and ocean-going steamships, there were well over 300 craft lying at the various wharves.

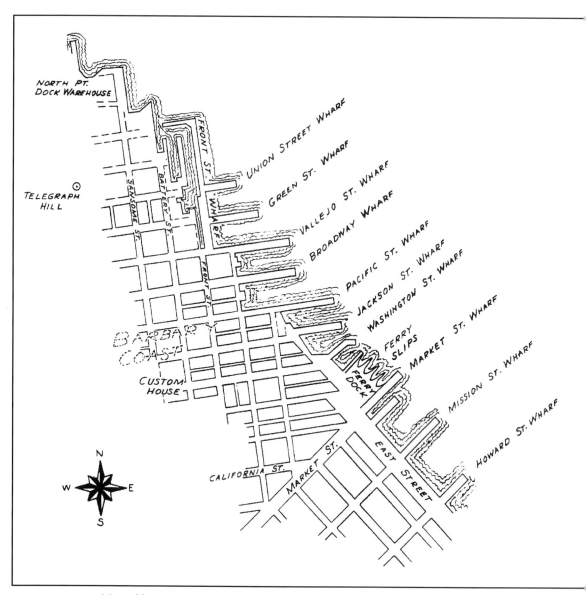

Map of San Francisco waterfront based on U.S. Coast Survey (NOAA) charts by the author, ca. 1875.

Although the Transcontinental Railroad imported a large number of passengers from the East beginning in 1869, the major mercantile activity at San Francisco still related to ocean-going, bay, and coastal water transportation. A wide variety of occupations was represented on the waterfront: stevedores, warehousemen, draymen, day laborers, shipping clerks, executives, and mariners, both coastal and deep-water. The region literally hummed with activity.[1]

Boasting a population of 270,000, many of whom were immigrants, San Francisco was the largest and busiest city on the West Coast of the United States. Although the infamous Barbary Coast section with its criminal element, sleazy merchants, and women of ill-repute was just as notorious as twenty-five years before, the city now contained a degree of more refined culture including museums, libraries, the beginnings of a major municipal park system and two large opera houses.

The *Glory of the Seas* arrived on August 23, 1876, completing a fine passage of 114 days from Liverpool. She was laden with 2,500 tons of steam coal for shipping merchants Rodgers, Meyer & Company.[2] Although her passage was not a record, she won that season's race from the British Isles by way of Cape Horn, beating a number of her competitors.

Showing the friendly, competitive spirit between ocean-going, first-class, squarerigger shipmasters of this period, one of the senior officers of the Boston ship *Triumphant* previously bragged in print that his ship would win the race to San Francisco from Liverpool.[3] To the chagrin of the money backers of the *Triumphant*, however, the *Glory of the Seas* beat her by six days.

Captain Knowles was publicly silent on the "race," other than briefly stating in his published memorandum in the *Daily Alta* that he had "passed ship *Triumphant* in lat[itude] 15º 46', lon[gitude]. 34º 42'W." Nothing more needed to be said because the latter vessel sailed the day before the *Glory* from Liverpool.[4]

On August 31st, a tug hauled the *Glory* alongside Front Street Wharf, situated just north of Union Street on the northeastern waterfront. There, stevedore gangs began unloading her cargo,

The ship America *at Front Street Wharf, San Francisco, ca. 1875. Courtesy San Francisco Maritime NHP, Fireman's Fund Collection.*

There, stevedore gangs began unloading her cargo, using the ship's cockbilled lower yards as booms to discharge wooden tub-loads of steam coal from her hold into portable hoppers located on the adjoining wharf. The coal was then slowly hauled off by large horse-drawn wagons to local storage yards.

A week later, the *Glory of the Seas* was joined at Front Street Wharf by the Boston ship *America,* a vessel nearly her size, which had just arrived with general cargo, 143 days from New York.[5]

Unloading the *Glory* quickly was not considered a priority by Captain Knowles or by Rodgers, Meyer & Company, her cargo consignees. She had not as yet been chartered for her next cargo, grain and still had 1,200 tons of coal aboard by the third week of September, a month after her arrival.

Captain Knowles, acting on behalf of J. Henry Sears & Company, finally received a grain charter for the *Glory of the Seas* during the last week of September. Her charterers were the Grangers Warehousing and Business Association of Contra Costa County; her freight rate was fifty-seven shillings, six pence per long ton ($13.88).[6] This was slightly above the average price received by vessels during the 1876-1877 grain year which ran from July 1, 1876, to June 30, 1877.

The Grangers Warehousing and Business Association had recently completed two warehouses of 8,900-ton capacity as well as a wooden wharf at Martinez on Carquinez Strait, situated at the eastern edge of San Pablo Bay. The wharf was connected by tramway to the warehouses, which permitted convenient loading of grain ships.[7]

The first grain vessel to load at Martinez was the ship *St. Charles* which arrived there on September 19th. Her crew was given "Freedom of the Town," as proclaimed by the town fathers.[8] Local shipping circles assumed that the *Glory of the Seas* would likewise load at Martinez. However, the charterers ultimately made the decision to load her at the Central Pacific Railroad Long Wharf at Oakland.[9] No doubt, the limited depth of the new loading facilities at Martinez was a factor, because the *Glory* was nearly double the *St. Charles'* tonnage and drew between four and five feet more than the latter craft when fully laden.

Figurehead of the Glory of the Seas, *July 22, 1900, San Francisco, Courtesy San Francisco Maritime NHP, Albert Gilberg Collection.*

By September 25th, the *America* had been hauled off Front Street Wharf to an anchorage to await her turn to load wheat. In the meantime, a gang of men thoroughly caulked the *Glory* on her upper decks and topsides. They were followed by local workmen who painted her sides with a fresh coat of black paint above her copper (yellow metal sheathing).[10]

Following their arrival at San Francisco, Captain McLaughlin and his wife were introduced to their new floating home — the *Glory of the Seas*. The McLaughlins first view of their new vessel showed her freshly painted and lying in ballast alongside Front Street Wharf with every line in order and yards squared to a "T," the dress-up position of an aristocratic, first-class squarerigger in port.

The captain especially appreciated the beautiful figurehead at the *Glory*'s prow, an unclad Grecian goddess, painted all in white with her right arm outstretched and her left holding flowing Grecian draperies between her breasts.

The ship drew only about thirteen feet of water, with twelve feet of copper sheathing showing above the water line. Her wooden yards were coated with linseed oil, and the lower masts were varnished except for six-inch wide, red lead-painted iron bands which held her "built" masts together. These lower masts on the *Glory of the Seas* were huge. For example, her lower main mast was forty-one inches in diameter and ninety-four feet from keelson to cap; the full height from keelson to main-skysail truck was 188 feet.[11]

The *Glory* was rigged for a suit of studdingsails on her fore and main. Thousands of square-rigged craft had been rigged in this manner, and full-bodied ships as well as smaller vessels set studdingsails. In the mid-1870s, this light-weather canvas was being eliminated by many American and foreign shipping companies. The sisters *Triumphant* and *America*, built in 1873 and 1874 respectively, had no studdingsails.

Captain Knowles and Captain McLaughlin, however, were "drivers" of the California gold rush clipper ship era. They favored the additional canvas and retained this rig on the *Glory*, at least for the present.

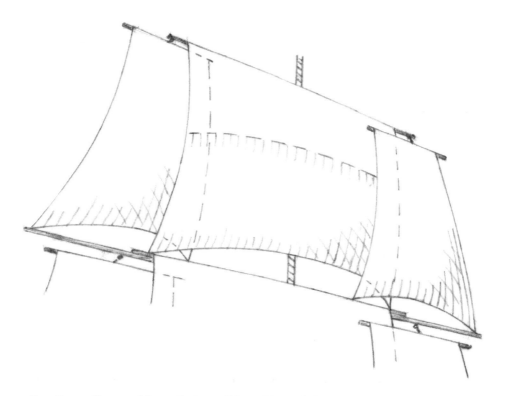

Set of topgallant studdingsails (stuns'ls) on Glory of the Seas. *Ship is on the wind with weather stuns'l abaft and lee stuns'l before the topgallant sail. Drawing by the author.*

The *Glory of the Seas* was also rigged with Manila hemp standing rigging. Her lower shrouds were especially huge with a diameter of over three inches[12] and were freshly coated with Stockholm tar. Later-built American vessels like the *Triumphant* and the *America* had standing rigging made of galvanized wire rope, a material which was becoming standard on many American sailing ships of the 1870s, not only because of its lower cost, but also because it had less tendency to stretch.[13]

In sharp contrast to the *Glory of the Seas* was the British ship *Seaforth*, a main skysail-yarder like the *Glory*, but nearly half her tonnage. Iron-hulled "lime-juicers" like the *Seaforth* were giving American vessels very stiff competition in the European grain trade. This ship's masts and yards were made of steel, and her standing rigging was wire rope. The British merchant marine generally viewed the *Seaforth* as the first ship to be fitted with metal spars,[14] one of many innovations which slowly but perceptibly led to worldwide British supremacy in the battle of wood construction versus iron. These continuing advancements led to the eventual demise of American sailing ships in the European grain trade. Shipbuilding was encouraged by political leaders in the United Kingdom where metal products were inexpensive. The cost of imported iron was prohibitive for building sailing ships on American soil. Because of the generally "no-growth" attitude prevailing in the U.S. political scene and the fact that wooden American ships received lower shipping rates, there was little chance that the average American full-rigger would make a reasonable profit in the grain trade in less than ten years.[15]

The *Seaforth*, formerly in the East Indian trade, was diverted to California to take advantage of the high rates for carrying wheat. She was one of the vessels beaten by the *Glory* in the race from England. She arrived at San Francisco the day after the *Glory of the Seas*, 148 days from Liverpool. A possible contributing factor to the *Seaforth*'s long run may have been a fouled bottom, because, before returning to Europe in October, 1876, her master had her hauled out and painted.

One of the disadvantages of iron hulls in this period of maritime history was the relative inefficiency of copper-based, antifouling paints applied to their underwater bodies. Within two years, marine growth on iron vessels could become, literally, a dense forest. In contrast, a wooden ship with a copper-sheathed bottom, according to insurance underwriters, did not have to be re-coppered for forty months, and its effectiveness, excluding damage to individual copper sheets, could last for five years and more.[16] The *Glory of the Seas'* record was a good example of the relative efficiency of copper sheathing on the bottom of a wooden-hulled vessel. She had not been hauled out for nearly three years.

In the 1870s, the major means of water transportation between San Francisco and the United Kingdom was vessels powered by sail alone. It was not economically feasible for steamships to haul grain to Europe from California due to the high cost of coal. Even though tramp steamers were not totally dependent on the winds, it still took them nearly four months to make the voyage from San Francisco to England via Cape Horn. During this era, deep-water steamers still carried auxiliary sail. Although steam conquered the Atlantic between Europe and America, as well as dominating the European and India trade via the Suez Canal, sail was still "queen" over the long haul grain trade from San Francisco. It would be another forty years before the Panama Canal opened, halving the distance between the North Atlantic and the North Pacific and making steam cost effective.[17]

Charter rates during the mid-1870s for grain ships varied measurably, especially due to the preferential treatment given by grain shippers to British iron ships over the American fleet, which were almost all of wood construction.[18] For example, although the rate for the *Glory of the Seas* was £2 17s 6d ($13.88) [in 1870 dollars] per long ton, both the *America* and the *Triumphant* were chartered for slightly more at £2 18s 0d ($14.09). The British ships *Borrowdale, The Douglas,* and *Seaforth,* (all chartered within several weeks of the American vessels), received rates of £3 2s 6d ($15.09). However, the California grain trade was one of the most profitable in the entire world still open to square-rigged sailing ships. Despite her lower rate, the owners of the *Glory of the Seas* would gross $42,103 [approximately $375,000 in 1990 dollars] in profits from her forthcoming voyage to Liverpool.[19]

The *Glory* (2,103 tons), the *America* (2,054 tons), and the *Triumphant* (2,046 tons) were larger than the average full-riggers of the 1870s. Most first-class American sailing ships were in the 1,200 to 1,500-ton range, but their British counterparts, on the average, were even smaller in tonnage. Of those regularly engaged in the wheat trade, the only vessels which were larger than the *Glory*, the *America*, and the *Triumphant* in the entire American merchant marine were the ex-steamship *Three Brothers*, the ex-steamship *Baltic*, and the J. Henry Sears-managed four-masted bark *Ocean King*—all wooden-hulled craft. However, larger ships were in the offing. Two 2,000-ton-plus down-Easters, newly built in 1876, the *Eureka* and the *Harvey Mills*, would enter the California grain trade the following year.

In 1876, the grain fleet loaded at a variety of wharves and piers on or near San Francisco Bay. The *America*, the *Seaforth*, and the American ship *Sterling* all loaded at the Starr Flouring Mills at South Vallejo, lying east of San Pablo Bay. The British iron ship *Blengfell* took on grain at San Francisco at the North Point Dock situated at the corner of Sansome and Chestnut Street. The *Triumphant* and the *Glory* — both chartered by the Grangers Warehousing — loaded at the Central Pacific Railroad Long Wharf. This two-mile-long wooden wharf, also called the Oakland Long Wharf, had been in operation since 1871 and represented the western terminus of the Transcontinental Railroad from which passengers went over to San Francisco.[20]

Following his arrival at San Francisco in October, Captain McLaughlin quickly attended to hiring additional afterguard; this was because all of Captain Knowles' officers quit the ship following his decision to leave the sea. The only crew the *Glory of the Seas* had on board was a chief mate, a carpenter, and a steward, all of whom joined the ship on September 14th.

Every captain had his own opinion as to how many crew were needed to properly handle a vessel. The mix McLaughlin preferred was slightly different from that of Captain Knowles.

McLaughlin's full complement on the *Herald of the Morning*, a ship nearly half the tonnage of the *Glory*, was only twenty-one beside the captain and his wife.[21] In contrast, on Knowles's final voyage from Liverpool, he had a crew of thirty-four besides himself, including eighteen able-bodied seamen, four ordinary seamen, four ship's boys, and eight in the afterguard.[22]

Captain McLaughlin's crew would ultimately be thirty-two plus himself. He would ship twenty able-bodied seamen, four ordinary seamen, and no ship's boys. This group of two dozen men, commonly termed "shipping before the mast," the "foremast hands" or the "foremast crowd," would join the ship just before sailing.[23] The absence of ship's boys on this initial voyage in the *Glory* showed McLaughlin's unwillingness to ship youngsters with no sea experience. He apparently equated the work experience level of two ordinary seamen with four ship's boys based on the eventual complement of thirty-three men.

By the third week of October 1876, a boatswain, two carpenters, a second steward, a cook, and a second and third mate had been hired for the *Glory of the Seas*. The most experienced man on board besides the captain was his chief mate, Thomas N. Rogers, a thirty-six-year-old down-Easter, who in a few years would be given his own command.

To obtain a high quality afterguard wasn't much of a problem for Captain McLaughlin. His reputation, as well as the *Glory*'s under Captain Knowles, followed her. This was considered important to the deep-water sailor.

Chief mates customarily were paid from $60 to $70 per month in the 1870s, and the ship's cook made $45. A first-class sailing ship captain's monthly wages were about $175. In addition, he also received primage, a gratuity customarily given to captains which was a small percentage of the gross freight profits.[24]

The *Glory of the Seas* began loading at Oakland Long Wharf on October 13, 1876. Five days later she had a full cargo on board consisting of 67,996 centals of wheat (3,035 long tons) valued at $116,241. This meant that one 100-pound sack of wheat (a cental) was valued at $1.71.[25] Everyone along the commercial production and servicing line from farmer, to shipper, and then to sailing ship made a reasonable profit in the grain trade this year. For instance, the *St. Charles'* cargo of 1,800 tons had been purchased from the farmers at $1.47-1/2 per cental.[26]

It cost about sixty cents to haul one sack of grain to the British Isles via the *Glory of the Seas*. The *Contra Costa Gazette* briefly reported on the general satisfaction of all involved in the grain-shipping chain:

> The ship *Glory of the Seas*, over two thousand tons register, char-tered by the Grangers' Business Association for shipment of wheat to Liverpool on Farmers' account has completed her cargo, which em-braces some two or three hundred tons belonging to farmers of our county and district, who are likely, with the advance of the market and prospects of further rise, to do well with their venture.[27]

During that part of the 1876-1877 grain year from July 1, 1876, to the end of October, the *Glory of the Seas* had the distinc-tion of loading the largest cargo to date on San Francisco Bay. Before the end of the grain year — June 30, 1877 — ninety-four American ships and 213 vessels of other nations would haul grain from San Francisco to Europe at an average freight rate of 52 shil-lings, six pence ($12.66) per long ton.[28]

Captain Daniel McLaughlin now busied himself provision-ing the *Glory of the Seas* for her coming voyage.

CHAPTER V
Dead Horse and Blood Money

By mid-October 1876, Captain Daniel McLaughlin had made changes in the appearance of the *Glory of the Seas*— changes which definitely showed a new master was in charge.

One of the most noticeable modifications was the change in her stable, located on the main deck in the after part of her fifty-three-foot-long forward house. Captain Knowles customarily carried several head of cattle for his long voyages. These provided fresh milk and butter for the afterguard and the captain's wife and three young children.

Although Knowles' family didn't accompany him on his last voyage from Liverpool, the stable housed two Alderney cows and a calf direct from Queen Victoria's farm at Windsor, England. Shortly after arrival at San Francisco, Knowles sold them at a good profit.[1]

Although the *Glory of the Seas* would no longer haul cattle, Captain McLaughlin planned on taking a few chickens (customarily carried on long sailing ship voyages to provide fresh eggs), pigs to provide fresh pork, and perhaps a nanny goat for fresh milk.

The other obvious changes were in the paint scheme. The hulls of most American deep sea sailing vessels of this period were painted black with white deck houses. Each captain, however, had his own opinion as to what color scheme should be used on deck furniture and other items, such as iron work.

Deck view of the Glory of the Seas *facing aft at Howard Street Wharf, San Francisco. ca. 1895. Capt. Knowles is farthest to the left. Courtesy of the author. Robert W. Weinstein Collection.*

Although the lower masts on the *Glory* were still brightly varnished, McLaughlin followed the custom of many shipmasters in having the "chapels" (notched grooves) in her built masts painted white.[2] In addition, he painted a white strip, three feet in width, just above her copper, and a six-inch-wide band of white along the line of her plank-sheer. The iron mast hoops remained red, but a large, double-acting capstan on her fo'c'sle-head, and the deck capstan, situated just forward of her mizzen hatch, were painted red. McLaughlin retained the rich red color that Captain Knowles used on the *Glory*'s large main pump wheels amidships. The deck houses remained white as did the insides of the bulwarks, while the waterways were blue. McLaughlin also made sure that the decks were freshly holystoned with all caulking in the seams well attended to. Now, the ship looked almost new.[3]

Obtaining able and ordinary seamen for the coming voyage was entirely different than hiring an afterguard. McLaughlin, as master of the *Glory*, and Captain Knowles, now acting as agent for J. Henry Sears, were at the mercy of the San Francisco boardinghouse landlord and shipping master system, an organization of extortioners who had robbed ship and seamen alike since California gold rush days.

In 1872, the "Shipping Commissioner's Act" established an official means of shipping and discharging American seamen engaged in trade on U.S. merchant ships at all domestic ports. Initially, this broke the power of the boardinghouse masters and shipping masters in San Francisco. In short order, however, they regained their power by continuing to levy so-called employment service fees against both seaman and ships.

The sailor on a deep-water sailing ship going to a foreign port was required by his boardinghouse master or landlord to pay an advance from future wages, termed "deadhorse" by sailors. This supposedly paid back the landlord the costs of housing and entertaining the sailor for the days or months he was ashore.

Until 1875, San Francisco's boardinghouse or shipping masters also levied a bounty or employment fee on ship captains. Commonly called "blood money," this fee was, in effect, the price

Deck view of the Glory of the Seas *facing forward at Howard Street Wharf, San Francisco, ca. 1895. The young man standing on the midship (boy's) house is unidentified. Courtesy of the author. Robert W. Weinstein Collection.*

paid for putting a sailor on board. Few seemed to care that the seaman was often shanghaied — that is, put on board without his full consent.[4]

In 1876, shanghaiing, dead horse, and blood money were still in vogue at most American ports. Although McLaughlin didn't pay blood money for his twenty-four foremast hands, they were extorted beyond reason. Able-bodied seamen paid a lump $60 (dead horse) from their future wages which would eventually be worked off at the rate of $25 per month. Dead horse was advanced by McLaughlin to twelve boardinghouse masters before he got his crew.[5]

The first set of crew shipping papers for this voyage were drawn up on Thursday, October 19, 1876, at the office of the U.S. Shipping Commissioner. The primary form, the Official Shipping Articles, was one single sheet, twenty-three by thirty-one inches, which contained the terms of employment, subject to U.S. Maritime law, between captain and crew. It necessitated obtaining name (or alias) of each seamen, his place of birth, and country of which he was a citizen. Also included were age, height, complexion, and color of hair.[6]

Although the information regarding the afterguard was easily obtained because this segment of the crew shipped voluntarily and had already made an appearance at the Shipping Commissioner's Office, it was a different matter with foremast hands. Although they, too, made an appearance, the boardinghouse landlord, one of his runners, or a shipping master accompanied the sailors to insure cooperation — especially since the crew members were shipping under a certain amount of duress, whether by threats and intimidation, or by the more treacherous shanghai system commonly used at San Francisco.

Boardinghouse masters customarily recruited sailors who had been at their establishment the longest, thereby running up their bill for lodging. This often meant getting the sailor half-drunk, perhaps doping him, and telling him that he was going to sea in the next few days. He was eventually delivered to the vessel half-sober or carried on board stone drunk and sometimes unconscious. The seaman was then dropped unceremoniously on deck with a donkey's breakfast (straw mattress), the clothes on his back, and his sailor's bag. This was shanghaiing. Sometimes, a qualified sailor couldn't be found and, to fill his quota, the boarding house master doped an unsuspecting landlubber and passed him off as an experienced hand. Once he awoke on board and found himself at sea, he learned how to be a sailor — this was also called shanghaiing.[7]

The Shipping Articles listed the names of those who were actually paid the advance. Some of these persons were notorious boardinghouse masters, most of whom were located on the waterfront in the vicinity of the infamous Barbary Coast. Alex Jackson provided one sailor for the *Glory*. Joseph Franklin (Columbia House) provided five men; and Shanghai Henry Brown (Scandinavian House), C.E. Peterson, and P. McMahon (New York and Brooklyn House) each provided a sailor. Tommy Chandler (Mariner's Home) made two hands available, and E.C. Lewis provided the largest number — six seamen.[8]

Twelve of the crew were listed on the Shipping Articles as already being "on board," and of that number, the mate, carpenter, and two sailors, didn't pay an advance to a boardinghouse.[9]

The life of a deep-water sailing ship hand of the mid-1870s was far from glamorous. In fact, it was much like being a U.S. Navy sailor of the period, except there was no standard issue, uniform clothing worn by the merchant seaman.[10]

When the foremast crew on the *Glory of the Seas* signed the official Shipping Articles on October 19, 1876, it was similar to enlisting for a prescribed period. The articles read as follows:

> It is agreed between the Master and Seaman or Mariners of the ship *Glory of the Seas* of Boston, whereof D. McLaughlin is at present Master, or whoever shall go for master, now bound for Liverpool; thence to such other foreign ports as the master may direct and return to a final port of discharge in the U.S. Voyage not to exceed 24 calendar months . . .

And in bold print:

NO SHEATH KNIVES OR PROFANE LANGUAGE ALLOWED
ON BOARD. NO GROG ALLOWED AND NONE TO BE PUT ON
BOARD BY THE CREW.

Then in smaller print, the contractual agreement went on:

> and the said crew agree to conduct themselves in an orderly, faith-
> ful, honest, and sober manner, and to be at all times diligent in their
> respective duties, and to be obedient to the lawful commands of the
> said master . . . and not to neglect or refuse doing their duty by day or
> night . . . [Punishments are as follows:] for desertion he shall be liable
> to imprisonment for any period not exceeding three months . . . for
> continued willful disobedience to lawful commands, or continued will-
> ful neglect of duty, he shall be liable to imprisonment for any period
> not exceeding six months;
>
> IN WITNESS THEREOF, the said parties have subscribed their
> names hereto on the days against their respective signatures. Signed
> by [signature] Danl McLaughlin, Master, on the 19th day of October,
> eighteen hundred and seventy-six.[11]

Whether it was factually true or not, the entire crew signed
an acknowledgment that they

> had read the foregoing instrument, [Shipping Articles] who each
> for himself Acknowledged to me [Deputy Shipping Commissioner]
> that he had read, or had heard read . . . and that while sober and not
> in a state of intoxication, he signed freely and voluntarily . . .[12]

The seamen had prescribed duties as specified in the navigation laws of the United States, and they had to obey all orders
(within the limits of maritime law) of the officers without question. Unlike the military, however, there was very little *esprit de
corps* on a merchant ship, and it was a rarity for foremast sailors to
develop any type of loyalty to a specific ship as would a U.S. Navy
sailor.[13]

Fourteen crew members, including the third mate, were
instructed (on the Shipping Articles) to report on board ship at

11 a.m., on Monday, October 23rd; four of the crew to report at 2 p.m. that day; and the balance of the crew were to report on board at 11 a.m. on sailing day, October 24th.

As the *Glory of the Seas* lay at anchor off the eastern waterfront, her remaining crew were transported out to the ship by Whitehall boat. On coming on board, either conscious or unconscious, the foremast crowd were introduced to their sleeping quarters for the next three and one-half months. These quarters, sometimes called the ship's forecastle or fo'c'sle, were in the forward end of the deck house located just abaft the foremast. The forecastle contained room for twenty-four men and was divided into two rooms, each eight-and-one-half feet wide and twenty-three feet long, separated by a fore-and-aft bulkhead which created a natural port and starboard watch for the crew. There were double-tier wooden bunks within each room and every bed was a standard size, two feet wide by six feet long. The only other pieces of furniture were two wooden benches down the center and a kerosene lamp hanging overhead. There the sailor ate his meal or smoked his pipe. Considering that the crew would be both sleeping and eating in this cramped space, the sparsely furnished fo'c'sle on the *Glory* could be likened to a floating barracks.[14]

The ship's crew was truly multinational. Only ten were U.S. citizens while fourteen were subjects of Queen Victoria. The remainder were Scandinavian and West European. There was also one Russian able-bodied seaman. The oldest man on board was Captain McLaughlin. The average age of the fo'c'sle crowd was twenty-seven, with the youngest crew member a seventeen-year-old ordinary seaman.[15]

In the year 1876, the average-sized American man was only five feet-six inches, and the average European was even shorter. This wasn't the case with Captain McLaughlin's first crew in the *Glory of the Seas.* The average height was five feet-eight inches, and the tallest man was six feet. The shortest, a nineteen-year-old ordinary seaman, was five feet-five inches tall.[16]

During the latter part of October, numerous sailing ships departed laden with grain bound for Liverpool and other United

British iron ship Brodick Castle *at anchor on San Francisco Bay, loaded with grain and ready to sail, ca. 1880. Courtesy San Francisco Maritime NHP, Fireman's Fund Collection.*

British ship Seaforth *under sail. Courtesy of the author.*

Kingdom ports. The *America* sailed on October 14th, and the *Sterling* sailed the following day.

On Friday, October 10th, a tug towed the *Glory* back to San Francisco from Oakland, and final stores were brought on board. On that day the British iron ship *Blengfell* and the *Triumphant* sailed for Liverpool. A number of other ships were nearly loaded with wheat and preparing to sail, among them the British iron ships *Brodick Castle, Seaforth,* and *The Douglas.*

The *Glory of the Seas* lay peacefully at anchor on October 23, 1876, the night before sailing day. Although he didn't publicly advertise it, McLaughlin quietly hoped to make the fastest run of every ship sailing to Liverpool that month. Would a ship of wood construction or iron win? Would a ship outfitted with studding-sails win or one without? Would the ship with the largest regular sail capacity win? Although they didn't have stuns'ls, both the *America* and the *Triumphant* were three skysail-yarders to the *Glory*'s single skysail on her main. The *Seaforth* and the *Brodick Castle* were the only British ships crossing a skysail.[17] Few if any of the British ships engaged in the race this month of October were rigged with stuns'ls. This was because of the general trend, especially among British shipping companies, to dispense with these light-weather sails. Ultimately it would be a combination of skill and good weather conditions that determined the outcome of the race.

Such was the anticipation of Captain McLaughlin on the night before sailing from San Francisco for the United Kingdom.

I, _D. McLaughlin_ .... Master of the said

Ship Glory of the Seas ...., do solemnly, sincerely, and truly

Swear .... that the within List contains the names of all the Crew of the said

Ship Glory of the Seas. ...., together with the places of their

birth and residence, as far as I can ascertain the same. _Danl McLaughlin_

Port of _San Francisco_

Sworn to and subscribed this ...... _24_ day of ...... _Oct_ ...... , 1876,

before me,

E Burke

.... Collector.

I do certify that the within is a true copy of the List of the Crew of the

Ship Glory of the Seas , of _Boston_

whereof ...... _D. McLaughlin_ ...... is Master, taken from the original

on file in this office.

Given under my hand and seal of office, at the Custom House,

this ...... _24_ day of ...... _Oct_ ...... in the year of our

Lord one thousand eight hundred and seventy- _six_

E Burke

.... Collector.

Certification of crew list by Daniel McLaughlin for Glory of the Seas, San Francisco, October 24, 1876, Courtesy National Archives and Records Administration, Washington D.C. San Francisco Custom House District.

CHAPTER VI
A Record Passage

Captain McLaughlin steered a westerly course to take the *Glory of the Seas* about 300 miles off shore. Prevailing fall winds and currents enabled her to make a good southing as she headed for the equator. Crossing the Line at about longitude 120° west, she steadily progressed into the South Pacific, passing eastward of Pitcairn Island. With a good press of sail, she steered a southeasterly course for Cape Horn.

While the northern hemisphere endured the extremes of winter, the *Glory of the Seas* rounded the Horn in December, midsummer for the southern hemisphere, when gales are at a minimum. With favorable winds and easterly-setting ocean currents near the Cape, Captain McLaughlin easily rounded the Horn. He then set his easterly course about eighty miles south of the Horn, approximately twenty miles north of the generally accepted course of vessels beating westward into the Pacific.[1]

Being the only woman on board, Margaret McLaughlin had to endure loneliness and monotony on a three-to-four month voyage. Other than an occasional word of greeting or acknowledgement to a sailor on duty at the wheel, hers was a "seen and not heard" existence as far as the foremast crew were concerned. By tradition Maggie's conversations were generally

The Glory of the Seas *off the Welsh Coast, ca. 1875. Oil painting by Charles J. Waldron, Liverpool Artist. Courtesy of the author.*

limited to the deck officers, stewards and petty officers such as the cook and carpenter.

The after cabin was viewed as the private quarters of Capt. and Mrs. McLaughlin (unless passengers were carried). Margaret McLaughlin followed the practice of other master's wives of first class Cape Horners in decorating it much like a home ashore. Her living space was the after half of the twenty-four by forty-five foot after house. This area consisted of two sleeping cabins, the captain's office (chart room), a full bath and a main living room. The latter, also called a "social hall," was beautifully paneled in combinations of mahogany, walnut and birds-eye maple. The social hall featured throw rugs on the deck, stuffed chairs (screwed to the deck), small bureaus covered with lace and ornately framed pictures on the cabin walls.

Margaret McLaughlin and the captain customarily took their meals with Chief Mate Rogers when it didn't conflict with the mate's watch duties. Starting at about seven a.m. the captain and his wife entered the dining area, called "dining saloon," just forward of the after cabin and were seated at the table by the ship's two stewards. By tradition, Capt. Daniel McLaughlin sat at the head, his wife, as a "guest" at his right, and Mate Rogers at his left. For breakfast they were attended to by Chief Steward Frank Chappell and his assistant, John Stewart, who served the various courses on the *Glory*'s unique dining table. Although the table edge was slightly raised to limit sliding of dishes in rough weather, which was common on deep water craft, it was unusual in that it was built around the ship's thirty-five-inch diameter mizzen mast. This dining saloon area was the steward's domain and Maggie's participation in the meals was limited other than helping plan some of the menus.

Ever careful of her place as wife of the captain, Margaret McLaughlin had to be above reproach in the eyes of the crew. Much of her days at sea were spent in the ship's after cabin (social Hall). Not having specific shipboard duties other than caring for her and her husband's clothing, keeping their bed made, cabin neat, clean and dusted, she had time for knitting, crocheting, reading and writing letters to family and friends. Depending on

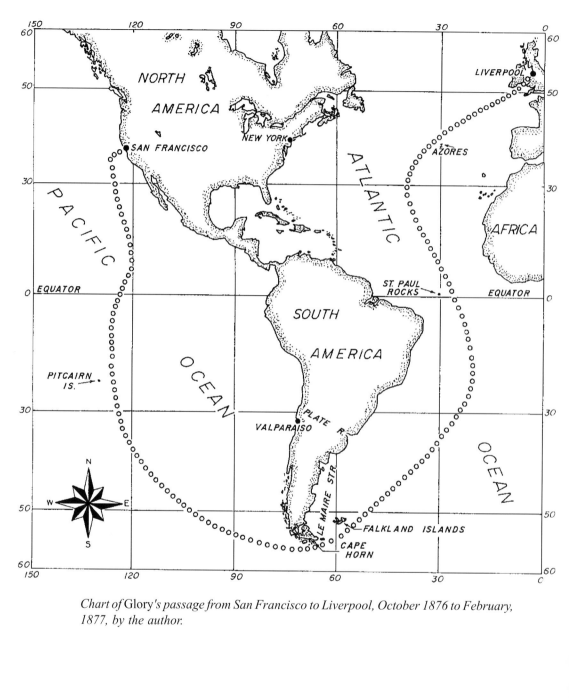

Chart of Glory's *passage from San Francisco to Liverpool, October 1876 to February, 1877, by the author.*

weather conditions she could break her day up by walks on the quarter deck or after cabin top as long as it didn't interfere with the work of the crew. When a ship, an unusual landmark, or possibly a school of whales was sighted, Capt. McLaughlin made sure that she was informed so she could come on deck. She well understoood and respected the fact that at any time, twenty-four hours of the day, her husband could be called on deck to attend to the ship. In the eyes of the crew Margaret McLaughlin was a good complement to their captain.

From the Horn, the *Glory of the Seas* passed eastward of the Falkland Islands and stayed generally mid-ocean. She made good progress as she sped northerly with the southeast trade winds toward the equator in the Atlantic, which was crossed at about longitude 25° west. From the Line, the *Glory* passed eastward of St. Paul Rocks and headed northerly, passing westward of the Azores as she made for St. George's Channel separating Great Britain from Ireland.

McLaughlin arrived at Liverpool on the morning of February 5, 1877, his 14,000-odd mile passage from San Francisco taking only 104 days. This voyage would prove to be the fastest eastward Cape Horn passage in the entire career of the *Glory of the Seas*.[2]

Compared with other vessels sailing to Liverpool from San Francisco in October 1876, the *Glory* was the fastest by a considerable margin. Not one ship came close to her speed of passage. Both the *Seaforth* and the *Brodick Castle*, which sailed on the day following the *Glory*, arrived twenty-seven days after her, and the British iron ships *Blengfell* and *The Douglas*, made passages of 135 and 130 days, respectively.

Of the six American vessels sailing in October, the only ship arriving before the *Glory* was the down-Easter *H.S. Gregory*, who sailed twenty days before the *Glory of the Seas*, for a total passage of 118 days. Both the Thayer and Lincoln-managed sister ships *America* and *Triumphant* were likewise beaten this trip. Captain Andrew Emerson in the *America* sailed ten days before the *Glory* and arrived at Liverpool the day after her, while the *Triumphant*,

Table 1 — Liverpool Departures from San Francisco, October, 1876

Date of Sailing	Flag	Name of Ship	Master	Gross Tonnage	Date of Arrival	Number of Days
Oct. 1	Am	*Louisiana*	Oliver	1,436	Feb. 10	132
Oct. 4	Am	*H.S. Gregory*	Anderson	1,653	Jan. 30	118
Oct. 14	Am	*America*	Emerson	2,054	Feb. 6	115
Oct. 15	Am	*Sterling*	Baker	1,732	Feb. 10	118
Oct. 21	Br	*Blengfell*	McCulloch	1,210	Mar. 5	135
Oct. 21	Am	*Triumphant*	Libbey	2,046	Feb. 15	117
Oct. 24	Am	*Glory of the Seas*	McLaughlin	2,103	Feb. 5	104
Oct. 25	Br	*Seaforth*	Woodward	1,190	Mar. 4	130
Oct. 25	Br	*Brodick Castle*	Thyne	1,785	Mar. 4	130
Oct. 26	Br	*The Douglas*	Wilson	1,428	Feb. 11	130

under command of Captain John B. Libbey, made a 117-day passage, sailing three days before the *Glory* and arriving ten days after her.

Comparing British iron against American wood, the U.S.-flag ships made a better showing than their British counterparts, with the exception of the down-Easter *Louisiana.* This vessel arrived five days after Glory, 132 days from San Francisco.

Table 1 provides a comparison of ships departing San Francisco for Liverpool in October 1876:[3]

Shortly after her arrival at Liverpool Bay, the *Glory of the Seas* was taken in tow by a steam sidewheel tug, which took her across the bar of the River Mersey at flood tide, up to Birkenhead on the west side of the river channel, through the East Float Dock gate and berthed her alongside a stone quay on the northern side. Adjacent to the quay was the Corn Warehouse, a multi-story, stone building which would receive the *Glory*'s 3,000-odd tons of grain cargo.

Within the confines of the River Mersey of the 1870s was a large variety of craft, most of which were powered by sail alone. Ranging from stately square-rigged sailing ships in ocean-going trade, ocean steamships, and coasting steamers, down to the hundreds of sailing barges, commonly called flats, there was a

CONSULATE OF THE
UNITED STATES OF AMERICA,
LIVERPOOL.

I _Lucius Fairchild_ Consul of the **United States of America for Liverpool and the Dependencies thereof**, do hereby make known and certify unto all whom it may concern, that on the day of the date hereof, personally appeared and came before me _J. McLaughlin_ Master of the _Glory of the Seas_ of _Boston_, and declared that all the officers and men of the Crew of the said vessel, who sailed in and with her on her last voyage from _San Francisco deserted at this Port as certified except Thos. N. Rogers, Jos. Tuetnel, Wm Sloman, J. Mathers, And Wilson, Frank Chappell, N. J. Williams, Walter Edwards, J. W. Lamy, Harry C. Hipple, and W. White, who are on board and Fred Thornton, Jas McTreat and John Ker who were discharged as certified_ and that he has shipped at Liverpool, to proceed on a voyage to _San Francisco_

Top and bottom, of ship's articles giving Capt. McLaughlin's statement as to desertion of crew members, those who did not desert and those signed on in Liverpool for the return voyage to San Francisco. At lower left can be seen part of the Consul's seal. Courtesy National Archives and Records Administration, Washington, D.C., San Francisco Custom House District.

Name	Country				Age				
H. Watson		3	0	0	38	5	—	9	
John Morris	Italy	3	0	0	31	5	—	9	
Paul Savy	Boston	3	0	0	34	5	—	8	
George Taylor	United States	3	0	0	23	5	—	9	
Francis Trainer	Do	3	0	0	23	5	—	9	
T. Sehs	Germany	3	0	0	27	5	—	8	
C. King	Holland	3	0	0	27	5	—	8	
Rich; Bennett	Baltimore	3	0	0	42	5	—	9	
John Pederson	Sweden	3	0	0	34	5	—	9	
George Brenner	N York	3	0	0	37	5	—	10	
Samuel Leven	France	3	0	0	32	5	—	9	
Thoms Guillon	France	3	0	0	25	5	—	10	
Louis Alex.	France	2	10	0	18	5	—	9	
George Eldridge	United States	2	10	0	20	5	—	8	

I also certify that said Master having produced to me his clearance, I have returned to him the papers of said vessel.

In testimony whereof, I have hereunto set my hand and affixed the Seal of the Consulate of the United States at LIVERPOOL aforesaid, this 29 day of March, in the Year of our Lord One Thousand Eight Hundred and Seventy 4 and in the Year of the Independence of the said United States.

Lucius Fairchild
U. S. Consul.

constant hustle and bustle of incoming and outgoing harbor traffic. This high level of activity peaked at flood tide when the great dock gates opened allowing vessels to enter and depart the dozens of wet docks on both sides of the river.[4]

On the day of the *Glory of the Seas'* arrival at Birkenhead, McLaughlin granted the crew shore leave and gave them an advance on their earned wages. Nineteen of their number, however, had something else in mind when they received their advance — desertion. This was a crime under American and British law, but rarely enforced in large foreign ports like Liverpool. In the eyes of U.S. lawmakers, to desert a merchant ship was technically as serious as if a man deserted the Army or Navy in peacetime. Desertion warranted a jail sentence if the man were caught — that is, if a captain had the time and inclination to force the issue.

Nevertheless, by midnight Monday, February 5, 1877, all nineteen foremast hands, along with their meager possessions, had been assisted ashore by boardinghouse runners who convinced the sailors that the delights of their particular establishments were far better than the drab, crowded quarters on the *Glory of the Seas.* The men left with no intention of returning and Captain McLaughlin was powerless to prevent it. The boardinghouse landlords and shipping masters at Liverpool were a law unto themselves and desertion was winked at by local government authorities. Moreover, making too much of an issue of his crew's desertion would have affected McLaughlin's ability to acquire a new crew.[5]

When deep-water sailing ship sailors were not attached to a specific vessel, they roomed in the local Sailortown, a ghetto-like slum area of boarding houses, pubs, and houses of ill-repute. One of the streets in Liverpool immortalized in the sea chanty "Blow the Man Down" relates to Paradise Street, a Sailortown street located two blocks from the Liverpool Custom House.[6] The familiar chanty begins: "When I was a-walking down Paradise Street. To my way, hey, Blow the Man Down!"

In Liverpool's Sailortown, the nineteen deserters were temporarily housed and entertained. Under the autocratic authority of the Liverpool boardinghouse landlords and their runners, the

Glory of the Seas *off Holyhead departing Liverpool on July 1, 1873. Water color painting by Mark H. Myers. Courtesy Mark H. Myers, Bude, Cornwall, England.*

counterparts of the Barbary Coast landlords at San Francisco, the deserter would be housed for a week or more and treated to wine, women, and song until he wore out his welcome, spent his meager funds, and incurred exorbitant debts to the boardinghouse master. Then the enterprising landlord shanghaied the sailor on some outgoing deep-water ship, perhaps heading back to San Francisco or a far eastern port. Of course, this was after the landlord extracted a dead horse advance from the new ship for the sailor's future wages — a never-ending, vicious cycle.

For the most part, these deep-water sailing ship men were seagoing wanderers and vagabonds. The only ones who ever amounted to anything or lived to an advanced age were those who rose to petty officer — boatswain, carpenter, sailmaker, or donkey man — or became deck officers; or completely left the sea.[7]

Most of the deserters left owing the *Glory of the Seas* money; an average of $8 based on their purchases of clothing, shoes, tobacco, etc., from the slop chest, the ship's seagoing general store, during their three month, twelve day passage. One extreme example involved an A.B. who bought supplies amounting to $34.75 and ended up owing the *Glory* $20.24 — nearly one month's wages. These amounts, however, were a pittance compared to the $60 advance extorted by the boardinghouse landlords at San Francisco the previous October.[8]

Another weakness in the sailing ship employment system of this era was that, by long-standing custom, deep-water sailors were not encouraged to stay by a ship when they reached foreign ports such as Liverpool. Captain McLaughlin, however, treated his crew humanely, unlike many captains who inflicted cruel and sadistic treatment on their crews to coerce them to desert upon arrival in foreign ports — thus reducing wage costs.

Only three men asked to be officially discharged, although eleven crew members stood by the *Glory of the Seas* until she returned to San Francisco. Actually, it benefited the ship to have a small crew remain on board. Because sailors were not allowed to unload or load cargo at Liverpool the remaining foremast hands assisted the mates in preparing the *Glory* for the following month's departure. This involved taking down all her sails and repairing them; roving off new leachlines, buntlines and clewlines to replace those showing signs of wear, overhauling broken ratlines and replacing footropes.[9]

Captain McLaughlin went about acquiring a homeward cargo as a normal part of his responsibilities. The best he could do was a charter for English steam coal from the nearby Lancashire mines. American Cape Horners of this period rarely obtained profit-making cargoes from British ports. About the only alternative to steam coal was a cargo of salt or caustic soda. Although sailing ships couldn't make large profits hauling coal on a four-month voyage, it provided a means by which the ship could at least pay for the cost of crew and supplies.

Eventually local stevedores loaded the *Glory*'s cargo at the coaling berths at Birkenhead.

By Thursday, March 29th, seven weeks after her arrival, the *Glory of the Seas* was fully loaded with a return cargo of 2,774 tons of steam coal.[10] The captain arranged through the hiring services of one of the local boardinghouse landlords to supply him with twenty-one sailors, replacing the deserters and men who were discharged. The new crew signed on in front of the U.S. Consul at Liverpool, who alone had the authority to enlist the services of merchant seamen.

The new A.B.s were to be paid at the rate of £3 ($14.48) per month, the standard wage offered deep-water sailors at Liverpool in the mid-1870s — more than $10 less than their counterparts received at San Francisco. This illustrates another of the many inequities of the sailing ship wage systems of that era in which the sailor was always the loser.[11]

In mid-March 1877, the *Daily Alta California* announced in its daily "Along the Wharves" column that McLaughlin's *Glory of the Seas* and Libbey's *Triumphant* would have another race to San Francisco. As usual, it was assumed that a number of other vessels would be involved.[12]

The *Glory of the Seas* sailed from Liverpool on Sunday, April 1st, followed by the British iron ship *Pizarro* two days later. The *Triumphant* departed on April 4th. The ship *Frolic*, which beat the *Glory* by just a few hours on her first eastward Cape Horn voyage in 1870, was also in the San Francisco-bound fleet.[13]

Glory of the Seas *at anchor, San Francisco Bay, ca. 1877. Her name appears on the port gangway. Courtesy San Francisco Maritime NHP, Fireman's Fund Collection.*

The marine reporter for the *Alta* made a forecast in mid-July 1877:

> If we are not very much mistaken, the ship *Glory of the Seas* will be
> the next arrival from Liverpool. The British ship *Pizarro* sailed two
> days after her, and will do her best to beat the *Glory*, but we think the
> *Glory* will beat her time by a large majority.[14]

The following week, the paper stated that ". . . they were
[daily] looking for the arrival" of these ships;[15] however, no vessels
making port in the next few days indicated that the Cape Horn
fleet was even close to San Francisco. Then on August 5th, with
the arrival from New York of the clipper ship *Young America*, reput-
edly the fastest overall vessel in the California-Cape Horn trade, it
had to be acknowledged by the San Francisco maritime community that the so-called race from the British Isles was over for all
practical purposes. Bad sailing conditions had drastically slowed
down all the participants.

The *Young America* was consistently fast on almost all her
Cape Horn voyages since the early 1850s, averaging 120 days in
eighteen passages. This time, however, she was 136 days from New
York, one of the longest voyages in her career.[16] On arrival at San
Francisco her master, Captain E.C. Baker, complained of experi-
encing bad sailing weather throughout the voyage except for his
rounding of Cape Horn, generally considered the most difficult
segment of a sailing ship's westward passage. Thereafter, it had to
be accepted that the entire Liverpool fleet would be extremely
late — certainly no reflection on any captain or vessel.

Finally, more than a month after she was expected, the *Glory
of the Seas* arrived at San Francisco in the early morning hours on
Wednesday, August 23, 1877, completing a 144-day passage from
Liverpool, the longest trip of her career.

Just prior to her arrival, McLaughlin composed a very
lengthy summary of his passage for the "Memoranda" column of
the newspapers which was also an obvious apology to his shipping
community friends for such a disappointing voyage. This detailed

account appeared in the *San Francisco Daily Evening Bulletin* as follows:

> Per *Glory of the Seas*. Sailed from Liverpool April [1st]l; crossed
> the equator in the Atlantic May 4th, 23 days out; crossed 50 degrees
> south in the Atlantic, June 13th, 73 days out, and 50 degrees south in
> the Pacific, June 26th, 85 days out; crossed equator in Pacific July 22,
> 112 days out. After leaving Liverpool, had light southwest to westerly
> winds for two weeks; was one week getting clear of the Channel; in
> latitude 28 N., got light S.E. trades, which we carried to lat. 2 45 north;
> then calms and light airs for 7 days, to the Equator; crossed in lon. 28
> 35 W. Got slight SSE and SE trades, which we carried to 20 deg. south;
> then to 43 deg. S lon. 60 W., had nothing but bad weather. Wind nearly
> all the time from SW to W. with strong gales and high sea. Then, the
> wind hauled to north, and after passing the Horn to NW and WNW
> which carried us to 59 deg. S,. long. 77 35 W. where we took SW to
> westerly wind. On June 19th, lat. 58 deg. S, lon. 75 34 W, had a very
> heavy gale from WSW, which only lasted seven hours; barometer in
> the gale standing at 28.16, which is the lowest Captain McLaughlin
> ever saw it; after crossing 50 S. in Pacific got NW and N winds which
> carried the ship well in on the West Coast [of South America]. In lat.
> 15 S, lon. 88 W, took the SE trades and carried them up to lat. [17] N,
> lon. 116 W. Then, got light N to NE winds which lasted 21 days. For
> the last three days light West and Northwest winds. The only fast time
> made was from latitude 43 deg. [south] in the Atlantic to latitude 25
> deg. south in the Pacific (25 days). On the whole, the passage has been
> a tedious one, the longest that Captain McLaughlin or the *Glory of the
> Seas* ever made; saw a ship in [lat.] 35 N, [lon.] 137 W, saw two ships
> for San Francisco.[17]

Arriving with the *Glory of the Seas* on August 23rd were three
other full-riggers: the American ship *Samaria*, the British iron ship
Grasmere, both from Liverpool, and the American ship *Joseph S.
Spinney* from New York.

McLaughlin apparently felt a need to explain in detail why
the *Glory* took so long on her passage. Captain Charles E. Patten,
master of the 217-foot *Samaria* made his passage in 125 days —
nineteen days faster than the *Glory of the Seas*. McLaughlin's pride

Table 2 — Liverpool cargoes entered at San Francisco, August-September, 1877.

Arrival Date	Constr.	Name of Vessel	Gross Tonnage	Cargo
Aug. 23	wood	*Glory of the Seas*	2,103	2,774 tons coal
Aug. 23	iron	*Grasmere*	1,304	1,680 tons tin plate, etc., 603 tons pig iron; 414 tons coke.
Aug. 23	wood	*Samaria*	1,509	1,650 tons coal; 199 tons coke
Aug. 25	iron	*Pizarro*	1,439	6,150 sacks salt; 205 tons pig iron; etc.
Aug. 25	wood	*Carondolet*	1,438	1,800 tons coal
Aug. 26	iron	*Sydney Dacres*	1,386	2,502 sacks salt, etc.
Sep. 2	wood	*Frolic*	1,368	1,750 tons coal
Sep. 3	wood	*Triumphant*	2,046	2,371 tons coal, 142 tons coke

was piqued. He felt strongly that his as well as the *Glory*'s reputation was tarnished. Clipper ship captains like McLaughlin and Knowles had the reputation of being hard drivers. They never passed up the opportunity to race their vessels against other ships. This style was known around the world as "carrying sail New York fashion." Although his peers (and the insurance underwriters) recognized and respected the fact that Daniel McLaughlin didn't take unnecessary risks, they knew him as a captain who used his long experience in fighting strong winds to get him to his destination before his competitors.[18]

The *Grasmere* made a 148-day passage from Liverpool, and the *Pizarro* arrived on the evening of August 25th, 144 days out, which nearly tied the Glory's long passage. That same day the American ship *Carondolet*, also from Liverpool, dropped anchor at San Francisco, 155 days out. The following day another ship arrived, the British iron ship *Sydney Dacres* completing a 176-day passage from Liverpool.

The next ship arriving from a British port was the *Frolic* on September 2, 155 days out. The proud *Triumphant* limped in the following day, 151 days from Liverpool. Captain Libbey, however, had a definite excuse for being so long on his passage. Off Cape Horn on June 25th an unusually heavy sea struck the *Triumphant* which badly damaged her rigging and spars and seriously twisted her hull. Ultimately, this necessitated major repairs amounting to $33,000.[19]

From a practical standpoint, not one of the sailing vessels arriving the latter part of August and first part of September at San Francisco from the British Isles or Eastern United States, including the *Samaria*, made a really good passage. For the indomitable *Young America* to have made a 136-day run from New York well illustrated the fact that the weather was definitely adverse to all westward-bound Cape Horners during that summer of 1877.

From an economic standpoint the important thing was the cargo each vessel carried and the profit her owners made after deducting costs from their unusually long passages. Table 2 lists the cargoes from Liverpool which were entered at the San Francisco Custom House in late August and early September 1877.

Since ocean-going steamships were fueled solely by coal at this time, steamship as well as railroad companies in the Bay region were the prime parties interested in acquiring cargoes of English steam coal. *Glory*'s full cargo was offered for sale by the consignee, Ammon, Gaspari & Company. By the second week of September 1877, it had been sold to the Central Pacific for $6.67 per ton, for a total of $18,503.[20]

To illustrate the margin of gross profit Captain McLaughlin obtained in 1877: Captain Knowles purchased 1,506 tons of steam coal at Liverpool for the *Glory of the Seas* in 1872 for $5,020 ($3.33 per ton) and sold it on arrival at San Francisco through an agent for $13,269.50.[21] In the absence of the ship's actual payable/receivable account, if one based the 1877 profits on these earlier figures, McLaughlin netted between $8,000 and $9,000 on her voyage from Liverpool. This was not high enough to make any profit for a first-class ship the size of the *Glory* — crew costs alone

Ship Young America *under full sail, ca. 1875. Courtesy San Francisco Maritime NHP. Fireman's Fund Collection.*

amounting to nearly $6,000 (not including possible blood money fees paid at Liverpool).

Before McLaughlin discharged his crew on August 23, 1877, an officer of the U.S. Shipping Commissioner's office at San Francisco went aboard as the *Glory* lay at anchor, verifying that the official crew list issued by the U.S. Consul at Liverpool and the original shipping articles, supplemented with deletions due to discharges and desertion, still corresponded exactly. Following this confirmation, the government official wrote on the return crew list:

> I certify that I have examined the crew on board the Am[erican] ship Glory of the Seas from Liverpool, whereof, Daniel McLaughlin is master and find them to correspond with the annexed list.
>
> Samuel Dodd, Acting Boarding Officer.[22]

CHAPTER VII

The Second Round Voyage

Following her arrival at San Francisco the *Glory of the Seas* lay at anchor for a week while arrangements were made to unload her cargo of steam coal at the Oakland Long Wharf. On Thursday, August 30, a tug towed the *Glory* across the Bay and berthed her alongside one of the finger piers situated at the outer end of Oakland Harbor.

Besides being a major grain-loading facility, the Oakland Long Wharf was also a freight unloading area. Sailing ships commonly came alongside to discharge cargo. Here, the *Glory of the Seas* was berthed next to a spur track lined with shallow, gondola railroad cars. Once alongside, stevedores rigged her cockbilled lower yards as cargo booms to discharge the steam coal directly into the cars.[1]

Within two weeks, the ship was fully discharged. McLaughlin had her ballasted with eighty tons of copper ore and towed off to an anchorage just east of Goat Island (Yerba Buena), an area becoming a popular lay-up ground for disengaged deep-water squareriggers.

The *Glory* lay quietly at anchor off Goat Island until the end of September 1877 when Captain Knowles chartered her to Rodgers, Meyer & Co., one of the major shipping and commission merchants at San Francisco. Although the *Glory of the Seas* had been in port only five weeks, Captain Knowles was able to charter her much more rapidly than other American vessels.

In general, managing shipowners were reluctant to accept California grain charters during the 1877-1878 grain year. Freight offerings were very low for both American and British vessels. The *Glory*'s freight rate for grain was £1 15s ($8.51) which was considered unprofitable if grain was all she was going to haul.[2] World grain shippers had already acknowledged that the California wheat crop for the 1877-1878 grain year would be poor; it ultimately provided employment for only fifty American vessels and fifty-nine foreign bottoms, representing a sixty-five percent drop in tonnage from the previous year.[3]

A number of vessels loaded on "owners' account," and others, such as the iron ship *Blengfall*, sailed up the Pacific Coast to load at Portland or Astoria, Oregon. In doing so they obtained a substantially higher freight rate of £2 17s 6d ($13.15), although other vessels' owners accepted the low rates prevailing at San Francisco. For instance, the new down-Easter *Palestine*, chartered several days after the *Glory of the Seas*, received a rate of £1 17s 6d ($9.01), and the American ship *Wm. H. Marcy* chartered several days later, received £1 17s 0d ($8.99) per long ton.[4]

The major difference between these latter vessels and the *Glory* was that the bulk of their cargo would be wheat, whereas, the *Glory of the Seas* had over twenty-five percent of her cargo in items other than grain, commonly called general cargo. This was unusual for ships sailing out of San Francisco for Europe.[5] It was the most expensive cargo the *Glory* carried in her entire career.

On Friday, October 5, 1877, the *Glory* left her anchorage under tow and was berthed alongside the Union Street Wharf at San Francisco. For the following month she took on board additional grain which was topped off with general cargo. The *Glory of the Seas* would be one of the few fortunate vessels in this disastrous grain year to make a substantial profit.

While Capt. McLaughlin attended to ship's business, Margaret took part in a variety of activities. Captain's wives on deep water ships of this period customarily become close friends with each other. The long periods of isolation at sea (unless there were children aboard) and the lack of female company created a strong bond of empathy. Following her arrival at San Francisco, Margaret quickly made contact with other captains' wives and joined them in outings ashore. Maggie's shore activities usually involved carefully avoiding the Barbary Coast while taking the cable car system, horse-drawn waterfront trollies and/or other types of horse-drawn carriages to various cultural displays such as Golden Gate Park.

It was customary for first class sailing ship captains to entertain fellow shipmasters and their families. Since their first voyage together in the *Swallow* in 1868-1869, Daniel and Margaret McLaughlin had frequently invited friends and guests aboard ship in San Francisco. Now they had the opportunity to extend this hospitality on their new home, the *Glory of the Seas*. Shipping agents, including Capt. Knowles, reciprocated. It was common to have dinner invitations from fellow shipmasters or shipping associates ashore. The McLaughlins were a popular couple and well thought of in the local maritime community.

On Saturday, November 10th, the day her cargo manifest was filed at the Custom House, the *Glory* had the following items on board:[6]

Assayer Sweeps [unrefined ore], sacks,	84
Borax, centals,	1,027
Canned Beef, cases,	1,850
Canned Fruit, do.,	420
Cotton, Foreign, lbs.,	3,319
Dry Goods, cases,	8
Mustard Seed, centals,	395
Copper Ore, tons,	80
Personal Effects, pkg.,	6
Pearl Shells, cases,	136
Silver Plates,	1
Salmon, domestic, cases	9,245
Do. Foreign, do,	4,056
Wheat, cen.,	50,393
Orchilla [purple dye from lichens], bales,	649
Total Value	$242,665

On this voyage Daniel McLaughlin had even fewer American sailors on board than the previous year. Seven men, including the captain, his three mates, the boatswain, and two able-bodied seamen were the only non-Europeans on board. Thirteen men were British, and the balance of the crew was a mixture of Russian, Scandinavian and Asian. The articles were signed on November 10th at the Shipping Commissioner's office. At the time the Custom official noted that six of the crew were illiterate. Each of the six made his mark on the articles with an "X."[7]

Two of the men unable to read or write had positions of some responsibility on board — the ship's steward Ah On and the cook Ah Sing, both natives of China. Although apparently neither man knew anything about a food menu or how to read a recipe, Captain McLaughlin and Maggie felt they were qualified and competent. Unlike the foremast hands, these two had already gone through a trial period on board and proved their abilities. Their pay scale showed how important Ah On and Ah Sing were. The steward's monthly wage was almost double that of an able-bodied seaman, and the cook was paid at the rate of about $40 per month. Able-bodied seamen received only $25 per month.[8]

On Monday, November 12, 1877, the *Glory of the Seas* once more went to sea on an outgoing tide bound for Liverpool. She was followed two days later by the ship *Palestine*, Captain S.P. Emmons commanding, also bound for the British port. On November 15th, the American ship *Trojan* sailed for Liverpool, and two days later the British iron ship *Eller Bank* and the *Wm. H. Marcy* also departed San Francisco bound for the British Isles.

Three and one-half months later, on February 27, 1878, the *Glory of the Seas* arrived at Liverpool, 107 days from San Francisco. This year, the overall length of voyages of the grain fleet arriving at Liverpool was much closer than in the winter of 1877. Comparing elapsed voyage times for November 1877 sailings from San Francisco, the British iron ship *Eller Bank*, under Captain Lane, beat the *Glory*'s elapsed time by one day. The *Eller Bank* arrived at the British port on March 3, 1878, 106 days out. The *Palestine*'s passage was 115 days, while the *Wm. H. Marcy* made her run in 109 days. The only exception to these fine voyages was the down-Easter *Trojan* which made the longest passage of the fleet, arriving at Liverpool on April 5th, 141 days from San Francisco.[9]

Captain McLaughlin's stay at Liverpool was marred by the *Glory of the Seas'* collision with a River Mersey flat — a single-masted, shallow draft sailing barge — on Monday, March 4, four days after his arrival. As a tug towed the *Glory* into the East Waterloo Dock on the east side of the River Mersey, she collided with the flat *Invincible*. The *Glory* was only slightly damaged, but the *Invincible* emerged from the fracas with loss of her "mainboom gaff."[10]

Waterloo Dock was one of the major grain-handling areas on the east side of the Mersey but smaller than the general grain warehouse area at Birkenhead. The East Waterloo [wet] Dock consisted of two acres (an acre being 208.57 feet square) with a dock gate entrance sixty feet wide. It was no wonder that a ship 240 feet long and forty-four feet wide stood a good chance of colliding with another vessel in such a restricted area.[11]

The *Glory of the Seas* was berthed alongside the east face of the Waterloo Dock where the contents of her hold were discharged into the Waterloo Dock Corn Warehouse, a six-story stone building with round-headed windows, rusticated arches, and large cornices. This structure, with its lifting machinery and weighing machines, was considered state of the art in the 1870s.[12]

With automated unloading methods, even at this early date, about 100 tons of wheat were supposed to be discharged per hour from the *Glory of the Seas*. Complicating the unloading of sailing ships was the fact that each sack of grain (the *Glory* had over 50,000 on board) was slit by a stevedore while on board the craft, emptied into an elevator bin and automatically lifted into the adjoining warehouse for storage. Another factor which slowed down the unloading was the general rule respecting unloading priority which steamers had even at this early date. A steamer with bulk grain could come alongside, and the *Glory*, by the terms of her charter, had to make way temporarily for quick unloading of the steamer. Then the sailing ship would be warped back into her discharging berth and resume unloading. It ultimately took about eight days to unload the *Glory of the Seas'* grain.[13]

Following discharge of the remainder of her cargo, McLaughlin arranged to have the *Glory of the Seas* overhauled at Liverpool, where repair costs were generally less expensive than in the United States. She was re-coppered and re-rigged with wire rope replacing her Manila hemp standing rigging. Another decision was made at this time respecting her rig which ultimately affected her future sailing performance — removal of the studding-sail irons from her main and foremasts. This decision was made by the J. Henry Sears Company at Boston which was concerned with net profits, not speed. With general profit margins dropping in the California trade, less sail area meant lower labor and maintenance costs.

While the *Glory of the Seas* was on the overhaul berth, McLaughlin worked with local agents to obtain a return cargo. Consisting of 1,711 tons of steam coal, 517 tons of coke, 150 drums of caustic soda, 221 casks of bleaching powder, and fifty-eight casks of soda ash, it was much more diversified than the previous year's cargo. Despite the variety, the overall value was nearly the same as her previous year's coal. For cargo insurance and for purposes of setting a ceiling for U.S. Custom's import fees, McLaughlin placed the value at $18,000.[14]

Before sailing back to San Francisco, Captain McLaughlin dealt once again with the acquisition of a foremast crew. Once the *Glory* was made secure in the East Waterloo Dock, twenty-two men jumped ship, followed by two more several days later. Only one sailor asked to be discharged. The remaining crew, including the Chinese steward and cook, stood by the ship while she was unloaded and reloaded with homeward cargo.[15]

On April 27, 1878, replacement sailors were officially signed on by the U.S. Consul at Liverpool. Among the crew replacements was a new second steward whose name, interestingly, was Ah Sing, the same as the ship's cook. Orientals of this period are commonly pictured as being very short in stature, but such was not the case with the new steward. Ah Sing was twenty-two years old and five feet, nine inches tall. His wages were £3 ($14.58) per month — ten shillings ($2.43) more than the newly shipped able-bodied seamen were paid. Even at that, the Liverpool wage scale was more than forty percent less than at San Francisco.[16]

On Monday, April 29, two months after her arrival at Liverpool, a paddle-wheel steam tug towed the *Glory of the Seas* down the River Mersey and out into Liverpool Bay. Topsails and jibs were loosed, the mates gave orders to set sail and brace the yards to catch the prevailing breeze. As the *Glory* slowly gained way, the tug soon had her out far enough that she could be on her own. The towboat captain signaled the ship to drop the tug's hawser, and Captain McLaughlin commenced his second westward passage to San Francisco. He had high hopes of making a better run this year in spite of his reduced rig.

The next day the British iron ship *Borrowdale* sailed from Liverpool, and a week later the British iron ship *Victoria Nyanza* departed, followed by the ship *Palestine* four days later. Then on May 18, the fleet-mate of the *Borrowdale*, the Dale-liner *Mitredale*, also sailed from Liverpool bound for San Francisco. Five first-class Cape Horners were competing to see which vessel would make the best elapsed voyage time to the West Coast of the United States.

In spite of Captain McLaughlin's many years of experience successfully combating Cape Horn, the winds and currents were in literal opposition to him this year. It took the *Glory of the Seas* a week to clear St. George's Channel, and a full thirty-seven days to reach the Line in the Atlantic. McLaughlin later commented in his voyage summary about the *Glory* as she headed from the Equator:

> . . . got a breeze from N which in time hauled to SSE, where it hung, so we had to beat all the way along the Brazil coast; after passing lat. 42 S, lon. 60 W, the wind came up from SW and S where it hung for 13 days, blowing a gale with lots of snow and hail."[17]

Fortunately, the *Glory* was able to pass through the Strait of Le Maire, the preferred route, on July 14th instead of having to sail around the eastward side of Staten Island, but to this point she was already seventy-six and-a half days out. That same evening at 10 p.m., the *Glory of the Seas* passed Cape Horn with the well-known

British iron ship Borrowdale *under full sail, ca. 1878. Water color by William G. Hartman, Birmingham, England, Courtesy of the author.*

landmark only three miles to the north. Shortly thereafter, McLaughlin vainly attempted steering north into the Pacific. Winds and weather were both against him. He stated in his voyage summary:

> . . . could not get north, the wind between NW and N for 17 days; [until August 1, 1878] stormy, bad weather, and I may say, the darkest and most disagreeable month I ever spent at sea.[18]

By the time Captain McLaughlin reached the Equator in the Pacific on August 22, 115 days out, the *Borrowdale* had almost caught him. The *Victoria Nyanza* was a week behind the *Glory*, the *Palestine* five days and the *Mitredale* ten days behind. Every vessel, however, made a long passage.

On September 4 McLaughlin identified a full-rigged sailing ship in the distance. It was the *Borrowdale*, Captain Kelly commanding. Kelly had experienced much the same weather as McLaughlin and made just as poor a passage. Captain Kelly established an excellent reputation over the years as master of the pioneer unit of Newton's Liverpool-based Dale Line fleet of iron packets. In three consecutive voyages from Liverpool, the *Borrowdale* made 107-, 108-, and 109-day passages to San Francisco, and returned home to Liverpool in 101, 107, and 105 days respectively.[19]

The *Glory of the Seas* and the *Borrowdale* sailed in company for fifteen days as they headed northerly into the North Pacific Ocean. The *Borrowdale* was only half the tonnage of the *Glory* and had a length of 226.4 and breadth of 36.4 feet. Unlike the *Glory*, she crossed royals only above single topgallants. Moreover, her paint scheme was entirely different from the American ship. She had white lower masts and doublings, and her topsides were black to the sheer strake where there was a wide white stripe. Then she was gray down to the load line, and below that her brown copper bottom paint stood out.[20]

As to existing sailing conditions, the *Glory* and the *Borrowdale* were almost equal this passage. The Dale-Liner, however, had a reputation of being much faster than American vessels of her size. For instance, she was once credited with a day's run of 360 miles, which is about the maximum (as documented) that the *Glory of the Seas* made in her career. It was surprising that the *Glory*, although 800 tons larger, and with much fuller lines, was able to compete with the *Borrowdale* on this lengthy passage.[21]

On September 19, the two vessels parted company, the *Glory* to head toward San Francisco, while the *Borrowdale's* destination was Portland, Oregon, which she reached several weeks later.

On Sunday, September 29th, twelve deep-water squareriggers arrived at San Francisco. Although the *Glory of the Seas'* name was at the top of the ship arrival list in the local papers, by no means had she made a faster passage than the other vessels. She was followed on the list by the vessels *Mitredale, Palestine,* and the *Victoria Nyanza,* all of which sailed after her from Liverpool. The *Glory's* passage was an embarrassing 153 days, which gave McLaughlin reason to write up an even longer account than the previous year. In his summary of the voyage it was evident that the winds and ocean currents were against the *Glory of the Seas.*[22]

Daniel McLaughlin, however, had a bedfellow this year. Captain Kelly and the *Borrowdale* didn't arrive at Portland until October 2nd, 155 days out from Liverpool.

Some vessels in the fleet made slightly better passages, but not by much. The *Victoria Nyanza's* passage was 147 days, the *Palestine's* 143 days, and the *Mitredale's* 134 days. The *Wm. H. Marcy's* passage was even longer, 167 days from Liverpool.

Five of the Cape Horn fleet arriving on September 29th were from the East Coast of the United States, and the fastest voyage of that particular group of vessels was that of the *H.S. Gregory,* 130 days from New York.

Like the *Glory,* the *Wm. H. Marcy* had been unable to make a northing into the Pacific after passing Cape Horn, but the latter vessel took thirty-two days to round Cape Horn from latitude 50° south in the Atlantic to 50° south in the Pacific. The *Glory of the Seas* took sixteen days over the same segment. Moreover, it is worth noting that the vessels *Glory, Victoria Nyanza* and *Wm. H. Marcy* crossed 50° south in the Pacific on August 1st, whereas, the *Palestine* and the *Mitredale* crossed on August 3rd, and 6,000-odd miles later all five vessels arrived at San Francisco on the same day.

Following their arrival, the twelve-vessel Cape Horn fleet was dispersed throughout the Bay waterfront. The ships from the U.S. East Coast, most of which had general cargoes, were docked at various wharves at San Francisco. The *Wm. H. Marcy* had a 2,000-ton cargo of Lancashire steam coal consigned to Josiah N. Knowles. The cargo for the *Glory of the Seas* was consigned to Balfour, Guthrie & Co.

Captain Josiah Knowles was becoming quite diversified, acting as San Francisco agent for the J. Henry Sears-managed ships *Ocean King, Glory of the Seas, Grecian, Spartan, Titan,* and other vessels in which they held an interest. This was a challenging process due to his being a relative newcomer in the San Francisco shipping and commission business. He advertised himself as a "Shipping and Commission Agent" and also as "Sole Agent on this coast for New Bedford Yellow Metal.*"[23]

In 1877, Captain Knowles listed himself as master of the ex-lumber bark *Jenny Pitts* on her Custom House Register following her acquisition for conversion to a whaling bark. This was only a temporary measure until a new master could be appointed.[24] In the years to come he would become agent for marine insurance companies as well as for other East Coast shipping firms.

In addition to his other interests, Captain Knowles retained his 1/16 interest in the *Glory of the Seas*. The captain and his family, which now consisted of his wife Mary and five children including two sets of twins, lived in Oakland. His business offices were situated at 10 California Street, a block from the San Francisco waterfront.

Although their relationship was technically supervisor and employee, Captain Knowles and Captain McLaughlin remained close friends. Hospitality was extended to the McLaughlins by the Knowles family following the arrival of the *Glory* at San Francisco.

The *Glory of the Seas*' cargo was discharged once more at Oakland. On Sunday, October 6, 1878, a tug towed her to the Long Wharf to unload. Following discharge she was towed to the anchorage east of Goat Island.

British four-mast ship County of Kinross *in San Francisco Bay, ca. 1880, Courtesy San Francisco Maritime NHP, Fireman's Fund Collection.*

In the coming months more than a dozen deep-water vessels joined the *Glory of the Seas* in lay-up awaiting cargoes. The
depressed condition of the California grain-shipping market during the fall of 1878 and winter of 1879 caused more ships than
usual to be laid up. Many sailing shipowners found it was totally
unprofitable for them to accept the charter rates offered by the
local grain shipping merchants.

In mid-November 1878, part of the sailing ship fleet on the
Bay consisted of four unusual vessels — four-masted iron vessels,
square-rigged on all masts. These vessels — the *County of Inverness*,
the *County of Kinross*, the *County of Dumfries*, and the *Simla* — arrived at San Francisco in October and early November. The three
County ships, although smaller in gross tonnage than the *Glory of
the Seas*, were all relatively new, and the *Simla*, the oldest of the
four, was a converted steamship.

The ships *County of Kinross, County of Dumfries* and *County of
Inverness* were making their first appearance at San Francisco. To
illustrate the relative size of the three County ships, the *County of
Kinross* had dimensions of 267 x 38.9 x 23.7 feet. Compared to an
American ship like the *Glory of the Seas*, the *County of Kinross* looked
much larger even though she was only about twenty-seven feet
longer. The *Glory*'s beam of forty-four feet was five feet greater
than that of the *County of Kinross*, and the three full decks on the
Glory compared with two on the *Kinross* somewhat explained the
400-ton difference in tonnage. Large iron ships like the *County of
Kinross* would soon give the American-owned grain fleet especially
stiff competition in the depressed charter market.

On November 14, 1878, the *San Francisco Commercial Herald*
reported on the shipping depression:

> We have now a large number of disengaged American [and Brit-
> ish] ships at anchor waiting the turn of the tide when owners hope
> with confidence that grain freights will rule much higher than at
> present; certainly one would suppose, that with our immense wheat
> surplus in store, and the small amount of tonnage en route to this
> port, that higher rates rise ere long.

Average grain-shipping freight rates, like the previous year (when there was a poor grain crop), continued in the 35 to 37 shilling range. The "Along the Wharves" column in the *Daily Alta* called them "starvation freights," that is, a below-profit margin.[25] An exception was the new ship *County of Kinross,* which was chartered prior to her arrival at San Francisco at £2 17s 6d ($13.87) for Cork (Queenstown) for orders. This figure, however, became a backlash to her charterers. The local shipping community generally conceded that, although the owners of the *Kinross* would do extremely well financially, the shipper would suffer a large loss — they had far exceeded market expectation. Fortunately both parties renegotiated a lower rate before the *Kinross* sailed.

By the 4th of December, 1878, the number of American ships laid up east of Goat Island rose to fifteen. There were enough inactive captains and their wives within rowing distance of each other to prompt the organization of group activities to break up the boredom of lay-up. They decided to have a clambake. The *Daily Alta* took notice of the festivity as follows:

> The American shipmasters who have laid up their vessels back of Goat Island, have put their heads together and are going to have a regular old-fashioned clambake today, to which all their friends are invited. It is unnecessary to say that it will be a grand success, as those boys come from the place that [sic] a regular old-fashioned clambake is understood and appreciated. The ships' boats will be at Oakland Wharf at 12:30 p.m. to carry the guests to the rendezvous.[26]

Following the clambake, the local newspapers referred to the laid-up fleet east of Goat Island as the "Clam Fleet."[27]

CHAPTER VIII

The Clam Fleet

By the first of the year 1879, forty-two full-rigged sailing ships and twelve barks were layed-up, anchored on San Francisco Bay. A monthly freight letter in the *Commercial Herald* told the story of the grain shipping depression in the region:

> San Francisco, January 2, 1879
>
> In reviewing the business of December, the closing month of the year, we find no relief from the depression experienced in previous months. In fact, the entire season has been an unprofitable one to shipowners here as well as elsewhere. Spot charters for wheat to Europe have ruled low all through the six months of the current harvest year. During this period of the year about one-half of the surplus wheat crop has been harvested, and we now have perhaps 300,000 tons of grain to be marketed .... The condition of the European continental markets does not seem to be favorable to exports of wheat at current rates demanded for our wheat, and freights at 35 shillings. The shipping outlook is therefore far from cheery to those having ships here out of business. We wish it were otherwise, but the business has not been profitable to any branch of the trade in a long time, and we fail to see now any silver lining to the cloud . . .[1]

Despite the prophets of gloom, the Clam Fleet shipmasters and their families enjoyed social affairs that raised their spirits and relieved the boredom of lay-up. In fact, the maritime social event of early 1879 on San Francisco Bay was held aboard the *Glory of the Seas* on the night of Saturday, January 4th. Captain McLaughlin and the masters of the ships *Chandos*, Captain Emory, *Palestine*, Captain Emmons, and *Thomas Dana*, Captain Cessam sponsored the event. Two of the guests attending this party, in addition to the marine reporter for the *Daily Alta*,[2] were Captain and Mrs. Jonathan Dow of Searsport, Maine, whose ship the *Clarissa B. Carver*, lay idle nearby. The *Carver* had been riding at anchor for three months. The day following the party, Mrs. Dow wrote down her impressions of the event:

> Last night we had the first ball of the season on board the ship *Glory of the Seas*. She lay in our fleet. It was given by four captains: Captain McGlanthilin [sic], Captain Emery, Captain Emmons and Captain Cessam. 150 guests were invited; nearly all came. Had music and dancing and dinner at six o'clock. The between-decks were fitted up very nice. The sides and stanchions were all covered with flags aft from the mizzen to the mainmast; had three tables set and flags hung festooned all around and lanterns hung all around. Forward of the mainmast was the dancing floor. Had a very nice time and chance to get acquainted. We shall be ready for another if it comes around.[3]

On January 15th, local newspapers reported that several units of the Clam Fleet, including the *Glory of the Seas*, had been fined $200 for noncompliance with harbor rules requiring the display of anchor lights at night. The ships named were *Glory of the Seas, Clarissa B. Carver, Wm. H. Marcy, Brown Brothers, Pharos*, and the coasting schooner *Emilie Schroeder*. Several days later the captains of these craft threatened to take the matter to the local Admiralty Court, disclosing that several of the fined vessels, including the *Glory of the Seas*, actually had the proper lights burning at the time in question.[4]

One outfall of this incident was an item appearing in the "Along the Wharves" column of the *Daily Alta*. It briefly mentioned that the clam fleet captains had added a new verse to the sea chanty normally sung when working the windlass capstan or pump brake

Although of poor quality, this photo, taken in 1911, shows the upper 'tween deck of Glory of the Seas *with a deck height of eight feet, two inches. Note diagonal bracing between hanging knees. This is where the first Clam Fleet ball took place in 1879. Courtesy of the author.*

situated on their respective ship's fo'c'sle-heads. The chorus now ended with "Where was *Marcy* when the light went out!"[5]

The adverse publicity had a desired effect and on January 31 the harbor authorities dismissed the charges and penalties against the *Glory of the Seas* and the *Wm. H. Marcy*; the other fines were never enforced.[6]

On February 19, 1879, Captain McLaughlin became something of a hero when he helped avert a serious disaster between two Central Pacific passenger ferries. On that foggy day just prior to 3:30 p.m., the captains of four American ships — Daniel McLaughlin of the *Glory of the Seas*, Edwin O. Day of the *Hecla*, Albert H. Dunbar of the *Grecian*, and William Ross, Jr., of the *Granite State* — boarded the steam passenger ferry *Alameda* at the San Francisco ferry terminal, situated at the foot of East Street between Clay and Market Streets. Their destination was the Oakland Long Wharf, about a half hour away. Shortly after they boarded, the *Alameda*, a double-ended, wooden-hulled vessel, steamed cautiously into the Bay with some 400 passengers aboard.[7]

About the same time, the passenger ferry *El Capitan*, a somewhat larger side-wheeler with 100 people aboard, set out from the Oakland ferry slip bound for San Francisco. Visibility was ten to twenty feet, but the officers in charge on the ferries were experienced and regularly blew their steam whistles to alert other vessels of their presence. Unbeknownst to them, however, the *Alameda* and *El Capitan* were on a collision course. Although visibility was almost zero and Captain McLaughlin had no particular reason for doing so, he positioned himself on the foredeck of the *Alameda* which proved to be "the right spot at the right time."[8] McLaughlin described the event to a newspaper reporter:[9]

> I left San Francisco on the 3:30 boat, and when about half way over, while standing forward on the *Alameda*, I heard the whistle blow and the signal given to "stop her!" and immediately after to "back her!" I then saw *El Capitan*. This was about seven minutes after leaving the slip. Seeing that a collision was inevitable, I tried to get out life-pre-servers, but they were wedged in so tightly that I broke the straps in

Steam ferry El Capitan *following her collision with ferry* Alameda *on February 19, 1879. Courtesy San Francisco Maritime NHP, Fireman's Fund Collection.*

trying to get them out. With Captain Ross, I broke down the stanchions in several places and assisted in distributing them.

With the *Alameda*'s officers attending their injured ship, McLaughlin immediately thought of the safety of the passengers and crew of the sinking *El Capitan*. Observers saw the fifty-five-year-old captain take off his dress coat and hand his gold pocket watch to a brother shipmaster.[10]

> We struck the *El Capitan* on her port side just forward of the wheel, our vessel going under her guards, crushing her side below the water line from twenty to thirty feet. Our vessel was then swung clear around by the tide so that we lay alongside of *El Capitan*. A large number of people on *El Capitan* – I should say between 40 or 50 – were in the water. I threw over a number of preservers, and then with Captain Ross, went on the other steamer. Finding her sinking, he and I took three gangway rails and laid them to make a bridge from boat to boat. From 50 to 100 persons passed on it to the *Alameda*. A good gangplank would have enabled every one to have passed.
>
> *El Capitan* sank to her hurricane deck, and drifted off. Boats were lowered, and every one in sight was picked up. The tug *Anasha* also lowered boats and rescued some. Everything in man's power was done by Captain Brown and the officers of the *Alameda*. No blame can possibly be attached to them. It is impossible to say that every one was saved, owing to so many being in the water at the time. The boats lay side by side for three or four minutes before *El Capitan* began to sink.

The *Alameda* suffered relatively minor damage: loss of bulwarks, a stove-in boat, and the loss of her forward rudder. But the *El Capitan*, which by this time was awash, had to be towed to shore to keep her from breaking up and sinking.[11]

The following Wednesday, February 26th, officers of the Steamboat Inspection Service held an inquiry at San Francisco. Captain McLaughlin was called as a material witness to testify as to the facts of the case. After the testimony of the master of the *El Capitan*, Captain McLaughlin gave the following account:[12]

Capt. Millen Griffith's steam tug Rescue *at Vallejo Street Wharf, ca. 1881. San Francisco Maritime NHP, Accession No. A1.1963n.*

I never in all my life saw a denser fog, and I have been a shipmaster since 1848. The masters, in my opinion, used due care and diligence. I know something about engines [earlier in his career he was master of the *Cassandra*] and never saw engines handled so well and rapidly as those on the *Alameda* were. It was a peculiarity that the atmosphere seemed to reverberate back our own whistles. I was greatly surprised when I saw *El Capitan*, having heard her whistle just previously, and then she seemed a long distance off.

Captain McLaughlin and Captain Ross won the praise of the shipping community for their quick thinking in the face of disaster which no doubt helped to save dozens of lives.

In the meantime, during the third week of February 1879, the patience of Captain J.N. Knowles in holding off chartering the *Glory of the Seas* for grain paid off. George W. McNear, San Francisco grain dealer, chartered her for £2 2s 6d ($10.21) for Queenstown for orders. However, other vessels were not as fortunate. The *Wm. H. Marcy*, chartered in January received only £1 15s ($8.51), and the ship *America*, chartered in February, received even less — £1 13s ($8.02).[13]

On February 28th, the *Glory of the Seas* left her anchorage and was towed to the Oakland Long Wharf to load sacked grain. During the following three and one-half weeks stevedores loaded 67,208 centals of grain (3,360 short tons), valued at $116,640, and 23,000 board feet of lumber. Following completion of her cargo, a tug towed the *Glory* to San Francisco where she anchored on March 25th.[14]

There, the *Glory of the Seas* lay until April 7th. In the meantime McLaughlin hired an entirely new afterguard. The old one, including Chief Mate Rogers, was discharged when Captain Knowles decided the *Glory* would be laid up for an indefinite time (lasting six months). Having the McLaughlins act as ship-keepers was a way to reduce ship expenses.

Mate Rogers soon became Captain Rogers, taking command of the 900-ton bark *Daniel Draper*. In 1882, Thomas Rogers succeeded his brother, William A. Rogers, as captain of the ship *Josephus*.[15]

One former crew member returned. Frank Chappell, ship's steward on McLaughlin's first voyage on the *Glory*, again signed on. Chappell was a forty-six-year-old Englishman who had followed the sea for a number of years on deep-water sailing ships. Evidently there was mutual respect between captain and steward for him to be re-employed two years later. A new cook and mess boy, both Chinese, also signed on — Ah John and Long Eng.[16]

This year Captain McLaughlin experienced a different labor problem at San Francisco, that of acquiring foremast hands. However, he wasn't alone. On March 17th, the United States Shipping Commissioner held a meeting in his offices in the Federal Building with about thirty-five local consignees and shipowners. The subject was payment of blood money to boardinghouse landlords. In 1875, the shipowners temporarily broke the power of the local boardinghouse masters by paying a direct bounty to individual sailors, thereby breaking the landlord's hold as middleman.[17] The problem, though, re-surfaced. Henceforth, an official notice from the commissioner was to be given to the master of each vessel entering the Port of San Francisco that said, in part:

> You are not to allow any sailor boardinghouse keeper or runner to come alongside or on board the ship as soon as she can be reached from shore . . . The object of these regulations have become absolutely necessary at this time to prevent a lawless association of sailor boardinghouse runners who demand $40 bounty or blood money for each sailor shipped on board vessels requiring crews.[18]

Although the boardinghouse keepers grudgingly complied with the resolution, they soon made it difficult for shipmasters to obtain crews. To illustrate, on March 25th, the *Glory* was anchored in the stream at San Francisco and ready to sail. It was twelve days before Captain McLaughlin received his full complement of hands consisting of seventeen able-bodied seamen and two men rated as quartermasters.[19]

With the crew problem solved, it was time once again for Capt. and Mrs. McLaughlin to say farewell to their friends. The captain could finally say, "This is sailing day."

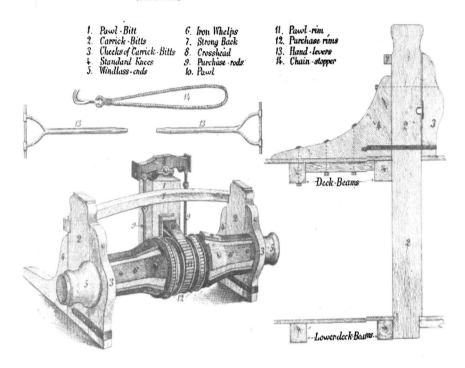

1. Pawl-Bitt
2. Carrick-Bitts
3. Cheeks of Carrick-Bitts
4. Standard Knees
5. Windlass-ends
6. Iron Whelps
7. Strong Back
8. Crosshead
9. Purchase-rods
10. Pawl
11. Pawl-rim
12. Purchase rims
13. Hand-levers
14. Chain-stopper

Wooden anchor windlass with operating equipment. Brake handles are labeled "hand levers." Courtesy of the author. Copied from Patterson's Illustrated Nautical Encyclopedia.

Tuesday, April 8, 1879, was a clear, spring day with the wind blowing from the west. The *Glory of the Seas'* sails were loosed so that when the anchor was up they could be set. One of Millen Griffiths' steam tugs came alongside and passed her hawser which was made fast on the fo'c'sle-head of the *Glory*. Captain McLaughlin next gave the command to his new down-Easter Mate, J.C. Cooper, to "Man the windlass!"

Cooper responded, "Aye, aye, Sir! Man the windlass!" This meant that he acknowledged he now had the responsibility of overseeing the job of weighing anchor.

Crew members hurried to the fo'c'sle-head and repeated the command, "Man the windlass, Sir!"

The *Glory of the Seas* was equipped with a wooden, twelve-foot-long barrel windlass located immediately below the fo'c'sle-head. It was activated by two T-shaped brake handles (metal levers) shipped into two square-shaped holes situated on the crossheads. The next step in weighing anchor was to "Heave away" on the levers. Eight men, four on each side, led by a chantyman, soon worked them up and down like a seesaw, to his rhythmic tune "Heave Away, My Johnnies." Their initial exertion was to heave the cable up short — a backbreaking task. As they heaved down, and then back up with all their strength on the lever handles, the great log windlass directly below slowly turned on a strongly-built iron ratchet connected to a geared windlass rim.

Though this unique mechanism saved manpower and was a big improvement over windlasses on sailing ships of a century before, it still required a lot of muscle from the eight seamen at the levers, most of whom were still suffering from the hangover effects of their last night ashore on the Barbary Coast. Once the cable was up short, it was no easy job to break loose the 5,700 pound iron and wood anchor from the muddy bay bottom. With the aid of the towboat, however, and with the seamen heaving away at the lever handles, the anchor finally broke free.

The *Glory of the Seas* forged ahead. Mate Cooper notified Captain McLaughlin, "Anchor's aweigh, Sir!"

The captain responded, "Very well, Sir!"

The men on the fo'c'sle-head now heaved to the chantyman's faster song pace and to the further accompaniment of the steady clank! clank! clank! of the windlass pawl, as the *Glory's* anchor slowly came up from the bottom. Meanwhile, directly below on the main deck, several seamen with a handy-billy (a small pump) and hose flushed mud from the heavy iron chain (each link 7 x 11-1/4 inches) as it came up through the hawsepipe.

The tug and the *Glory*, connected by a long tow rope, headed out the Golden Gate on the ebb tide. Her anchor ring was soon up to the hawsepipe ready to be "catted," that is, hauled up to the cathead, a job that had to be done quickly so the anchor's great mass of wood and metal would not unduly bang under the bows and scar her yellow metal sheathing.

With a large fish hook, one of the crew caught the anchor ring, making it fast to a fish tackle, a large temporary block-and-tackle arrangement. With the aid of the large double-headed fo'c'sle-head capstan just forward of the windlass levers, the *Glory's* sailors used the fish tackle to cat her anchor. Once the crew secured the anchor ring to the cathead, the fish tackle again came into play and the sailors hauled the nearly three-ton anchor inboard over the buffalo rail. When the wooden stock was almost vertical, they lashed the anchor securely.[20]

By this time, the *Glory* was well outside the San Francisco Heads and under easy sail. With these operations completed, the tug left far astern and the pilot dropped, Captain Daniel McLaughlin began his third voyage in command of the *Glory of the Seas* bound for the United Kingdom.

CHAPTER IX

Queenstown, Le Havre and New York

Captain McLaughlin reclaimed his reputation after the long westward Cape Horn voyage by making a 110-day passage from San Francisco to Queenstown (now named Cobh), Ireland, arriving on July 27, 1879. The *Glory of the Seas* beat Queenstown-bound vessels such as the American ships *Clarissa B. Carver* and *Ivanhoe*, the New Brunswick-built ship *Governor Tilley*, and the British bark *Hecla*. The *Ivanhoe*'s voyage took 134 days and the *Clarissa B. Carver*'s, 131. The *Governor Tilley* sailed a week before the *Glory* but arrived the day after, while the *Ivanhoe* sailed a week afterward and arrived at the Irish port a month later than the *Glory*. The *Hecla* departed San Francisco two days before the *Ivanhoe* and made a 135-day passage.

The only vessel making a better overall passage to the United Kingdom in April's sailings from San Francisco was the American ship *St. Stephen*, a three-skysail-yarder of 1,392 tons. She arrived at Liverpool on July 27th, the same day the *Glory of the Seas* arrived at Queenstown. However, the *St. Stephen*'s excellent run was 101 days, which became the best eastward voyage in this vessel's entire career (her average: 113 days).[1] Still, McLaughlin was pleased with the *Glory's* run which made his average 107 days.

At Queenstown the captain received orders to proceed to Le Havre for final cargo discharge. Sailing on July 29, he arrived three days later. Le Havre is located at the mouth of the Seine

Ship St. Stephen *at Front Street Wharf, ca. 1880.   San Francisco Maritime NHP. Fireman's Fund Collection.*

River and although berthing capacity was much smaller than Liverpool, the grain warehouses at Le Havre were located alongside wet docks similar to those at the great British port. At high water, the *Glory of the Seas* was towed into the outer wet dock facilities where she unloaded over a period of several weeks.

Unlike her four previous voyages from Europe, the *Glory of the Seas* did not load a return cargo for San Francisco. J. Henry Sears & Company chartered her, instead, for the first time since 1873, to load general cargo at New York City. Captain McLaughlin arranged for 650 tons of stone rubble ballast to be taken aboard and on September 12, 1879, the *Glory* departed the Le Havre wet docks under tow, only to ground in the Outer Harbor. This forced him to wait until evening high tide to float her off. Damage was minimal and she departed immediately for sea.[2]

Six days out, McLaughlin spoke the Canadian ship *Cumberland*, Captain McCarthy, which sailed from Le Havre the same day as the *Glory*. This Nova Scotian-built vessel was bound for Hampton Roads, Virginia. On his tenth day at sea Capt. McLaughlin spoke the British bark *Arcadia* bound for the Delaware Breakwater. The *Glory* subsequently left both ships far astern. On October 12th, the *Glory of the Seas* arrived at New York, thirty days out, and 3,000-odd miles from Le Havre.[3]

Although her fall passage was not considered a record, the *Glory* made the fastest crossing of any sailing vessel arriving at New York within a few days of October 12th. Captain McLaughlin modestly described the overall voyage conditions in the maritime column of the *New York Herald* as "had fine weather."[4]

The American ship *Charles Dennis*, likewise in ballast, made a thirty-five-day crossing from Le Havre, and the American ship *Palmyra*, which arrived the day before the *Glory* at New York, made a thirty-seven-day passage from the French port. Moreover, the former Thayer and Lincoln ship *Friedlander* (now under the German flag) was thirty-seven days from Bremen. McLaughlin's passage spoke for itself.

Captain McLaughlin was also pleased with the *Glory*'s performance in comparison with the two vessels she spoke during this passage. The *Cumberland* arrived at Philadelphia, Pennsylvania, ten days after her, and the *Arcadia* made Baltimore, Maryland, on October 18th, six days after the *Glory* arrived at New York. Even the Cape Horner *America*, arrived the day after the *Glory of the Seas*, thirty-four days from Liverpool.

The general maritime community viewed this voyage of the *Glory of the Seas* as unimportant. Steam was king in New York. Decades before, steamships totally eclipsed sail in the lucrative passenger and cargo New York-European trades. Even so, as of October 15, 1879, the "Directory of Shipping" column of the *New York Maritime Register* listed seventy-seven full-rigged ships as loading in the Port of New York (including New York, Brooklyn, and New Jersey), besides hundreds of other vessels, including coasters.

Sears & Company chartered the *Glory* to the New York shipping and commission firm, Simonson and Howes, to load general cargo for San Francisco.[5] She had to wait her turn, however, for a berth on the crowded South Street waterfront located at the southern end of Manhattan Island.

The *America* was also chartered by the Simonson and Howes Line and was to load first. Immediately following her arrival on October 13th, she was towed to Pier 11 on the East River, located at the foot of Old Slip, where she began taking on general cargo. The *Glory of the Seas* was towed to Prentice's Basin in Brooklyn for temporary lay-up until berthing space was available for her on the crowded East River. A number of sailing vessels were there with her: the American ships *Centennial*, *Eureka*, and *Loretto Fish*, the British ship *Aminta*, and the German ship *Meta*, to name a few. The *Glory* remained there until Friday, November 7th, when the fully-loaded *America* was hauled off and towed to sea.

Later that same day a coal-powered steam tug took the *Glory of the Seas* in tow and escorted her across the East River to Pier 11. Here she was berthed carefully alongside a narrow wooden wharf which was only about thirty feet wide and 475 feet long. Soon, the *Glory*'s bowsprit and jibboom projected out over South Street focusing the eyes of passing admirers on her beautiful figurehead. Her tall spars and furled canvas now became a part of the vast

Lower Manhattan from Brooklyn Bridge Tower, 1876. "Beale's New York Panorama," Image No. One. Courtesy of the Museum of the City of New York.

forest of sailing ship masts fronting the Manhattan side of the East River.

In the year 1879, New York, boasting a population of about 1,200,000, was the largest city in the United States. The maritime life of the port was carried on along the East and North (Hudson) Rivers. Most of the transatlantic steamship lines were situated on the east side of the North River. The Manhattan side of the East River, however, was covered by dozens of small nondescript wharves that were built when the average sailing ship was less than half the size of the *Glory.*

Before 1850, almost all transatlantic and east coastal packet lines were located in this region. Now, the California trade sailing ships loaded in the area south of the Brooklyn Bridge, which was then under construction. However, the number of vessels so engaged was far less than ten years before when the Transcontinental Railroad began operations. When the *Glory of the Seas* berthed at Pier 11, there were only four other San Francisco-bound ships loading, three of which were at Pier 19 for Sutton & Co. Also, an R.B. Van Vieck-chartered vessel was located at Pier 13.

Not only were there sailing ships in this area, but commuter ferry terminals to Brooklyn and Staten Island and major steamship piers sprang up in the last decade. Although there had been some South Street wharf modernization with the erection of covered piers such as the steamship lines of C.L. Mallory & Co. at Pier 20 and the Morgan's Line at Pier 18, much of South Street remained the haven of square-rigged sailing ships, coasting schooners, and fishing smacks.

The Manhattan of 1879 was not an island of skyscrapers. The largest buildings fronting South Street reached five stories. The majority of the occupants of these buildings relied on the maritime commerce of the Port of New York for income, as did shipping and commission merchants, ship grocers, chandlery firms, sail lofts and the other businesses that catered to ships. Also located in the area were the less savory elements of the city; sailors' boardinghouses, saloons, whorehouses, and the like. These preyed on sailors when they arrived in port. Sailing ship officers, however, were a breed apart. Instead of congregating in the disreputable

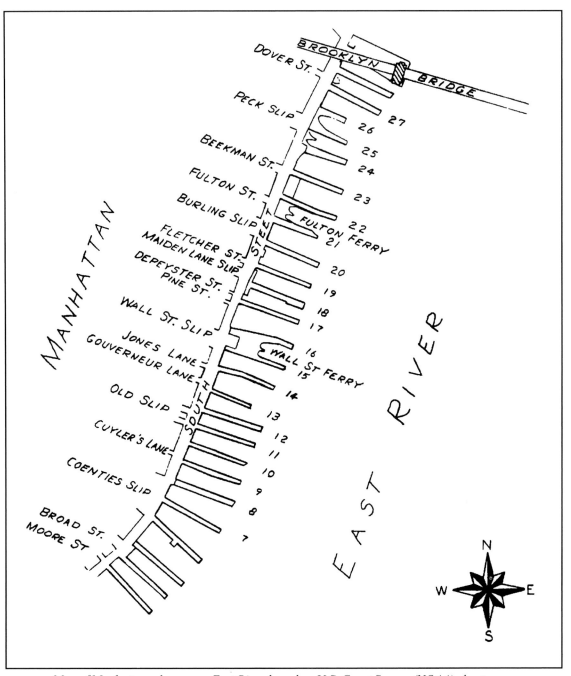

Map of Manhattan wharves on East River based on U.S. Coast Survey (NOAA) charts by the author, 1887.

bars in this region, they socialized in the coffee shops around Peck Slip and opposite Pier 19 on the East River.[6]

On November 18th, eighty-eight full-rigged ships were in port, but part of this number were at Brooklyn and on the New Jersey side. Of that number, a big sister of *Glory of the Seas*, the 258-foot medium clipper *Donald McKay* of 2,408 tons, was berthed at Hoboken, New Jersey, taking on cargo. An Australian Black Ball Line passenger ship in the 1850s and 1860s, she now carried case oil, regularly plying the route between New York and Germany under the German flag.

Throughout the remainder of November 1879, the *Glory of the Seas* loaded cargo at Pier 11. Stevedores rigged a wire stay between her masts with a single block over each hatch[7] and loaded over 4,000 barrels of cement, 661 tons of coal, cases of petroleum, 2,550 kegs of nails and casks of whiskey. In previous decades farm implements were a major item in the California clipper trade but with the increased competition of the Transcontinental Railroad, charterers found it increasingly difficult to acquire San Francisco consignees willing to wait for agricultural items delivered by ship. The *Glory* was the exception this year, because her cargo also included a large variety of farm implements.[8]

Although many passenger carriages and freight carts were used along South Street, the main freight-hauling vehicles around Old Slip were large wooden wagons drawn by draft horses in pairs and driven by teamsters. These wagons transported various items of cargo alongside the *Glory of the Seas*, which cargo was loaded on board by stevedores under the nominal direction of Chief Mate Cooper.

The month-and-a-half period during which the *Glory* lay at New York gave Captain McLaughlin and his wife sufficient time to travel to Malden, Eastport, and Grand Manan to visit family for the first time in three years. The captain's children, now all grown, lived in New England, and Maggie's family lived on Grand Manan. Also, McLaughlin's eighty-four-year-old mother still lived on Grand Manan, along with some of his brothers and sisters.

It was difficult for Captain McLaughlin's children to accept Maggie as a stepmother. In fact, there were few close relationships

Ship Sovereign of the Seas *at foot of Telegraph Hill, ca. 1875. Courtesy San Francisco Maritime NHP, Fireman's Fund Collection.*

between her and most of them.[9] Unfortunately, this caused a strain through the years whenever there were family gatherings. In spite of this, the McLaughlins visited many relatives in 1879 while they were on the East Coast, and generally had a pleasant reunion.

Throughout his years of long periods at sea, Captain McLaughlin regularly wrote to his children. Although he wasn't able to spend a great deal of time with his youngest son during his teen years, the captain's many fatherly letters to Carl brought the two as close as people can get under such circumstances. It was not the same as living day-to-day under the same roof, but it helped fill a paternal void in Carl's adolescent years.

On November 17th, the ship *Sovereign of the Seas*, a smaller sister of the *Glory*, arrived at New York, twenty-six days from Liverpool. A tug berthed her alongside Pier 27 just south of the nearly completed West Tower of the Brooklyn Bridge soon to be spanning the East River. The *Sovereign* was built the year before the *Glory of the Seas* by Donald McKay at East Boston. Managed by Lawrence, Giles & Co., major operators of steamships and sailing vessels at New York, she regularly traded in the triangle route between New York, San Francisco, and the United Kingdom. Unlike the *Glory*, the *Sovereign* was full-bodied in design, 199.5 feet in length and measured 1,502 tons (40 feet shorter and 600 less tons). Also, unlike the *Glory*, the *Sovereign* had a male figurehead at her prow whose countenance gave the ship the aura of a true sovereign of the seas. Nevertheless, there were similarities between the two craft. Like the *Glory of the Seas*, the *Sovereign* crossed a skysail on the main, had "built" lower masts, and had the same style of decorative joiner work on her main deck and at her stern. The exterior surfaces of her deck houses were the same design and were a combination of paneling and horizontal planking. In further contrast to the other Donald McKay-built ships then loading in the vicinity of the port of New York was the *New World*. Constructed for the Atlantic packet trade in 1846, she had a length of 187.7 feet and measured 1,417 tons. Unlike her bigger sisters, the *Sovereign of the Seas*, the *Glory of the Seas*, and the *Donald McKay*, the *New World* had a square stern, an old-fashioned beak-head, and a man-

o'-war type white stripe on her sides. Following her arrival at New
York, twenty-four days from London, the *New World* was docked at
Pier 13, two wharves immediately north of the *Glory of the Seas.*

The *New World* was a regular part of the Grinnell, Minturn
& Co. fleet, which, until steamships usurped the passenger trade
between the United Kingdom and the United States, was a regular
passenger carrier between London and New York. For many years
she made regularly-scheduled sailings three times a year with other
first-class vessels of the Grinnell-Minturn packet fleet. However,
by the year 1879 the *New World* had to be content with hauling
marginal-profit cargoes such as paper, wool, chalk, and scrap iron
on return passages from London, once her prime general cargoes
from New York were delivered to the British port.[10]

Manning standards were quite different between the three
McKay-built American flag vessels berthed on the East River. The
Glory of the Seas normally carried a full complement of thirty-three
men;[11] *Sovereign of the Seas*, twenty-five men,[12] including her captain, A. H. Wood; and the *New World*, under command of Capt. W.
C. Hammond, likewise, had a full crew of twenty-five men on her
just-completed voyage from London.[13]

The *New World* loaded general cargo for London once again,
but the *Sovereign of the Seas*, like the *Glory*, loaded general cargo for
San Francisco. In some shipping circles the 1879-1880 grain year
was being viewed very optimistically by California grain shippers
and owners of ships in the grain trade. This optimism was fueled
in part by a news story from San Francisco that appeared in the
New York Shipping Guide, representing a complete reversal of the
California shipping depression of the previous two grain seasons:

San Francisco, Oct. 9. — By reason of an unexpected demand for
wheat tonnage, and numerous charters at steadily advancing prices, ships
may now be said to be booming. There are few, very few ships disengaged; ships either here or to arrive for a month to come; hence, freight
may be said to be kiting [sic]. Vessels to arrive have been chartered at
60s @ 65s [$14.58 to $15.80] and on the spot engagements have been
concluded at even higher figures. The fact is, ship owners are afraid to

name rates for fear of being snapped up – 67 @ 70s [$16.28 to $17.01] is now the ruling rate for wheat to the United Kingdom . . .[14]

With such profit-making prospects in view, J. Henry Sears & Company pressed the charterers to get the *Glory*'s cargo completed as soon as possible so she could sail for San Francisco to take advantage of the anticipated boom.

Meanwhile, routine expenses for the *Glory of the Seas* mounted. They were all necessary, but general ship services cost more at New York than at San Francisco.

The *San Francisco Bulletin* published an interesting comparison of port charges for the ship *Young America* for her stay at New York in January 1879, and at San Francisco in May and early June of 1879 which well-illustrate relative costs of vessels at the two ports:[15]

Description of Service	New York	San Francisco
Inward [Towage]	$182.81	$170.00
Towage in harbor and to sea	250.00	300.00
[Towage at San Francisco included a 30-mile tow to Vallejo and return]		
Wharfage	784.57	462.00
Loading and Discharging rate per ton	60 cents	35 cents
Loading at New York	$1,306.80	
Discharging at San Francisco		$849.40
	$2,524.18	$1,781.40

The *Young America* arrived at New York from San Francisco on September 3, 1879, and didn't start loading for George Howes & Co. at Pier 19 on the East River until December. As she was towed over from Prentice's Basin, preparations were underway for the *Glory of the Seas* to complete her cargo and sail for San Francisco.

CHAPTER X

The Cape Horn Road

On December 6, 1879, Captain McLaughlin received his official crew list from the Office of the U.S. Shipping Commissioner at New York. Because it was an intercoastal voyage to San Francisco, the vessel came under the jurisdiction of the Commissioner. The crew had to sign a shipping agreement similar to a foreign voyage, legally binding them for a specific period, subject to terms of dismissal at the eventual port of discharge.

Thirty-three persons signed the agreement, including McLaughlin in his capacity as master, but there was an unusual addition to the official crew list. Only eight of the *Glory*'s crew were viewed as bona fide American citizens. In the column "Of What Country Citizens or Subjects," the Customs clerk put "No Proof" for twenty-five of the names, which meant he could levy an extra fee of fifty cents per ton against the ship. This was because she did not have "two thirds of the crew . . . proved citizens of the United States."[1]

The fact that almost the entire crew claimed to reside in New York, of course, did not prove citizenship. This was probably the case with many of the *Glory*'s foremast sailors supplied by boardinghouse landlords at New York, but it definitely did not apply to several of the afterguard. For example, the cook Ah John, a Chinaman, and Frank Chappell, chief steward, who came over

Office of the U. S. SHIPPING COMMISSIONER,
Port of New York.

LIST OF PERSONS

Composing the Crew of the Ship "Glory of the Seas" of Boston whereof
D McLaughlin is Master, bound for San Francisco, Cala

NAMES	PLACES OF BIRTH.	PLACES OF RESIDENCE.	OF WHAT COUNTRY CITIZENS OR SUBJECTS.	AGE.	HEIGHT FEET.	INCHES.	COMPLEXION.	HAIR.	EYES.
John C. Cooper	Maine		United States	59	5	10	Light	Brown	Grey
William McClellan	Mass		United States	33	6	—	Light	Brown	Grey
M Freeman	Boston		" "	32	5	10	"	"	"
John Gimion	Newburyport Mass		" "	35	5	7	"	"	"
John Anderson	Norway		No Proof	30	5	9	Light	Brown	Grey
Frank Chappell	England		" "	46	5	8	"	Grey	Blue
Millie Chappell	China		" "	30	5	4	"	Brown	Grey
All John	China		" "	35	5	4	Yellow	Black	"
A. F. Rydberg	Sweden		No Proof	44	5	7	Light	Brown	Grey
John Bolan	"		"	28	5	8	"	"	"
Emil Carlsson	"		"	23	5	7	"	"	"
William Franklin	Finland		"	27	5	9	"	"	"
F. Wle Baer	Holland		"	27	5	8	"	"	"
Charles Wagner	Me		United States	24	5	8	"	"	"
Wm Levine	Austria		No Proof	26	5	10	Dark	Dark	Dark
John Claude	Glasgow Scot		" "	38	5	9	Light	Brown	Grey
Wr Theorson	Sweden		" "	23	5	7	"	"	"
M. Paulson	Norway		" "	28	5	7	"	"	"
A Johansen	"		" "	33	5	7	"	"	Blue
			" "	72	5				

Crew list for Glory of the Seas *from New York towards San Francisco, December 6, 1879. Courtesy National Archives and Records Administration, Washington, D.C., San Francisco Custom House District.*

22	John Wilson	Russia		" "	29	5	10	"	"	Blue
23	Peter Lundqvist	Sweden		" "	30	5	10	"	"	Grey
24	Karlsen Larsen	Norway		" "	22	5	9	"	"	Lt Brown
25	John Smith	Austria		" "	25	5	8	"	"	Grey
26	William Leabitt	Me		United States	42	5	9	"	"	"
27	Oleary Burgess	Sweden		No Proof	26	5	9	"	"	"
28	O. Hansen	Germ		" "	39	5	8	—	"	"
29	August Bachman	Russia		" "	26	5	8	Dark	Dark	Dark
30	J Wagerstrom	Sweden		" "	24	5	8	Light	Brown	Grey
31	Thomas Cassidy	Canada		" "	21	5	6	Light	Brown	Grey
32	J B Hayden	Mass		United States	20	5	7			

A TRUE COPY OF THE
ORIGINAL IN MY
POSSESSION.

Fra C... can
U. S. SHIPPING COMMISSIONER.

Donl M Laughlin

PORT OF NEW YORK,
STATE OF NEW YORK, } ss.

That on the day of the date hereof, before me personally came and appeared Danl McLaughlin do hereby certify
Master or Commander of the Ship Glory of the Seas
now about clearing out for San Francisco &co who being duly sworn, did solemnly and sincerely
declare that the above List contains the names of the Officers and Crew of the said Ship together with
the places of their Birth and Residence, as far as he hath been able to ascertain the same.

Given under my Hand and Seal of Office, at the Port of New York, this 6 day of Decr 1879

on the ship from Le Havre were obviously not "residents of New York."[2]

Long Eng, the ship's mess boy, was replaced by Frank Chappell's wife, Millie, a thirty-year-old Englishwoman, who signed on as stewardess. The Chappells would continue as crew members for the next two years.

Although the *Glory of the Seas* officially cleared at the New York Custom House on Friday, December 6, she didn't sail until the following Monday at 4:20 p.m. McLaughlin's subsequent passage of 118 days proved to be a vast improvement over his previous Cape Horn voyages. Showing his satisfaction in the *Glory*'s performance, McLaughlin's summary, published in the "memoranda" columns in the San Francisco newspapers the week of April 5, 1880, was to the point. It read in the *Alta* as follows:[3]

> Per *Glory of the Seas* — Sailed Dec. 9th, and crossed the Equator in Atlantic in lon 28 44 W., 22 days out; 50 S., 51 days out, [The *Chronicle* adds two lines omitted by the *Alta*: Pacific 10 days; crossed equator in Pacific in lon 111 26 W (92) days out, and 26 days] thence to port; winds the entire passage very light with exception of one gale in 46 S, lon 62 W.; ship has not had topgallant sails off of her for 67 days; got calm weather in 9 S., long. 107 W., and had nothing but light baffling airs and calms for 19 days; took NE trades in lat 9 N., long 114 W., and lost them in Lat 21 N., lon 125 W.; then light winds up to lat 33 N., lon 32 W.; then NW to SW winds two days, which run us up near the Farallones, where we lay becalmed for 24 hours; took a pilot at midnight, 4th inst.

On arrival at San Francisco, McLaughlin found that the *Glory of the Seas* was once again bettered by the *St. Stephen*, this time by five days. The latter vessel arrived two days before the *Glory*, 113 days from Philadelphia.

Capt. William E. Douglas, the *St. Stephen*'s commander, was known as a daring ship driver and on this passage he took his vessel to her limits recording the best westward Cape Horn voyage of her entire career.[4]

Water color of Glory of the Seas *with* Young America *in background by Carl G. Evers. Entitled "Conquerors of Cape Horn" it depicts the two ships in 1879. Courtesy Carl G. Evers.*

There was some very close sailing between the *Glory* and *St. Stephen*. The winds were fairly light for both vessels, except for one gale about 100 miles off the east coast of Argentina. They crossed latitude 50° south in the Atlantic on the same day. Thereafter, Captain McLaughlin kept his topgallant sails set until he reached San Francisco. Captain Douglas kept his royals set from the Falkland Islands to port. Both ships rounded Cape Horn from 50° south in the Atlantic to 50° south in the Pacific in the excellent time of ten days; however, the *St. Stephen* beat the *Glory* to the equator by two days. As they approached San Francisco, the *Glory* had nearly caught up with the *St. Stephen*, only to be becalmed for twenty-four hours.[5]

Three days after the *Glory of the Seas'* arrival, the still indomitable *Young America* arrived 102-1/2 days from New York, beating the elapsed time of both her competitors. This became the best westward passage in the *Young America*'s career, a remarkable feat for a twenty-seven-year-old wooden ship on her twenty-fourth voyage from the East Coast.[6] A second vessel arriving a week after the *Glory* was the down-Easter *Thrasher* which also made a 118-day passage.

The problem of crews being pirated off deep-water craft immediately after entering San Francisco Bay still existed. The *Glory*'s crew became fair game to boardinghouse runners. A statement by Joseph Malcolm Perry, a seaman aboard the Boston medium clipper *Southern Cross* which arrived about this time from Hong Kong, described the continuing victimization of sailors:

> One morning we sighted the Farallones and a towboat soon took [*Southern Cross*] through the Golden Gate, the entrance to San Francisco Bay [on April 15, 1880]. We were hardly fastened to the towboat and sails furled, before the boardinghouse runners were climbing over the ship's sides well supplied with whiskey bottles, which were forced on the crew, with invitations to come to their [boarding] houses.
>
> This was the usual order of things, and the captain and officers of the ship were powerless to prevent it, as they were dependent on the boardinghouses to furnish a new crew when the ship sailed again. In a short time the sailors were led over the side by the runners, and we

Ship Young America *at Vallejo Street Wharf, ca. 1877.* Sovereign of the Seas *is on other side of the wharf. Courtesy San Francisco NHP. Fireman's Fund Collection.*

did not see them again until they were paid off in the office of the U.S. [Shipping] Commissioner.

One of the evils of those days was that a sailor had very few real friends ashore, but fell into the hands of crimps and harpies who robbed him of his wages and advance money, then shipped him aboard another vessel within a few days of his arrival in port.[7]

Two days after the arrival of the *Glory* at San Francisco, the following consignee notice appeared in the *Daily Alta*:[8]

> Ship *Glory of the Seas* Captain D. McLaughlin, will commence discharging on WEDNESDAY MORNING, April 7, at Green Street wharf. Consignee will please call at the office of the undersigned, pay freight, and receive their orders. All merchandise when landed on the wharf, will be at the risk of the owners thereof, without regard to weather, and if not removed before five o'clock p.m. of each day, will be stored at their risk and expense.
>
> J. N. KNOWLES, 36 California Street

In four years, Captain Knowles had become an important shipping and commission merchant at San Francisco. Not only was he West Coast agent for the *Glory* and the other Sears Company fleet, but two Cape Horners, the ships *Louisiana* and *Mariposa*, both enroute to San Francisco with general cargo from New York, were also represented by his office.

Captain Knowles arranged for the *Glory of the Seas* to be berthed at Green Street Wharf, a 70 x 600-foot wooden pier adjoining Front Street on the northeastern waterfront. Like the wharf area fronting South Street at New York, the San Francisco waterfront was a forest of tall masts interspersed with shorter steamer and fore-and-aft rigged masts. However, at San Francisco there was far less congestion and a great deal more space between piers.

On April 8th, the marine reporter of the *Daily Alta* wrote in his column:

> We paid a visit to the ship *Glory of the Seas* yesterday. She was discharging at Green Street, is in splendid condition and looks well . . . May she live long under "Old Glory."[9]

Glory of the Seas *at Green Street Wharf, April 1880. Courtesy San Francisco Maritime NHP. Fireman's Fund Collection.*

All of the New York arrivals, along with the *Southern Cross*, were located within a quarter of a mile on the San Francisco waterfront. Starting at the Vallejo Street Wharf three vessels were berthed—*Young America, Seminole,* and *Southern Cross.* At Green Street, the *Glory of the Seas* lay berthed on the south side, and along the south side of the Union Street Wharf were the ships *Eureka* and *Thrasher.* The *St. Stephen* was berthed alongside Front Street.

Although J.N. Knowles was agent for the *Glory,* several local shipping and commission merchants acted as San Francisco agents for various other Cape Horners in port. George Howes & Co. represented the *Eureka, Seminole, Young America* and *St. Stephen.* Williams, Dimond & Co., one of the oldest shipping firms at San Francisco, was agent for *Thrasher* and *Southern Cross.*

A striking photographic record was preserved by a professional photographer[10] of some of these aristocratic sailing vessels in mid-April 1880. Two of the ships singled out were the *Glory of the Seas* and the *Southern Cross.* The glass image of the *Glory* caught her at her very best. Every line was in order, and her yards were crossed to a "T." A large, wooden-stock bower anchor hung from her port cathead, and the gilded scrollwork at her bows complemented the pale white of her beautiful figurehead.

The photograph of the *Southern Cross* berthed on the south side of the Vallejo Street Wharf illustrated a distinct contrast in design to the *Glory of the Seas.* Although nearly half the *Glory's* tonnage with a length of 176.8 feet, this vessel, built the year before the *Glory of the Seas* by Curtis and Smith at East Boston, was a good example of the typical American medium clipper constructed after the Civil War. The *Southern Cross* crossed a main-skysail like the *Glory* and appeared in first-class condition, even though she was twelve years old. She was managed by Baker and Morrill, one of the major sailing shipowners at Boston. Capt. Nathan F. Gibbs, her master, had squared all her yards to a "T" with the exception of her mainyard which was cockbilled for use as a cargo boom. As on the *Glory,* a bower anchor hung from her port cathead, and everything in her appearance looked neat and in good repair. Unlike the *Glory,* however, the *Southern Cross* had an ornate billethead which was the forward termination of two elaborately-

Ship Southern Cross *at Vallejo Street Wharf, April 1880.* Glory of the Seas *is to the left at Green Street Wharf. Courtesy San Francisco Maritime NHP. Fireman's Fund Collection.*

carved trailboards. Also, she had less sheer than the McKay-designed craft and less concavity in her upper body lines at the bow. To the left of this image the photographer caught the *Glory* at Green Street.

Captain Knowles had high expectations of obtaining a boom grain rate as predicted by the *New York Shipping Guide* the previous October. He fully understood, however, that "supply and demand" could easily raise or lower charter rates. In April 1880 he dealt with rates that had dropped considerably, although still at a profit-making level. Knowles accepted a reduced freight rate of £2 2s 6d ($10.23) per long ton from George W. McNear to load for Queenstown for orders during the last week of April.

Interestingly, the *Young America* was chartered for £2 6s 0d ($11.18), truly remarkable for a vessel her age. It was a tribute to her builder, William H. Webb of New York, as well as to her officers, crews, and owners, who maintained her in first-class condition for so many years.[11]

On May 6, a tug took the *Glory of the Seas* in tow, making a thirty-mile trip up San Francisco Bay to Vallejo on Carquinez Strait. Here the *Glory* loaded at the Starr Flouring Mills. This mill and grain-loading facility was situated at South Vallejo on the east side of the Mare Island Channel, and had been in operation since 1869. The main building was a seven-story grain elevator constructed of wood. It was built on a wooden wharf which carried railroad spur lines. The wharf jutted out into sufficiently deep water to allow ships the size of the *Glory of the Seas* to come alongside.[12] Here she loaded the greater quantity of her 1880 grain cargo in 100-pound sacks. Ten days later a tug towed the ship back to San Francisco and berthed her alongside the large grain-loading terminal at Mission Rock where she received the balance of her cargo.

Meanwhile, on May 20, the *Young America* sailed for Liverpool. The major differences in the overall hull design of the two ships *Young America* and *Glory of the Seas* — that of extreme clipper and medium clipper — could be readily seen by the cargo manifests published in the *Daily Alta* for the two vessels. It showed that the *Young America*'s cargo was almost half that of the *Glory of the Seas*.

The following shows the distinct differences in cargo capacity:[13]

Vessel	Cargo	Short Tons	Value
Young America	36,988 centals	1,850	$ 64,728
Glory of the Seas	68,149 centals	3,407	$112,400
	39,000 board feet lumber		$ 580

Although the *Young America* was just inches shorter than the *Glory*, she measured 664 gross tons less. Meanwhile, managing owners of other vessels held off on accepting charters for grain and in the hopes that freight rates would rise. This is how the ships *St. Stephen* and *Thrasher* came to be chartered for single voyages in which they hauled coal for the Pacific Mail Steamship Company from Nanaimo, British Columbia, to San Francisco at the rate of $2.75 per ton.[14] Unfortunately, the *Thrasher*, a three-year-old vessel, didn't complete her voyage. As she was being towed coal-laden to sea from Nanaimo, she accidentally went ashore and became a total loss. The wreck was sold for $500.[15]

Although the *Young America* and the *Glory of the Seas* were successful in obtaining profitable charter rates, acquiring foremast crews was still a problem. Seamen were noticeably scarce on the San Francisco waterfront in the spring of 1880. Even Captain H.T. Baker, master of the *Young America*, had been unable to get a crew in a timely fashion in spite of his vessel's fine reputation.[16] The boardinghouse runners and shipping masters claimed they had difficulty recruiting qualified men for departing Cape Horners. In fact, every shipmaster except Capt. Baker waited until the latter part of May before they were able to ship foremast hands. From the time the *Young America* cleared San Francisco on May 19th until the *Glory* cleared ten days later, only one grain ship, the British bark (ex-ship) *Middlesex*, received a deep-water crew.

On Friday, May 28, Captain McLaughlin finally had a crew on board consisting of fifteen A.B.s, five O.S.s and one shanghaied ship's boy. Five of the men were last-minute replacements

*View of San Francisco waterfront from Telegraph Hill, ca. 1881. Vallejo Street Wharf
is third from left. San Francisco Panorama, No. 6. I.W. Tabor, photographer. Courtesy
San Francisco Maritime NHP, Accession No. a11.15,550n.*

Bark Penguin, *ships* Sovereign of the Seas *and* Mariposa *all laden with cargo at anchor on San Francisco Bay, ca. 1880. Courtesy San Francisco Maritime NHP, Fireman's Fund Collection.*

(pierhead jumps) for sailors who signed Articles but failed to join the ship.[17]

The shanghaied boy was an unwilling recruit on the *Glory of the Seas*. Eighteen-year-old William B. Joseph, son of a Boston sea captain, happened to be on the waterfront on sailing day and was coerced by several crimps to join the *Glory*. Although he was from a maritime family, Joseph had little sea experience. He was stocky, big-boned, and of medium height, but was in delicate health because of tuberculosis. Through intimidation and threat of a beating, the crimps forced Joseph to sign shipping articles. He allowed himself to be transported out to the ship lying at anchor awaiting last minute crew replacements. Unfortunately, neither the crimps, government officials, nor ship's officers cared to listen when Joseph tried telling them he had tuberculosis and no hope of a cure.

On May 30, the *Glory of the Seas* was towed out to sea in the face of a west wind, bound for "Cork for orders" [actually Queenstown (Cobh) Ireland]. From the first days at sea, William Joseph, the new ship's boy, found that the general nineteenth century cure for tuberculosis — complete bed rest with a carefully balanced diet — was not included in his job description.

The standard watch system on board sailing ships, four hours on, four hours off, with two two-hour dog-watches — a twelve hour work day — was seven days a week. Joseph would not get more than four hours' rest at a time. He wondered whether he would live to complete the voyage.

After a few days at sea, Joseph's hands were badly blistered, but he endured the hardening-up period like any novice. He constantly swept down the decks, washed paint work, holystoned, coiled ropes and performed other ship's boy duties. The mates required William Joseph to learn the fundamentals of working a big square-rigger at sea. Moreover, he endured the traditional verbal and physical abuse of his shipmates as a part of the learning process. It was almost unheard of for a ship's boy to be told "Job well done!"

As his hands began to callous, he found himself able to stand such hard duty as hauling on a rope, completely different from merely pulling on a rope. At first, not knowing the technique,

Joseph, with his limited strength, hauled his guts out and quivered with exhaustion. However, he finally learned how to haul as one along with his shipmates in rhythm to chantyman's songs such as "What do you do with a drunken sailor." In time, young Joseph toughened up and his emaciated frame filled out.

As required under the existing U.S. maritime laws, the sailors were fed a standard shipboard diet, one usually devoid of fresh fruits and vegetables. Because refrigeration was nonexistent aboard the *Glory of the Seas* a limited variety of salt beef, pork, fish, dried vegetables, and ship's biscuit were the main fare in the fo'c'sle.

By the time the four-month voyage was over, a seeming miracle had occurred. Willam B. Joseph was completely cured of his tuberculosis.[19] Had he not been in good health, Captain McLaughlin would have been required to pay for his extended treatment at a British hospital.

The *Glory of the Seas* arrived at Queenstown on Monday, September 27, 120 uneventful days from San Francisco. Of the previous May's sailings the only vessel making a better run from San Francisco was the *Young America* which arrived at Liverpool on September 3, 106 days out. Fortunately, McLaughlin experienced no mishaps, unlike the British bark *Middlesex* which made the disaster columns of the shipping newspapers on several occasions. The British ship *Cannanore*, also listed in the mishap columns, sailed from San Francisco on May 13th, two and one-half weeks before the *Glory*. Both ships suffered frequent storm damage. The *Cannanore* made a 153-day passage to Queenstown. The British bark *Springwood*, which sailed ten days after the *Glory*, made a 166-day passage. All in all, Daniel McLaughlin had good reason to be pleased with the *Glory*'s voyage to Queenstown in the year 1880.

CHAPTER XI

A Close Call

Following her arrival at Queenstown, Ireland, the *Glory of the Seas* lay at anchor for nearly a week awaiting orders from the grain consignee. It was Sunday, October 3, 1880, before Captain McLaughlin weighed anchor, took on a St. George's Channel pilot and sailed for Dublin, about 200 miles distant, her final port of discharge.

On October 4th, the *Glory* arrived off Kish Bank, a narrow sand and rock reef about fifteen miles east of Dublin Bay. Here the ship was caught in a sudden gale in restricted waters. Dublin Bay, at the mouth of the River Liffey, was generally shallow. At a distance of nearly a mile east from shore the bay was only eighteen feet deep at low water, except for the dredged ship channel located in the center of the Bay. Heading west toward Dublin, the pilot found it impossible for the *Glory* to cross the bar to the narrow ship channel because of a heavy sea running into the Bay. Furthermore, the *Glory of the Seas* drew twenty-five feet[1] and the Dublin Bar was only twenty feet at low water.

The next day, the St. George's pilot instructed Captain McLaughlin to make for Kingstown (Dun Laoghaire) Harbor on the south side of Dublin Bay. Formed by two large granite breakwaters jutting in a northerly direction about a quarter of a mile from the south shore of the Bay, it has a narrow entry only 760 feet wide. McLaughlin and his crew, however, aided by the Channel pilot, brought the *Glory* to a supposedly safe anchorage within the confines of the Kingstown breakwater.[2]

Unfortunately, the location had very poor holding ground, especially for a three-decked sailing ship with 3,400-tons of cargo on board. With easterly gale winds fiercely blowing and heavy seas running into the harbor, the *Glory of the Seas* dragged her anchors. Suddenly, one anchor chain snapped. Out of control and dragging her remaining anchor, she struck the sandy bottom. For about an hour the *Glory* pounded on the bottom with each wave. A small steam tug came to her assistance and attempted, without immediate success, to haul her off into deeper water.[3]

After about three hours, the tug repositioned the *Glory of the Seas* in the harbor; however, with the next low tide the big square-rigger grounded again on the sandy bottom. Finally, on Wednesday morning, two tugs from Dublin steamed over to Kingstown harbor, passed their hawsers, and by 1:00 p.m. towed the *Glory* to a safe anchorage near the guard ship at Kingstown.[4]

During the following week storm winds abated and seas became relatively calm, enabling Captain McLaughlin to arrange to have his cargo unloaded. McLaughlin made a formal request to the Dublin port engineer to bring the ship directly up the River Liffey to unload alongside one of the quays fronting the river. However, since the depth of the main channel and alongside the quays was five to ten feet less than the *Glory*'s draft, it was decided to lighter out a portion of her cargo.[5]

Rather than hire a local lightering service, McLaughlin temporarily chartered the 417-ton barkentine *Nereide* which lay at anchor in Kingstown Harbor. Unfortunately, his effort to save the ship money became more complex and expensive than it was worth. Within several days of the *Glory* anchoring near the Kingstown guard ship, the *Nereide* was brought alongside. Subsequently, about 650 tons of sacked grain were transferred to the smaller vessel and discharged alongside the quays. Once sufficient grain was removed, a tug towed the *Glory* up the River Liffey to a Dublin quay.[6]

Instead of using automated unloading facilities such as were used at Liverpool, Dublin stevedores unloaded "according to custom;" that is, in the same manner as half century before. Two of

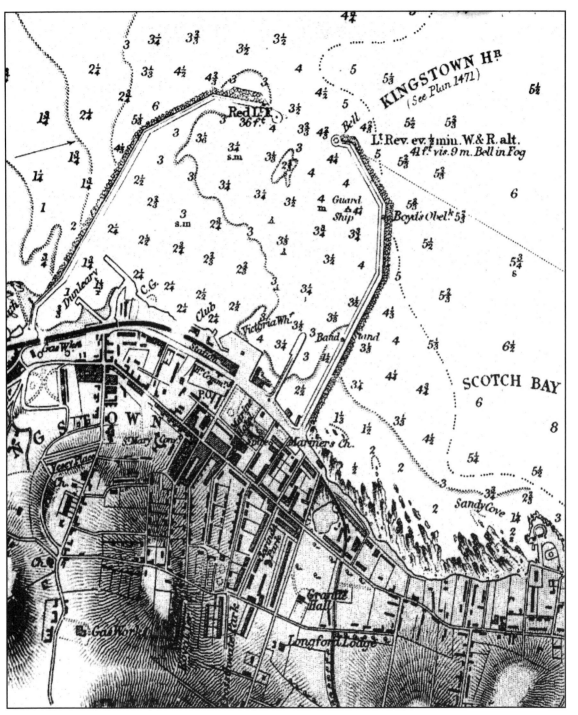

Chart of Kingstown Harbor, Admiralty Chart for Dublin Bay, 1874. Author's collection.

the *Glory's* hatches were worked at the same time. Each unloading area was rigged separately but the ship's yards were not used as cargo booms. Initially, the Dublin stevedores rigged a wire stay between the masts along with a single block over the center of the hatch with a single rope fall. Next, they secured a hand-operated winch to the hatch coaming and led a rope fall to the winch. A beam scale installed on a wooden platform at the *Glory's* bulwarks allowed clearance of the ship's six-foot bulwarks as the grain left the ship.[7]

When their unloading gear was in place, the gangs took a tea break, which, according to custom, was always done before the hatches were opened. After they finally removed the hatch covers, part of the longshore gang went below and began unloading the remaining wheat from the upper 'tween decks. But instead of unloading the 100-pound sacks, they cut each sack open and dumped the contents in the square of the 'tween deck hatch. The grain was then scooped up in buckets and poured it into large, narrow sacks. A rope fall was tied to each sack and it was winched up to the main deck where it was transferred onto a scale beam and weighed under the direction of a weigh master — dressed in a long, green coat and a top hat — who tied the top of each sack with a red band and sealed it with wax.[8] The final step in unloading consisted of swinging the sack (attached to the scale beam) over the adjoining quay where it was dropped into a wooden cart which took it to a nearby grain storage building. Discharging the entire cargo took about five weeks.

On October 27 Captain McLaughlin was startled to learn he was being double taxed for his cargo. The Custom House collector charged a tonnage tax for the *Nereide* for her portion of the cargo which she loaded alongside the *Glory* and discharged at the quay. The Custom House collector then charged the *Glory* for the tax on her full cargo, explaining that "tolls were due by Act of Parliament." McLaughlin strenuously objected. The Port and Docks Board was entirely separate from the Custom House authority and the Board of Works eventually paid a refund to the grain consignee, thereby saving the *Glory* from paying the extra tax.[9]

Although none of the *Glory of the Seas'* cargo became water-damaged at Kingstown, the ship's insurance carrier instructed that she be thoroughly surveyed for possible damage to her metal fastenings due to her brief pounding. Even without a thorough marine survey, they assumed that some of her copper sheathing was damaged and needed replacing. When her cargo was unloaded, McLaughlin, under instructions from J. Henry Sears & Company, arranged to have the *Glory* docked and coppered. Fortunately, Dublin had a 432-foot graving dock on the north bank of the River Liffey that could be used for this purpose.

In the dock, marine surveyors thoroughly inspected her bottom. Although her yellow metal sheathing was not extensively damaged, they decided, because the sheathing was thirty months old, the *Glory* should be completely re-coppered. Actually, the estimated damage to her hull was minor — $4,000 — considering the insurance underwriters valued the *Glory of the Seas* at $65,000 and insured her for $61,438.[10]

While the *Glory* was in the graving dock, the surveyors opened her up in specified areas to determine whether she still rated a special insurance classification "A-1 in Red" which was initially assigned her by the American Shipmasters Association. This required a rigid inspection of hull, spars, sails and other equipment. These rules said in part:

> . . . all outside plank deemed necessary by the Surveyor to be removed, to an extent equal to three strakes all around the vessel, and sufficient at the ends to expose all the cants, apron, sternpost and transoms, bolts, and tree-nails to be driven out according to the Surveyor's judgment, in number sufficient to determine the exact condition of the fastenings; . . . masts to be bored, spars, standing and running rigging, and sails, to be in perfect order.[11]

The *Glory of the Seas* passed inspection. The marine surveyor recommended that her special classification be extended to the fifteen-year mark dating from October 1869. This was an excellent rating for a large wooden-hulled vessel, especially since many similar ships were not rated beyond ten years. It was a further tribute to Donald McKay, and to the *Glory*'s managing owners and masters who carefully maintained and repaired her through the years.

When the marine surveyor completed his inspection, shipwrights replaced the planking and the *Glory*'s bottom was covered with ship felt. Then workers installed a new suit of copper sheets (yellow metal) up to her load line.

On November 27, 1880, almost two months after her arrival at Dublin, the *Glory of the Seas* came out of the graving dock newly sheathed and freshly painted. In the days that followed she was ballasted, then crossed St. George's Channel to Cardiff, Wales, where she received her homeward cargo for San Francisco.

McLaughlin hired four ship runners — temporary hands hired solely as crew replacements — to help sail the *Glory* the 230 miles to Cardiff. This was done on December 4, 1880, with the U.S. Consul at Dublin acting as a shipping commissioner.[12] However, due to delays in departure, the *Glory* did not arrive at the Welsh port for another six days.

Following arrival at Cardiff, the *Glory of the Seas* loaded 1,732 tons of coke and 600 tons of pig iron, the total value of her cargo being $10,399,[13] the least valuable cargo she had carried to date. The next two-and-a-half weeks were taken up with loading cargo, provisioning the ship, and acquiring a replacement crew for her return voyage.

In the meantime, seventeen seamen, including the ship's boy, William B. Joseph, deserted.[14] Unlike the other seamen, Joseph returned to San Francisco with but one thought in mind — to leave the world of deep-water sailing ships. Following his return to the Bay area, he married and settled in Oakland. Eventually he became a stationary steam engineer in commercial buildings in the downtown Oakland area.

In his later years, Joseph built a detailed model of the *Glory of the Seas* using his distinct memories of the vessel and her outfit. Although not professionally done, his attention to specific deck details gave the model a realistic appearance. Starting forward, Joseph showed the two brake handles on her fo'c'sle-head. On the aft end of the fo'c'sle-head he attached a miniature ship's brass bell which undoubtedly reminded him that he actually heard and rang the *Glory*'s bell many times marking each half hour through the day. William Joseph painted the model's capstans — one located on the fo'c'sle-head and the other immediately forward of the mizzen hatch — bright red. The large main pump wheels also were painted the same color as were the fire buckets situated on the aft end of the forward house. Moreover, the model had deck furniture such as a boarding ladder and a large, red-painted balsa life raft located on the forward house top along with three white-painted ship's boats. These details reflect distinct memories of Joseph's first deep-water voyage. His model of the *Glory of the Seas* took twenty-eight months to build.

William B. Joseph lived until 1942, sixty-two years after his 1880 passage aboard the *Glory of the Seas*.[15]

On December 27, 1880, the *Glory* departed Cardiff bound for San Francisco. Bad weather in the North Atlantic adversely affected her passage to the equator. Bad weather also affected all vessels sailing within a week of her from the British Isles. The *Glory of the Seas* crossed the Line in the Atlantic, thirty-five days out on January 31, 1881, but made a very fast run of twenty-two days to 50º South, crossing that latitude on February 22. Four days later she passed Cape Horn. Rounding the Horn, the weather was extreme as the *Glory* headed westerly and then northerly, battling gale winds and blinding sheets of rain. Amazingly, Captain McLaughlin made the passage from 50º south in the Atlantic to 50º south in the Pacific in eleven days; thence northerly, having to tack and wear constantly with winds from the north which continued for fifteen days. The *Glory of the Seas* reached the southeast tradewinds in latitude 25º south. McLaughlin carried the trades up to the doldrums in the Pacific just south of the equator. Another week of light airs and calms took her to latitude 6º north where northerly winds again slowed her progress. The final voyage segment from the Line to San Francisco was twenty-eight days, totalling 129 days for the entire passage. She arrived there on May 5, 1881.[16]

Despite a fairly long voyage, the *Glory of the Seas* made the best run of any sailing ship departing the United Kingdom in the

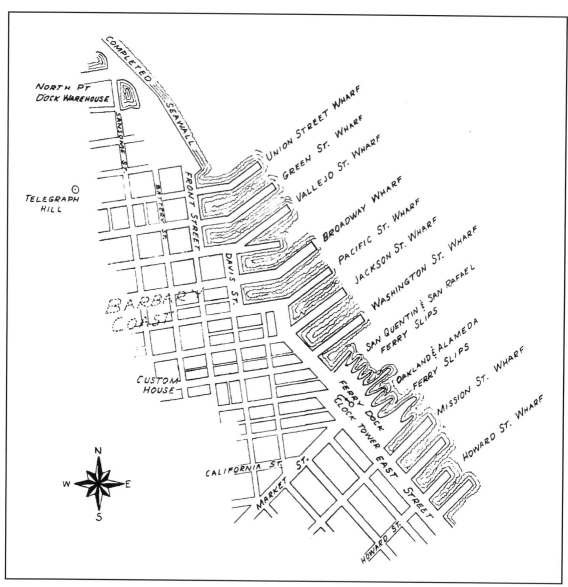

*Map of northern San Francisco waterfront by the author based on U.S. Coast Survey
(NOAA) charts, 1881.*

latter half of December 1880 and the early part of January 1881. Three other vessels arrived at San Francisco from the British Isles on May 5th: the *Hecla*, 135 days from Liverpool; the iron ship *Chinsura*, 138 days from Liverpool; and the four-mast bark *Glencairn*, 135 days from Glasgow, Scotland.

All four of these vessels made long runs to the equator in the Atlantic, but the *Glory*'s 35-day segment to the Line was the shortest of the fleet, *Chinsura*'s 40 days being the longest. Each of these ships experienced strong gales off Cape Horn but made good roundings of the Horn despite the adverse weather. The *Glory* forged ahead of all three vessels by the time 50° south in the Pacific was reached and, with the exception of the *Chinsura*, which crossed one day before, stayed in the lead until the equator was passed.[17]

The *Glencairn* was a fine example of the type of sailing vessel fast supplanting the *Glory of the Seas*, other similar wooden-hulled vessels, and smaller vessels of iron, of course — all being full-riggers in the California grain trade. Built of iron in 1878, the *Glencairn*, length, 252.4 feet and tonnage, 1,620, was a unit of the popular Shire Line, with the typical gunport-painted color scheme of many British vessels. She was neither as lofty nor as heavily-sparred as the *Glory*. The *Glencairn*'s master, Captain Tannock, had a reputation as a hard shipdriver.[18]

The *Glencairn* and her four-masted iron sisters in the British merchant marine had a distinct advantage over the *Glory*. They were newer and their iron construction made them less costly to maintain. Most deep-water sailors, however, viewed the *Glory of the Seas*, with her deep draft and six-foot-high bulwarks as a safer and more comfortable sea vessel, especially when the tempestuous seas of the southern latitudes were roaring high and sweeping over the decks.

Most four-masted barks had open wheels aft. With their low silhouettes and relatively short bulwarks, they were considered wet vessels. Not until the mid-1880s would some of the larger British sailing ships be designed with midship houses. This made them much safer in breaking up the heavy seas thrown on deck and more comfortable, so far as their crews were concerned.

An exception to most iron four-masted bark rigs was the *Glencairn*'s suit of studdingsails. Whereas, McLaughlin in the *Glory* dispensed with these light-weather sails, the *Glencairn* came to the Shire Line with stuns'l booms as high as her top-gallant yards. This use of studdingsails may have accounted for the four-day-shorter run of the *Glencairn* in very light winds from the Line in the Pacific to San Francisco in comparison to the *Glory*. In rough weather, however, the *Glory of the Seas* proved to be the more weatherly vessel. In matter of fact, she beat all three British vessels in rounding the Horn.[19]

Four days after her arrival at San Francisco, the *Glory* lay at Oakland Long Wharf discharging her cargo. Balfour, Guthrie & Co., San Francisco shipping and commission merchants, directed her cargo discharge.

Capt. and Mrs. McLaughlin traveled down the coast to Fresno County to look at large tracts of property. At fifty-eight years of age, Captain McLaughlin was beginning to think of eventual retirement. They purchased sixty acres of soil-rich land in the San Joaquin Valley, situated about five miles outside Fresno at the little community of Oleander.[20] The captain decided to become a grape grower once he permanently retired from the sea.

Captain McLaughlin's son, Carl, described his father's and Maggie's efforts as novice wine grape producers:

> The land had been leveled and planted to Muscat grape vines, and had the jack rabbits been possessed with any decent regard for other's property at that early date, it would not have been necessary to replant the vineyard nor to get some fast greyhounds to kill the jacks faster than the jacks could eat the vines.[21]

By the end of May 1881, Captain Knowles chartered the *Glory* a third time to G.W. McNear. This year her destination was Le Havre, France. Knowles obtained a rate of £3 13 s 6d ($17.76), the highest grain rate she received in over six years. This offered the potential for higher net profits as long as no mishaps occurred on the voyage.[22]

While the McLaughlins worked on their new vineyard project, a tug towed the *Glory of the Seas* up the Bay to Port Costa to the large grain-loading facilities located on the south side of Carquinez Strait. A major boom in commercial warehouse construction took place in this region beginning in 1879, a preview of future developments.

The Central Pacific Railroad shortened its track route west from Sacramento by constructing a huge railroad ferry to traverse mile-wide Carquinez Strait. This gave grain merchants the impetus to construct large warehouses and wooden wharves on the south shore of Carquinez Strait adjoining the landing.

The 3,549-gross-ton ferry *Solano,* the largest sidewheeler in the world, began service on December 28, 1879. Not until 1880, however, did she start carrying train loads of grain at Benicia on the four sets of tracks laid on her 420-foot wooden deck. From there, she chugged across the Strait to the massive ferry landing just east of the newly-built grain warehouses. The nearly 68,000 sacks of grain loaded aboard the *Glory of the Seas* in 1881 were brought over on the *Solano.*[23]

Port Costa, located at the foot of a steep bluff across from Benicia, had no roads leading to it at this early date. It was simply a place to load grain ships. By the end of the 1881-1882 grain year, Port Costa would outstrip San Francisco, Vallejo, and Oakland by loading more ships than any other single place on San Francisco Bay. Over 100 ships would load there.[24]

In the grain year beginning June 30, 1882, 559 vessels, 154 of them American, carried 1,128,031 tons of wheat and barley and 919,898 barrels of flour from the various loading areas on San Francisco Bay to Europe. It was a boom year for shippers and sailing ship owners.[25]

CHAPTER XII
Disaster Averted

On July 9, 1881, Captain Daniel McLaughlin's foremast sailors signed on before a deputy U.S. Shipping commissioner at the Custom House at San Francisco. This voyage, the ratio of American citizens in his crew was about one-third those of foreign birth. An even dozen subjects of Queen Victoria signed articles, including both stewards and one of the boatswains. This was an indication of the numerous United Kingdom bottoms that arrived in San Francisco Bay and would eventually haul a large amount of California grain to Europe during the 1881-1882 boom year.[1] It likewise proved many subjects of the Crown still preferred shipping on American sailing ships with their better food and living conditions. The sailor's common viewpoint was if he were going to be shanghaied at San Francisco, he'd fight such impressment less if his ship were an American vessel.

The monthly wages for deep-water sailors shipping foreign out of San Francisco continued at $25. But with a dead horse of about $60 deducted from his future wages, the sailor's incentive to excel was generally lacking. This anachronistic ship employment system increasingly affected the ability of deep-water shipmasters to attract qualified seamen and officers to their craft.

As the use of steamships increasingly became a predominant force in many ocean trades, sailors looking to the future had to admit that sail would eventually lose out to steam. Thus, as each decade passed, especially after the American Civil War, square-rig sail under the U.S. flag continued a slow decline.

Captain McLaughlin departed San Francisco on July 11, bound for Le Havre. Thirty squareriggers cleared from the Bay for the United Kingdom and continental Europe that month. The down-Easter *Hagarstown* left the same day as the *Glory*, bound for Antwerp, Belgium, with 3,012 short tons of grain on board. In comparison, the *Glory of the Seas* had 3,372 tons on board. The total value of the *Glory*'s cargo was $94,560. Although not the most valuable cargo she ever carried, it was the largest as well as the most valuable cargo of the fleet sailing from San Francisco that month.[2]

Captain Dexter Whitmore, master of the *Hagarstown*, previously sailed on July 9, but returned to port the following morning after suffering damage to the iron work on his main yard. After repairs, tugs towed both the *Hagarstown* and the *Glory* beyond the San Francisco Bar and let them go on the following morning.[3]

Captain McLaughlin had only two mates this voyage. Instead of a third officer, he shipped two men rated as boatswains, more commonly called bo'suns. One of these petty officers came from Australia, and the other was a native of Germany. Bo'suns were intermediaries between officers and foremast hands. They administered much of the actual follow-through of the mate's orders aboard ship and were expected to be the best practical sailors on board. They acted as foreman of each watch under the nominal supervision of the two mates. It was not uncommon for a bo'sun to knock a man down with his fist for failure to step lively when given an order. Although Captain McLaughlin did not generally allow "bucko" brutality (such as beating a man with a belaying pin or kicking him while he was down), he did not tolerate insubordination, either verbally or in action. A seaman could easily find himself in irons (handcuffs) for disobedience of orders.[4]

Twenty-three men made up the foremast hands, six of whom were ordinary seamen, while the remainder were able-bodied seamen. Of this group, eight were American citizens, nine British and the balance German, Russian, Scandinavian, Austrian and

Belgian. Most of these sailors were "hard-case," that is, semi-wild, tough, hardened men used to the most bitter weather conditions imaginable. They expected rough treatment from officers for any attempt at insubordination even though American maritime authorities viewed such treatment as illegal. They were fortunate to have shipped aboard the *Glory of the Seas* — a vessel whose master didn't tolerate any type of extreme methods to maintain shipboard discipline unless extenuating circumstances arose.[5]

Most deep-water sailors of this post-Civil War period had simple requirements — a wooden frame bunk bed, a straw-filled mattress, three good meals a day, including sailor's grade coffee ("freshly brewed" at 5 a.m. every morning), tobacco and pipe, and sufficient work clothes, including rain gear. Their plans when ashore were vague, and even more so on board ship — get to the next seaport and its Sailortown sometime in the distant future. Tomorrow would take care of itself. Today was what counted. They were a wild, brutal, restless breed, and very few of these deep-water vagabonds amounted to anything or lived to an advanced age.[6]

An exception to the general rule was John Gribble. Born on the Isle of Jersey in 1852, he was twenty-nine years old in 1881. A stocky, broad-shouldered man, five feet-five inches in height, and utterly fearless, he was a hard-case sailor.[7] There was one major and important difference. Gribble kept a day-to-day diary during his seagoing days which enabled him to describe his voyage on the *Glory* in detail. He was a merchant sailor, but his earlier experiences aboard the ill-fated man-o'-war HMS *Captain* literally saved the *Glory of the Seas* on her forthcoming voyage.[8]

Gribble arrived at San Francisco on May 23, 1881, on the British bark *Inglewood*, Captain Brockelbank, completing a seventy-eight-day passage from Newcastle, New South Wales. He joined the *Inglewood* at Le Havre in June 1880 for a voyage to Algoa Bay, South Africa "and farther" [As was stated in the shipping articles.] John Gribble, however, decided that San Francisco was far enough on a lime-juicer and jumped ship just before the *Inglewood* sailed for Queenstown on June 23. Gribble indulged in two weeks of Barbary Coast wine, women, and song before being told by his boardinghouse master that he expected him to sail as an Able-

John Gribble, able-bodied seaman on Glory of the Seas *in 1881. Pencil sketch by Sharla R. Mjelde shows Gribble in Royal Navy uniform. Courtesy of the author.*

Bodied seaman on the *Glory of the Seas.* On July 9, 1881, John Gribble, who used the alias "Henry Myers" when he signed articles,[9] went on board with the rest of the crew. The ship sailed south from San Francisco on July 11 towards a rendezvous with near disaster.

By August 22, the *Glory* was at latitude 41° 15' south, longitude 106° 30' west, heading south under shortened sail (she was about a week ahead of the *Hagarstown*). Suddenly a hurricane struck, throwing the heavily-laden vessel on her port side. Her bulwarks were fully engulfed and she was forced over more than forty-five degrees. Although she came back partially upright, the abrupt lateral motion shifted her cargo. For nearly sixteen hours she remained on her beam ends in a hove-to condition, with lower yards and topsail yardarms dipping into the storm-tossed Pacific.[10] John Gribble's memory of this situation, reconstructed from his diary, goes on to say:[11]

We passed Pitcairn's Island, and all went well with us until we encountered a gale off Cape Horn.

It was August 22, 1881. A southerly gale was blowing at the time, and by 8 a.m., we were running with close-reefed topsails [set] and [we] had stowed the jib and mainsail . . . One big monster of a sea swept nine men overboard, but the heavy roll of the ship scooped up piles of water and threw us all back on board. I found myself with piles of loose ropes about 20 feet up on the main rigging. Not one man was lost! . . . The ship was laboring heavy and heavy seas were breaking over her. At ten a.m. while hands were pumping her out (we have four pumps), a heavy sea swept the deck, smashing a boat, drew the bolts out of the skids; this shifted our cargo to one side, throwing the ship onto her beam ends with heavy seas breaking clean over her. The seams of the deck [planking] opened, and the water poured down below. We had 3,000 [long] tons of wheat on board.

[The captain] called all hands to wear ship and trim cargo with one watch on the pumps. [We] sounded the pumps and found four feet of water. The men lined up to windward to knound [haul hand over hand] in the braces.

A rope was slipped over the second mate [Samuel Sawyer's shoulders] to lower him down to leeward to slack off the lee braces. He

flung the rope off and refused to go — the lee side of the ship was
under water. The rope was then put over one of the boatswains and he
and the other [boatswain] refused to go. The ship was in a bad position and it would not take many minutes to put her clean over.

As Gribble stood on the slanting deck of the *Glory of the
Seas,* memories of the HMS *Captain* in the Bay of Biscay flooded
over him. During a training cruise on September 7, 1870, the
Captain turned turtle in a severe squall and sank with the loss of
472 men.[12] It happened so suddenly that Gribble, inexperienced
in such a situation, was helpless. Only eighteen men, including
Gribble, survived the disaster. As he recounted in his journal eleven
years before:

> . . . I let go the brace and made a jump for the hammock netting,
> but only succeeded in catching hold with my hands. I looked over my
> shoulder and could see the lower yards under water and the sea ap-
> peared like a boiling cauldron, and a very heavy sea was coming from
> the lee side. I could hear them to windward. The sea broke on board.
> I was frightened and shut my eyes.

This memory, the cries of his shipmates, and the sounds of
a dying ship haunted him. The disaster that befell the *Captain*
seemed about to happen again to the *Glory of the Seas.*

> Captain McLauchlan [sic], an old man with long, grey curly hair,
> was in a very serious mood. No officer to venture down to leeward?
> He was almost crying when he said, "Have I no one who will go?" I
> looked up and said, "Captain, you have a dozen men waiting to go, but
> it is the officer's duty."
>
> I realized that there would be no ship or men unless we could
> bring the ship around, so I said, "I am number one!" Little did I think
> that I would ever come back; so the captain said, "Volunteer!" I jumped.
>
> They put a rope around me but I flung it off and said that I would
> go if the mate [J.C. Cooper] would watch for one [a heavy sea coming
> aboard], and not let me get caught unprepared. Right here I want to
> say that the seas off Cape Horn are long and regular, not like the At-
> lantic and Bay of Biscay.

The mate said that he would look out for me — which he did well. The stewardess [Millie Chappell] was watching through the glass cabin door and told me afterwards that she could see my teeth clench, and I went as white as a sheet (you must remember that I had been through a deal like this once before). She told me after it was all over that they expected to see me killed with the first sea that broke over me, and I never expected anything else; but there was a chance there, but none if we did not try to get the ship around.

. . . so I marched down [the deck of the *Glory*], and when the mate would call out, "Look Out! Look Out!" I prepared for the shock by belaying the braces and would take a half hitch over the pin and wind both my arms close up to the pins. Then I took hold, one hand on top of the other under the rail and lay right up against the ship's side; but when the sea broke 20 feet high, it smothered me. It would have smashed me to bits if it had caught me away from the ship's side. I slacked the braces, inch by inch, and the men gathered in, and finally got the ship around with the wind on the other side. My arms were badly skinned [to the elbows] and my ribs sore, but no damage done.

Because of Gribble's efforts, the crew hauled the *Glory*'s yards around and brought her around on the other tack. Then Gribble went below to clear the pumps which were choked with loose grain when dozens of sacks in the lower hold burst as the *Glory* went over on her beam ends making it impossible to keep the water level down in her bilges.[13]

As Gribble tells it:

The next thing was to pump her out. The ship was still in a very dangerous position: on her beam ends, so we found all the pumps were choked. The captain called for a volunteer to go below and try to clear them. The men were all afraid that she would turn over while they were down there and none would go; so the captain asked me, would I go? He said, "I hate to ask you, but if you will go, I'll do anything for you, and you need not do another tap of work during the voyage." I pointed to my arms, and he said, "if you go and we get out of this, we'll nurse you;" so I went. It meant diving down among all that hot wheat and getting it away from the [pump] suction [area] . . .

I was fortunate in getting the main pump cleaned and started again. Then all hands were put to work trimming the cargo.

This continued until the crew, feverishly working below in her listing 'tween decks, were able to partially re-stow enough cargo to bring her back to a fairly even keel. At the same time, men worked at the pumps on her sloping main deck to remove the four feet of water in her hold.[14]

Gribble:

We won out. We were lying to under the main [lower] topsail. That was a close call for the *Glory of the Seas*; but I have never shirked my work. I never laid up, putting work on my shipmates. The captain and stewardess bandaged me up. It was only skin deep anyway . . . She told me that [her husband, Frank] had been watching when I went forward and thought that I would be killed, and asked me if I was not afraid. "Afraid," I exclaimed, "that is why I went! I was afraid not to go, because unless some person did, the ship would turn over, and everybody would be drowned." It was better to risk being washed overboard and have a chance for life than to hang back and [face] certain death.

It was a sad commentary that Captain Daniel McLaughlin, a seasoned shipmaster with forty-five years of maritime experience, had to ask for a foremast hand to volunteer for a life-threatening duty when both his mates and the two boatswains declined. Gribble, fortunately had the necessary experience — learned on the HMS *Captain* eleven years before — that enabled him to go "above and beyond the call of duty" — and it saved the *Glory of the Seas* and her crew from total disaster.

The following day, August 23, McLaughlin gave orders to make for Valparaiso, Chile, about 2,000 miles east. There was no way to save the cargo without hull repairs.

Gribble's diary continues:

The next day, I turned up to do my duty when my watch was called, and the captain asked me what I was doing, reminding me that I did not have to do any work. I told him that I did not want any reward for saving my own life.

Gribble tersely reported the further events of the day following her mishap:

> We set the topsails, squared yards, and ran for Valparaiso, Chile, for repairs and the next days got all the pumps clear. [Had] lots of hail squalls.

On August 30, his journal read, "sighted the Island of Juan Fernandez, Robinson Crusoe's Island which lies in lat. 33° 45' south, long. 78°, 52' west" and for the following four days the crew stayed by the pumps as the crippled ship sailed toward the South American port.

The *Glory of the Seas* arrived there on September 3 where, according to Gribble, she was "anchored in the Roads of Valparaiso." Valparaiso, the largest and most important seaport on the West Coast of South America, is laid out on the south side of the semicircular Bay of Valparaiso. A spur of barren hills terminating on the west at Penta Angeles sheltered the open harbor at Valparaiso from west and southerly winds. However, ships had little protection from winds from the north. Heavy winds from this direction (locally called a "Norther") could wreak havoc on a helpless sailing ship, so normal procedure was to anchor a vessel securely fore and aft in a north-south direction with bow pointed north.[15] With the harbor being two and one-half miles wide and very deep, McLaughlin experienced no difficulty in locating a safe anchorage for the *Glory*.

Once they had her secure, with two anchors forward, each with 120 fathoms cable and one anchor astern, the captain ordered a boat crew to row him ashore. The boat contained the mate, carpenter, and several seamen, including John Gribble. Subsequently, Captain McLaughlin entered the *Glory* through Valparaiso Customs. He also contacted the U.S. Consul and filed a protest — a legal report of her being damaged in the hurricane. She was technically a vessel in distress; however, because the vessel was not destroyed, no lives lost or men seriously injured, no other official reports were required.[16]

A bit of excitement occurred while McLaughlin and his men were ashore. John Gribble:

> While on shore a slight shock of an earthquake was felt, and the people all ran out of their houses, but as we were [normally] aboard ship, we had no back door [to slip out of].

In the next few days Captain McLaughlin contacted the local agent for the insurance companies to file claims. In turn, arrangements were made to have the *Glory of the Seas* surveyed to ascertain what it would take to make her seaworthy. A local marine surveyor was needed to determine the extent of damage to her cargo and to take appropriate steps to discharge the sea-damaged portion so as to minimize contamination of the remaining grain on board.

Shipmasters normally sent upper masts and yards down on deck in the winter season. Following the *Glory*'s arrival, McLaughlin made lengthy preparations to repair her. He kept his crew busy unbending all her sails and sending down upper spars. The *Glory of the Seas* would spend a prolonged time undergoing repairs.

In the meantime, marine surveyors made a preliminary inspection of hull and cargo. Their main purpose was to determine the source of the damage. Was it due to poor stowage or the hurricane? They decided that 2,800 short tons — 56,000 one-hundred pound sacks of grain — must be removed before a complete estimate of repairs could be made and before they could determine the cause of the disaster. Captain McLaughlin advertised in the Valparaiso newspapers to charter old sailing vessels, now relegated to storage hulk status, into which cargo could be temporarily transferred. Since the *Glory* was larger than the average sailing ship, McLaughlin needed three or four old hulks for storage.[17]

In the weeks that followed, McLaughlin kept his crew busy at the slow, tedious task of removing the thousands of sacks of grain to the hulks tied securely alongside. As late as September

27, nearly four weeks after arriving at Valparaiso, this labor-intensive work continued.[18]

Captain McLaughlin dispensed with the regular watch-on-watch system (four hours on, four hours off), so the crew could work through the day and have part of their evenings off. Shipmasters commonly granted shore leave to their crews at Valparaiso with restrictions. Because of the chance of an unexpected "Norther" he allowed one watch shore leave while the other stayed aboard.

As in San Francisco, Liverpool, and New York, Valparaiso had its Sailortown quarter. Here, the crews mixed with the lower element of the city in sailor's boardinghouses, the red light district and seaman's taverns. Valparaiso's downtown streets were narrow and crowded, typical of some South American cities. One Sailortown street was called Gafftop'sl Street, and another *Calle Clave* (Street of the Nail). Over a three-month period, the foremast sailors on the *Glory of the Seas* became steady customers.[19]

On October 18, John Gribble wrote:

> . . . a great national holiday [celebrated at Valparaiso commemorating Chile's Constitution being adopted in 1825]. The dead body of a man was picked up. He had been strangled, his eyes poked out, and his ears cut [off].

The day before [October 17th], a fight occurred aboard the *Glory* between an officer and a seaman. Gribble's diary:

> a big row in the cabin . . . [and the officers] were going to ill use him; but he drew his knife and stood them off." [Later that day] the man that had the row was put in irons.
>
> At one a.m. I broke the irons for him, so he is a little more comfortable, and the next day [October 19] when they let him up for his usual walk, they did not see that the irons were broken. He ran below and hid, but was soon found, and handcuffed behind his back. When the captain came on board, he had them changed to the front. The captain offered fifty dollars if he could find out who broke the irons. I

told him, "I did" but he would not believe me, so I did not get the money. They let the man out the next day.

Gribble's autobiography records another unforgettable incident that occurred one Sunday:

> Some of the men fished for whiskey, the bait being a dollar tied in a rag. A boat could come alongside, take the dollar, and tie on a bottle of whiskey. The men got quite a lot [drunk] and got fighting mad. The mate [Cooper] entered the forecastle and managed to get hold of one of the bottles; but one of the men, however, struck him with a bottle and drove him out. The officers soon came back all armed with revolvers. The mate fired at the crowd but missed hitting anybody. He then drew one of the iron belaying pins and split the man's head open alongside of me. They did not try to hurt me as they saw that I was doing my best to keep peace among the men, and none of the men would hurt [me] their friend. After a free [-for-all] fight, we got the men quieted. I told the officers that if they would go to their cabins, I could get the men quiet, which they did.
>
> The ship's deck was like a shambles – broken bottles, iron pins, and blood — all the way to the [after] cabin where the men drove the officers. So ended the happiest day that I've had on the *Glory of the Seas.*

By mid-October Captain McLaughlin had the *Glory*'s 'tween decks empty of cargo. In addition, the crew removed enough heat and water-damaged cargo from her lower hold to enable the surveyors to complete their respective insurance reports.

The insurance adjuster then had to determine whether the cargo shifted because of bad stowage at San Francisco or due to perils of the sea. Fortunately for Sears Company, Captain Knowles, an experienced insurance agent, had "Protection and Indemnity" (P & I) insurance to cover such a matter. Whatever the cause, the action constituted a cargo claim. Initially, the insurance adjuster estimated that only 2,000 sacks of grain were ruined. This figure, however, quickly swelled to 5,000, and by the time the *Glory of the Seas* reached Le Havre four months later, this too proved to be a gross error. Meanwhile, insurance adjusters auctioned off the damaged cargo for animal feed.[20]

A marine surveyor made a thorough hull survey. His task was to determine what it would take to make the *Glory of the Seas* seaworthy. The terrific twisting motion in being thrown on her beam ends caused minor damage to the *Glory of the Seas'* frame and fastenings. This necessitated tightening up her hull, which the surveyor felt could be accomplished by adding additional stanchions in her lower hold. He also specified that her main deck and portions of both starboard and port sides should be re-caulked. Further repairs included rigging and the replacement of a boat. The surveyor estimated the cost of repairs as $6,600, which the hull insurance underwriters viewed as not too serious for a vessel now valued at $60,000 and insured for $56,438. The hull insurer viewed this claim as a "particular average," meaning he bore the expense of the loss as opposed to "general average" in which hull *and* cargo insurers share the loss.[21]

The surveyor also decided that the *Glory's* hull should be hove down to accomplish the re-caulking on her sides. Shipwrights subsequently berthed the *Glory* alongside a wharf and heaved on her upper masts so that half of her bottom rose out of the water for easy repair. They then repeated the operation on the opposite side. Internally, the shipwrights added wooden stanchions in her lower hold.[22]

Once the hull repairs were complete, riggers overhauled the *Glory's* standing rigging. Being on her beam ends for sixteen hours in the hurricane stretched her starboard standing rigging. It had to be taken up before she could safely proceed to France.

On December 1, 1881, the *Glory of the Seas* lay out in the Bay of Valparaiso, reloaded with cargo and ready to sail. Repairs were complete and her wrecked boat was replaced. The ship passed survey, and retained her A-l in Red insurance classification. The *Glory* looked in first-class condition with a fresh coat of paint in preparation for departure. A total of twenty-five thousand dollars was spent, exclusive of hull and rigging repairs, over a three-month period at Valparaiso — the largest insurance loss in her twelve-year career.[23]

John Gribble summarized the remainder of the voyage:

> We started the 1st of December, passed Massa Fucias [sic], also Juan Fernandez [Island]. After losing some sails and heavy seas, we rounded Cape Horn; and after a few [more] fights and loss of a few sails, finally arrived at Havre de Grace . . .[24]

The *Glory* arrived there on February 16, 1882, 220 days from San Francisco and 131 sailing days out. The *Hagarstown* had arrived long before at Antwerp on November 13, 1881, in 125 days. She completely missed the storm that nearly sank the *Glory of the Seas*.

Following their arrival at Le Havre, John Gribble asked to be paid off and to receive a discharge. Captain McLaughlin told him "he had not forgotten what Gribble had done" to save the ship, and paid him the balance of seven-and-one-half months' wages, minus slops and dead horse.[25]

Gribble took passage on a steamer to Plymouth, England; thence worked as a steward for a "shilling a month" on a steamship bound to Australia by way of Cape Town. There he caught a mail steamer to San Francisco and finally made the maiden voyage of the steam whaler *Orca* (which was managed by Captain Knowles) to the Arctic. Following his return to San Francisco on November 9th, 1883, John Gribble quit seafaring and ended his now well-worn, fifteen-year-old journal with "Farewell to the Sea."[26]

Subsequently settling near Nanaimo, in the community of East Wellington, British Columbia, John Gribble married an English immigrant. More than forty years after the harrowing event of 1881, he wrote his autobiography utilizing the journal he kept during his seagoing years in which he recounted his experiences as a rough-and-tumble sailor on many ships including the *Glory of the Seas*.

He died at the age of seventy-six, satisfied that he was able to save the lives of his shipmates as well as keep the *Glory of the Seas* from turning turtle and thus dispel the tragedy of the HMS *Captain* and 472 lost shipmates.

CHAPTER XIII

Winter, North Atlantic

Several days after her arrival at Le Havre, the *Glory of the Seas* began unloading. Stevedores discovered that more grain was damaged than the cargo survey at Valparaiso revealed. Captain McLaughlin called for another insurance survey to determine the extent of the loss and to make sure the insurance underwriters didn't blame the ship for the damage. On March 31, 1882, an auction was held to sell the second spoiled portion as animal feed.[1]

Meanwhile, Capt. McLaughlin sailed in ballast on March 20, vainly attempting to sail into the Atlantic against strong head winds. A series of westerly gales inhibited his progress so much that after almost four days at sea he made for a safe harbor at Torbay on the southern Coast of Devon, England, about 200 miles northwest of Le Havre. Here he patiently waited until April 3 for the stiff head winds to moderate.

During that ten-day period at Torbay, McLaughlin composed an unusual letter addressed to the editor of the *New York Maritime Register*, the chief ship movement newspaper in the United States. In his letter he outlined his conclusions respecting safe ventilation of coal cargoes, strongly disagreeing with the British Board of Trade and some of the major cargo insurance companies on the subject.

Over the years many sailing ship coal cargoes caught fire by spontaneous ignition. The *Glory* herself was almost a casualty of such a fire in 1874. While enroute from the British Isles her coal cargo became heated. Capt. Knowles had the crew dig into the affected areas and hose them down. He then kept her hatches off for the balance of the voyage whenever possible. Only through these intensive efforts had the ship been saved. A number of American ships, including the Sears' ship *Mogul*, and the *Glory*'s smaller sister, the *Helen Morris*, were lost to fire while hauling steam coal from the United Kingdom to San Francisco via Cape Horn.

Capt. McLaughlin's comments on this controversial subject caught the eye of the editor of the *New York Maritime Register*, mainly because the *Maritime Register* editorialized on the subject in its issue of March 1, 1882. Captain McLaughlin's letter outlined the existing coal-loading practices in the British Isles, comparing them to the procedure by which he had personally made sure stevedores safely loaded the *Glory of the Seas* on his first voyage in 1876-1877.

Along with his treatise appeared a detailed sketch drawn by the captain showing how simple and relatively inexpensive ventilation could be accomplished. His letter, published under the heading of "Correspondence," read:

Ventilation of Ships

Editor *New York Maritime Register*:

I have seen in a number of English papers and also in your number of March 1st articles relating to the ventilation of coal cargoes, there seemingly being a difference of opinion between the Royal Commissioners and many of the [insurance] underwriters as to the utility of any ventilation. My opinion is decidedly in favor of the latter, as any sane man will easily understand, that with a ship's keelson ventilated fore and aft, and a good ventilator in each end and one in the main hatch, a current of fresh air, which tends to expel the [coal] gas and dry the wet coal, can be forced under and through the whole cargo.

I have carried large cargoes of coal around both Capes [Horn and Good Hope] and have found no trouble in keeping a good, even temperature by ventilating by the way stated. No doubt, the great cause

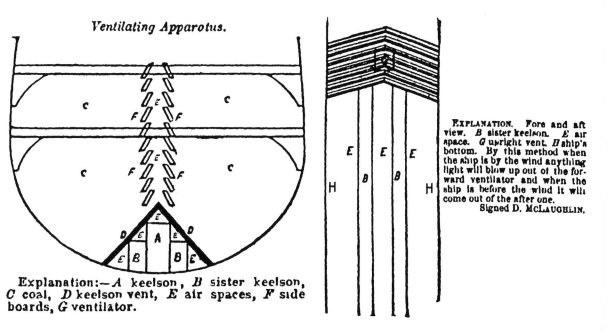

Ventilating Apparotus.

C *E* *C*
F *F*

C *E* *F* *C*

E
D *E* *D*
E *A* *E*
E *B* *B* *E*

Explanation:—*A* keelson, *B* sister keelson, *C* coal, *D* keelson vent, *E* air spaces, *F* side boards, *G* ventilator.

E *E* *E*

H *B* *B* *H*

EXPLANATION. Fore and aft view. *B* sister keelson. *E* air space. *G* upright vent. *H* ship's bottom. By this method when the ship is by the wind anything light will blow up out of the forward ventilator and when the ship is before the wind it will come out of the after one.
Signed D. McLAUGHLIN.

Sketch of "Ventilating Apparatus" by Capt. Daniel McLaughlin appearing in New York Maritime Register *on April 19, 1882. Courtesy Mystic Seaport Museum and Independence Seaport Museum Library.*

of coal cargoes igniting is for the great want of proper care being taken in the loading of them.

I will state a few of the facts which have frequently come under my notice. As soon as the coal is mined, it is bited [sic] out of the pit and deposited in open top [railroad] cars of about ten tons each. It then stands until a ship is ready for it, and down it goes to the docks well soaked with rain. The ship is ordered by the berthing master under the dump and this coal is dumped on board.

They usually begin in the after hatch, where, if the ship is about 1500 tons [register], they will dump about 550 tons, and then move to the main hatch, which they will fill and have 75 tons on deck to block it sit [sic]. A third move is made to the fore hatch, where the loading is finished. You will perceive that by this system of loading, there will be tons of fine wet coal in each hatch, which is the place where spontaneous combustion usually takes place.

At Birkenhead a few years ago [1877], [longshoremen] loaded in this ship [*Glory of the Seas*] 2600 tons of coal, which was wheeled on board, and the trimmers would not take a shovel full of it to trim until the top of it was up above the decks. In order to get them to level it in the hatches, so that I could put timbers across them and separate the fine coal, I had to pay them a pound for each hatch, making six in all, which I consider money well spent.

When a ship is loading coal, rain or shine, night or day, she must have all her hatches open, and as it usually rains half of the time in England, no small quantity of water goes below in that way, and it all helps to kindle the fire. My opinion is, that if the [British] Board of Trade paid a little more attention to the way coals should be loaded, and less to the Royal Commissioners, the Underwriters would have fewer ships and cargoes to pay for.

Yours truly,
DANIEL MCLAUGHLIN
Master of ship Glory of the Seas

Torbay, England, March 29, 1882.

On Thursday, May 4th, the *Sovereign of the Seas*, Captain Aaron H. Wood, arrived at New York, thirty-three days from Antwerp. She had on board a cargo of old railroad iron and empty wooden barrels for her owners, Lawrence, Giles & Co. The *Sovereign* crossed the Atlantic by way of the 3,000-mile Middle Passage, and for the most part experienced fair sailing weather. This was with the exception of the region between long. 42º west to 27º west where "heavy westerly gales and very rough weather," as Captain Wood described it, impeded her progress.[2]

Four days later the *Glory of the Seas* arrived at New York, thirty-five days from Torbay and forty-five days from Le Havre. This was the only voyage in the entire career of the *Sovereign of the Seas* where she bettered her bigger sister in elapsed days from port to port.

McLaughlin experienced an unusually eventful passage across the Atlantic in 1882. His voyage summary, published in the maritime columns of the *New York Herald*, tersely described her bout with extremely adverse weather. It also mentioned the *Glory*'s near contact with huge icebergs off the Grand Banks of Newfoundland.

> Ship *Glory of the Seas* (of Boston) McLaughlin, Havre, March 20 via Torbay; April 3, in ballast, to order. Had heavy westerly gales with snow and hail at times. April 17, lat. 43, lon. 40 27; had a hurricane from SSW lasting ten hours; [April] 19th, had a hurricane lasting four hours; from the 23rd, lat. 43 48, lon. 48 to [April] 27th, lat. 43, lon. 52 22, passed icebergs and broken ice; on the Banks saw three schooners and one brig at anchor, and a large iceberg within five miles of them. May 3, lat. 41 10, lon. 65 34, passed bark *Arcturus*, [Capt] Kelly, from Boston for San Francisco.[3]

Meanwhile, the *Maritime Register* had published Daniel McLaughlin's letter (which arrived by trans-Atlantic steamer) on April 19, 1882, while the *Glory* was en route to New York.

After the *Glory*'s arrival at New York on May 8, a tug towed the ship to the Atlantic Basin at Brooklyn, a large ship mooring area at the foot of Commercial Street Wharf. Here she lay until the end of May undergoing minor repairs by the shipbuilding firm of C. and R. Poillon. This included the making of new spars.[4]

Besides the *Sovereign of the Seas*, the McKay-built ship *New World* was also in port. Grinnell-Minturn and Co., her long-time owners, sold her in March 1881. Her new owner, in turn, sold her for $7,000 on May 15, 1882, to Austrian buyers who renamed her *Kaiser Rudolph.* The *Kaiser Rudolph* arrived at New York on March 26 from London with a cargo of chalk and empty barrels. Although rebuilt in 1876, she was an old ship and well past her prime. Her new owners planned to use her as a case-oil carrier for a few more years — quite a comedown from the crack transatlantic packet of the 1840s and 1850s.[5]

In mid-May the *Kaiser Rudolph, Glory of the Seas,* and *Sovereign of the Seas* were berthed near each other at Brooklyn but by mid-June, the *Sovereign of the Seas* had moved across the East River to Pier 19, loading general cargo for the Sutton and Company Line for San Francisco. The *Glory* lay farther south at Pier 10, loading California freight for R. B. Van Vieck & Co.[6]

On June 15th, the day the *Sovereign of the Seas* sailed for San Francisco, the former Grinnell-Minturn packet ship *Cornelius Grinnell,* another Donald McKay product, arrived from London with the same type cargo as the *Kaiser Rudolph* — chalk and empty barrels. She, too, was sold in 1881 and in her old age her new owner, Peter J. Nevius used her as a transatlantic freighter.[7]

The *Grinnell* and the *Kaiser Rudolph,* thirty-two and thirty-six years old respectively, had few years left in active trading. They were remnants of the now-dead Atlantic passenger trade which had almost totally been taken over by steamships. The *Glory* and the *Sovereign of the Seas,* active in the grain trade, were examples of distinctive New England-designed wooden-hulled vessels which were being slowly superseded by foreign-built iron-hulled squareriggers. American Cape Horners were a dying breed.

May and June 1882 in New York were significant because this was the last large assemblage of ships built by Donald McKay. The *Glory of the Seas* never again called at New York. The *Sovereign of the Seas* would soon be sold foreign, and McKay's former packet ships would retire. In a few short years the *Glory of the Seas* would be the only McKay-built merchant ship actively sailing under the American flag.

CHAPTER XIV

A Memorable Voyage

In May and June 1882, the *Glory of the Seas* underwent repairs and loaded general cargo at the Port of New York. Captain Daniel McLaughlin and his wife visited family and friends at Malden and Grand Manan Island.

Captain McLaughlin persuaded Carl, his twenty-one year old son, to move West where job opportunities would permit him to follow his chosen field of accounting and made arrangements for him to make the coming voyage to San Francisco. Carl had lived with relatives at Malden since the death of his mother when he was six. Although he spent time with his family at sea as a baby, he had no other maritime experience.

Carl had an aptitude for writing, especially poetry. "Around in the *Glory*" was a detailed account of his one and only voyage on the *Glory of the Seas*, for which he drew from his personal diary for factual information.

Captain McLaughlin filed the crew list for his forthcoming voyage on June 30, cleared the *Glory* at the Custom House[1] and departed two days later.

Carl McLaughlin's account began the night before sailing:

> On the ebb tide of the evening of July 1, 1882, the tugboat took
> hold of the *Glory*. We started on my first long voyage, our destination

Daniel Carlton "Carl" McLaughlin, ca. 1890. Courtesy Mary Ann Snedeker, Collection of Frances McLaughlin Savory.

being San Francisco . . . The poet so splendidly expressed it: "The feathers began to fall from the wings of night."

The tug turned us in the stream so that our bow faced away from little old New York. [At about eight p.m.] we beheld the beautiful sight of the lighted steamship *City of Rome*, the largest vessel afloat[2] at that time (about 8,000 tons register) majestically moving down the harbor. This tug stayed with us until we were off Sandy Hook Lightship. Then with everything set and drawing, and a fair wind off shore, we headed away from a dangerous coast out into the broad Atlantic. Our voyage began.

The *Glory* under full sail was a sight worth gazing upon . . . She was as graceful as a swan, her high sharp bow, well-rounded stern with its snow white taffrail, and the glorious figurehead, were not to be forgotten by one who loves such things.

Her canvas, if not brand new, was nearly so. The masts were very lofty, and she was heavily sparred. Her main yard alone being 96 [ninety-one] feet long and 36 [twenty-four] inches in diameter in the slings. The spread of canvas in the mainsail alone was 900 yards [about 700] yards, and all other sails in proportion. So, one can realize what a driving power forced the ship along in a fair and steady breeze.

We experienced what the captain claimed was the most pleasant voyage he had ever made in any ship around "Old blow me down." Our longest day's run from noon to noon was 352 knots with everything set.

For the enlightenment of some old people and many young ones, I will describe some of the fittings of a first-class American clipper, and state that few landlubbers ever dwelt in such luxurious quarters as were found aboard the *Glory*.

Her after cabin was paneled in lustrous polished rosewood[3] and bird's-eye maple. The captain's stateroom, furnished with a full-width bed, bureau and clothes' press, occupied the after part of the starboard part with the chronometer and chart room just forward of his stateroom.[4] On the port side, directly opposite the captain's room, was a smaller stateroom with two wide berths, one above the other. There were stationary wash bowls with running water in both rooms. Forward [Aft] of the port stateroom was the toilet and bathroom. Forward of that, the medicine closet and instrument drawer; for, in emergencies, the captain must act as doctor or surgeon.

The forward cabin was finished in white and gold with one state-room on the port side. Just forward of the forward cabin were the staterooms of the first and second mate where they could step onto the deck as their watch changed without entering the cabin.[5]

The steward and second steward, who was the steward's wife, occu-pied one of the cabins. Forward of the after house was the booby hatch, the main hatch and the mess room. The mess room was the quarters of the two boatswains, and carpenter. All three of these men (along with the second mate), took their meals there. The captain, first mate, stewardess, and any passenger who might be on board, ate in the forward cabin [dining saloon].

Glory of the Seas carried 24 men before the mast, a cook, carpenter, two boatswains, two mates, two stewards, captain, one dead-head [Carl McLaughlin], one cat, and a dog.

This happy band started out for the Golden Gate with a fair wind and favorable tide upon a never-to-be-forgotten day. By late morning, we were upon the broad Atlantic, out of sight of land, and well on our way.

Such splendid days, nights, and glorious weather as followed are seldom met with in succession. We had been provided with a supply of fireworks, and on the evening of July 3rd, they were set off from the deck of the wheelhouse. A few days later, far ahead on the port bow, we spied a sail and ran as close as it was safe. She was a bark and passed us to leeward so near, that both vessels were able to read each other's names. We exchanged our nautical positions by means of chalk and black-boards; then entered the event in our log book. The bark's officer on watch did the same thing in their log, as was the custom in such cases.

On the following night, we filled an old tar barrel with shavings, and after lighting them, carefully lowered it over the stern. We watched it burn brightly for more than an hour where we had left it over ten miles astern in our wake.

We saw no other vessels on the Atlantic side and had all that ocean to ourselves. But, we had plenty to interest us as we approached the Tropics. One evening, the captain said, "Now, look sharp and you will see the Portugee Man-of-War!" When they actually appeared, the sail-ors laughed when I remarked, "Oh, look at that big bunch of bubbles. Where did they come from?"

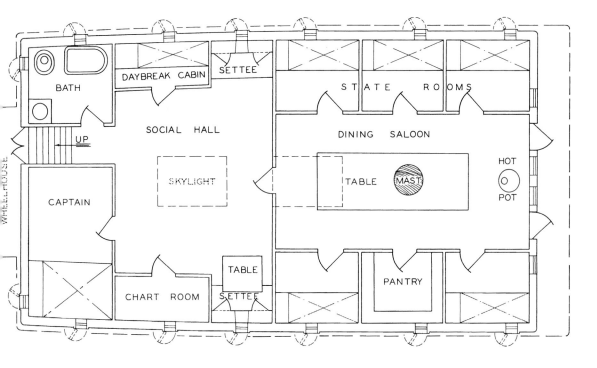

After house plan of Glory *as of 1876 by the author. Courtesy Mystic Seaport Museum.*

When we had reached the latitude of the Tropic of Cancer, I was told, that the following evening, we would be able to see the Southern Cross, that beautiful constellation which can't be seen in latitudes north of Cancer. It was certainly an inspiring sight and appeared high in the sky when darkness brought out all her splendid lanterns. The Cross remained in view until the showy Megellanic clouds, which cannot be observed until the equator is crossed, had come into full view.

One afternoon, one of the boatswains came aft with the information that a seaman was certainly looney. He had been discovered on the forecastle-head earnestly inviting imaginary mermaids to come aboard via the bobstays. The vision-seeing sailor was confined for a few days to not allow him to be on the lookout. All such persons were dangerous to others and themselves.

The following days were uneventful. We were nearing the equator and soon crossed it with a fair wind.

As day broke one morning, we found that we were becalmed, a predicament that is not at all unusual in the tropical latitudes. The sky was cloudless and the sea as smooth and glistening as a mirror for as far as the eye could see. Not a ripple marred its surface. Occasionally, it rose and fell in long undulating motions that caused the ship to gently lean to port or starboard, or to gracefully bow as would a lady to a gentleman in an old time square dance. Pitch from the deck seams rose from the caulking and the odor of pine could be plainly detected.

Towards evening, the first officer, who was scanning the oily expanse, joyously exclaimed, "Here she comes!" and handed his glass to the captain. Martins said, "A couple of miles off the starboard quarter, sir." There we could see a disturbance on the water. By the time the yards were braced to receive it, the breeze was upon us. We were on our way again, well pleased that the calm had been a short one. Very little bad weather was encountered. We escaped the storms entirely that are often met off the mouth of the River de la Plata.

[On August 24th, the *Glory of the Seas* crossed lat. 50° south, twenty-five days from the equator.] Steadily, we moved along at a ten or twelve-knot breeze [speed] hoping to make the Strait of Le Maire in latitude 55° south, longitude 65° west, in pleasant weather. This strait divides Tierra del Fuego and Staten land and is but seven miles wide and 14 long. It was named for the daring French voyager who first passed through there in 1665.

No land had been sighted since we had bade farewell to Sandy Hook. As we neared the Strait, the officers and crew knew that we must sight something before many days or hours. Many ducks and geese, wild fowl which hug the shores, were to be seen, and some little land birds came off and lit upon the yards. Seaweed drifted about us. For two full days we were enveloped in fog, but we knew that land was very close. The ship's dog knew it. He trotted up and down the deck with his nose in the air and wore a knowing smile. The first officer, Mr. Martins, a tall gentlemanly German, had been a ship captain, but had never passed through the Strait. He was to be excused for feeling nervous. He asked the captain if he felt quite safe to proceed in so thick a fog.

On the 27th of August, 57 days since we sailed, the captain said, "Well, Mr. Martins, if the fog doesn't lift by four o'clock this afternoon so that we can see land clearly, we will come about and go around the Island, meaning Staten land."

The mate was clearly nervous, as he paced the quarter deck near the wheelhouse. He looked first at his watch, then from side to side. He was constantly alert for signs of land, as we had been running for the last two days by dead reckoning.

The captain's judgement that the fog would lift was justified. At 3:45 p.m., the sun burst through the fog almost amidships on our starboard beam. Then, it shone all about us, lighting up the rugged hill tops of Tierra del Fuego. They were covered with snow, and lower down, displayed the first green of Antarctic spring. To port, we plainly viewed the rocky shore of Staten land, and all drew a long breath of thanks towards the power that had so far protected us. We were fairly in the middle of the Strait and about half-way through.

Mr. Martins placed his hand upon the captain's shoulder and said, "Captain, that was some navigation! I was certainly nervous with no observation for two days and not a sight of land for 57 days. I want to congratulate you!" The captain replied, "Thank you, sir. I felt sure that we were safe. I cannot blame you for feeling nervous. It shows that you are not a reckless man."

Good feeling dwelt aboard that ship. The dog raced up and down the deck with his head high in the air barking his best, and perhaps thinking that some poor castaway on shore might hear his voice and take hope, or answer him. He certainly listened for a reply.

The sun disappeared behind the hills of Tierra del Fuego, and the *Glory's* course changed a little to the eastward so that she might have plenty of room to safely clear the Cape. In all the captain's voyages around he had seen that low-lying point of rocks but twice, and was not anxious to glimpse it again.

Myriads of sea birds fell in with us in the lower southern latitudes. They escorted us on our way, constantly rising above the water or diving into it for scraps from the cook's galley, or for small fish which could not be plainly seen. There was the stately and graceful albatross, the king of them all, whom all sailors insist is sacred, and must not be killed; and the stormy petrel or mother cary's chicken, also included with the king. Then there were the molly hawks, and the cape pigeons, a few sea parrots, and Johnny penguins. We had a good ten-gauge shotgun and plenty of ammunition, and thought that we were wing shots. But these birds must have been wearing underclothes constructed from sole leather, or we were simply rotten shots.

Of course, we succeeded in killing a few pigeons, but not one fell on board. We also carried two old style rim-fire 44-cal Winchesters and plenty of cartridges. We surprised a school of seven or eight grampuses, which were foolish enough to approach at about 100 yards range. The captain said that they probably thought that a swarm of sea insects were biting them. At any rate, they dived a few times and we saw them no more. We could plainly hear the bullets as they struck the great fishes, but their vital parts were covered with blubber and they were not injured.

A fishing line trailed astern with an alarm ratchet attached for nearly our whole trip; but luck was against us. One dolphin and one bonito was all of the catch. The colors of a dying dolphin were here illustrated in the passing of the lonesome member of the tribe that took our trolling bait. The fish, which was about two and one-half feet in length, two and one-half inches through, and five inches deep, was placed in a deck tub where it could be observed until it ceased breathing. As the dolphin began to breathe in short gasps, and to throw itself about the tub, its colors changed from a silvery blue to the iridescent shades of pink; then violet and deeper blues — commencing at its gills and running downward-gradually becoming fainter until it died. Then, its original color returned.

The captain now said, "Look at that fish, boys! Wasn't he built for speed? Look at his draught and that tail he uses for a rudder on a sharp turn. No wonder they can follow a bunch of flying-fish as they rise from the water, and then be there to grab them when they hit the surface again, 100 yards to leeward, as I have seen a dolphin do!"

Of course, we cooked and ate the fish. First, we placed a silver coin in the frying [pan] to guard against copper poisoning. All sailors claim this will be shown by the coin turning black if poison is present. The flesh of the dolphin and bonito, while being very firm, was dry and not to be compared for flavor with salmon, mackerel, or any well-known saltwater fish.

A new main yard had been provided. Everything had been arranged to lower the old spar and hang the new one. The sail had been unbent and the carpenter had been aloft and had taken accurate measurements for the sheave holes and all necessary iron work. [Lines were made fast to] the main yard slings, as the center is called, and the yard was then lowered to the deck. The sheaves and the iron straps were then put on the new yard, and it was hoisted into place. All was safely handled by the crew with the main deck capstan in one short day without accident of any kind.

This spar replacement became an occasion of increasing a simple feud between George Jackson,[6] the old ivory-colored cook, on the one side and two members of the port watch, both gentlemen of Irish ancestry.

One of the last mentioned worthies, Charlie Donahoo[7] by name, took offense when Mr. Jackson verbally demonstrated that it was very easy for him to split up parts of the old spar, and that some of the sailors had made an awful mess of it. Jackson was one of the best formed and strongest men to be met anywhere. He was also a good cook and very peaceable, but Donahoo was spoiling for a fight. So, aided and abetted by his friend, Jim Smith,[8] he unwisely stated that he "hated a nigger anywhere, and had never met one that he couldn't lick!"

Now, Donahoo was only a welter at best, while Jackson was a tall heavy-weight. One back-handed slap across the mouth did for Donahoo. Smith's intentions to do Mr. Jackson great bodily harm were very strong, but he possessed more caution than did his fellow countryman, and so he escaped for the time being.

George Jackson was a friendly man and very reminiscent regarding his travels. He was so entertaining that he could be forgiven [his verbosity]. He had read many accounts of different events from a large bundle of newspapers; that is, until one person noticed that the copies he held before his eyes, as he lay at ease in his berth adjoining the galley, were frequently wrong-side-up, and impossible to read.

However, George was a good fellow and a square shooter. He feared nothing in the line of duty, on deck, or in the galley. His inquiry, "Captain, what shall I do if any of these fellows come in my galley to fix me as they say they will?" was answered: "Well, cook, with all the knives, stove wood, and hot water that a cook has on hand, I don't believe that he should let anyone hurt him very badly. I don't believe they will try anything." The captain, however, was mistaken.

Early one morning, we heard a commotion on deck while we were at breakfast. The mate immediately left the table and went forward to investigate. He soon came aft and informed the captain that Donahoo and Smith had tried to get inside the galley. The cook had run them out with a poker. Smith had cut the cook with a sheath knife, though not very badly. The cook came aft to the forward cabin. We saw that the knife point had been stopped by a rib which could be plainly seen after the wound was washed. Smith's intentions were murderous, but they failed. Upon arrival in port, he was convicted of assault with a deadly weapon and sent to the penitentiary for a year that he might think the matter over.[9]

At this point the *Glory of the Seas* was about to pass Cape Horn. Carl McLaughlin was about halfway to San Francisco.

CHAPTER XV

Cape Horn Weather

Capt. McLaughlin gradually caught up with vessels that departed the U.S. East Coast before him. The American ship *Norris*, a down-Easter half the tonnage of the *Glory of the Seas*, sailed from Philadelphia on June 14, and passed lat. 50º south in the Atlantic on her sixty-first day at sea, compared to the *Glory*'s fifty-three days to the same latitude. McLaughlin was now only ten days behind Captain George Barstow, master of the *Norris*.

Capt. Wood's *Sovereign of the Seas* sailed seventeen days before the *Glory* from New York, and at lat. 50º south, was only eight days ahead of her. Although Wood bettered McLaughlin in elapsed time across the Atlantic in the spring of 1882, the run to San Francisco would be a different matter. The *Glory* had much finer lines than the *Sovereign* besides being a much better overall sailer. In a fourteen-year career, the latter vessel's best westward passage to San Francisco was 138 days, whereas the *Glory*'s was ninety-five days.

Both the *Glory* and the *Sovereign* rounded the Horn from 50º south in the Atlantic to 50º south in the Pacific in eighteen days. McLaughlin well described the winds in this region in his voyage summary: ". . . after passing the Diego Rameriz [Islands], wind came up with stormy weather 'Westnorthwest'."[1]

Carl McLaughlin:

By the morning of August 28, we had safely rounded the Horn and with a fair wind were headed almost into the Pacific. We commenced overhauling several ships sailing in the same direction, but far to windward of us.

We could see a group of several small islands a few points off our port bow rising precipitously from the ocean. The water being very bold, we ran in toward them, probably about one-half mile from the largest one. Upon referring to his chart, the Captain declared that they were the Diego Ramirez in about 57 south lat and 68 west long, and approximately 60 miles southwest of Cape Horn.

The mate, Mr. Martins, was scanning the shore and remarked: "Take the glass, Captain, and look! I believe I can see a signal of distress!" The captain, after looking where the mate directed, said, "Certainly, it is!" He then gave the order to lay to, ran up the colors to the mizzen peak, and dipped them so that those on shore would know that we had seen their signal.

At this point there were five vessels directly to port of us, but the nearest one was three or four miles to windward, and the farthest two were so far away that we could only see their mast heads and yards above the horizon. Every one of the five vessels ran up their ensigns, and then began signalling to us to learn if we were in trouble. We were kept busy answering them through code with our signal pennants. When they learned what we were about, they all wished to help and share if possible in our efforts, asking, "Shall we stand by? Shall we run down to you?" When we had convinced them that we needed no assistance, they signaled a "good-bye" and filled away on their course.

Through the captain's splendid marine spy glass, as a sailor will always call it, we could plainly read the code flags on the ships which themselves were out of sight. The captain and mate agreed that [some of the ships] were probably twenty miles away from us; but they all understood our signals. [Many of them later] reported speaking to us, and what we were doing off the [Diego Ramirez] Islands.

Before we had finished signalling, we saw a boat approaching from the shore. At first, it was a small object upon the water, which gradually became clearer in view as it neared our ship. Through the glasses, we were soon able to see that it was a whaleboat. Its crew was made up of four men at the oars and one at the stern guiding it with a long steering oar. As soon as they were within hailing distance, our captain addressed them: "Boat ahoy!" The steersman replied, "Ship ahoy!" Our captain then asked, "Who are you?" The leader in the boat replied, "Americans from New Bedford, Massachusetts, down here hunting seal. Our supply vessel is long overdue, and we are in need of food."

Our captain then asked, "What is your name?" and when the reply came "John Smith," he said, "I have met that man in many places in this world, but never in a whaleboat off Cape Horn. John Smith, come aboard!"

The whaleboat came alongside and the spry little man at once grasped the man ropes beside the Jacob's Ladder. Like a hungry squirrel climbing a hickory tree, he nimbly came up the ship's side, and over the rail onto the main deck. After a warm handshake with our captain, he came by invitation into the cabin. He was not over five feet, six inches tall. His face was covered with a heavy beard as black and shiny as I ever saw. The other men in the boat were very dark, but wore no beards or mustaches. While their leader was on board ship, they occupied themselves by keeping the whaleboat from chafing against the ship's side. They were sailors, every one of them.

The leader explained that the party had been landed on Diego Ramirez to hunt the fur seal, and that the vessel that was to bring them provisions was now over a month behind time. She was to sail from Sandy Point, Magellan Straits, and the sealers feared that something had surely happened to her.

Six ships besides the *Glory* had passed close to the rocks during the past month, but none had seen their signals, a large Stars and Stripes waving to and fro, and a large bonfire on the shore. When they saw the good old flag at our mizzen peak, they were not long in getting out to us. They had not yet suffered for food, but were down to one hard-tack for each man per day. Their meat ration consisted of seal flesh, which was a poor substitute for good corned beef.

The leader was quick to say that they had no money, but that he had brought some baby seal skins to offer in exchange for whatever we could spare from our stores. Our captain told him to forget it — that they were not only human beings, but Americans in distress — and to state what they needed. If it was on board, it was theirs. The leader said that they needed nothing but bread and meat, and that they had plenty of coffee, brown sugar, and other luxuries.

Our steward stated that we had plenty of prime beef and pork, and also pilot bread, which is the trade term for the much maligned hardtack. With a barrel each of beef, pork and bread, which together weighed over 1,000 pounds, and five men in that whaleboat, the little band of 100 per cent Americans left us. With a "God bless you" and a wave of their greasy caps, they bent to their oars, the gunwales of their little craft not over three inches clear of the water.

When they were well on their way, we discovered a little roll of seal skins which John Smith had carefully laid upon the medicine locker in the after cabin. The skins were from baby seals. They had been carefully plucked of the long hairs which must be scraped from the inner sides. These must be removed by the application of wood ashes, or by some other process known to the seal hunters. There were three of them, enough for a lady's cap and trimming for a cloak. Their fur was a beautiful non-dyed brown. It was about one-half inch deep and as soft as could be imagined.

The order was now given to square [brace] the yards and resume the course that we had been sailing before Mr. Martins had caught sight of the signals for help. We had lain to for perhaps two hours. In that time the ships which we had seen to windward had steadily held on their course. They were now far in advance off our port bow.

Our captain declared that if nothing happened, we would soon overhaul them as we had done before. However, something did occur. No sooner had we passed from under the lee of the Diego Ramirez, when a strong breeze from the northwest caught us. We were obliged to come about and run for it in a southerly direction. The officers decided that we had run into the tail end of a heavy storm that was wearing out in the natural home of storms off the Cape.

By nightfall, the wind had increased to half a gale, and skysail and royals had all been taken in. The ship was running before it, and while the night was clear, the seas were running. She was taking some of them over her bows, passing overboard through the lee scuppers. The crew was in its glory. The weather was to their liking and they jumped to their tasks like boys at play.

When the watch was ordered to brace the yards as was done frequently during the next few days, the chanty man would open his face and the balance would join him in, "Blow, boys, blow for California. Oh, for there's heaps of gold, as I've been told, on the banks of the

Sac-a-ree-mento;" and the balance would join him until the bosun bawled out, "Belay there!" the trailing braces were then coiled and hung on the pins.

And so it continued for over a week, first on one tack, and then on the other, in trying to gain our northerly course again and make some latitude. We were driven 360 miles south of the Horn. It was two weeks before we were up even with the Diego Ramirez; but then, we were far to windward, and did not catch sight of them again. We had lost a lot of time by laying to and supplying the sealers with provisions, but in so doing, had perhaps saved their lives. We never regretted the act.

One morning, the captain, the first officer and the writer had just seated ourselves at the breakfast table. The stewardess had poured our coffee, and we had been helped to generous plates full of fish hash, and had broken and buttered our hot Parker House rolls. The *Glory* decided that as rolls were in order, she would help herself, and did so. Over the ship went to port; then, back to starboard. Before we could get back upon our feet, she was down to port again.

The captain, whose seat was always at the head of the table, could not free himself, and so landed without injury on the cabin floor. The mate, in his endeavor to save his hot coffee, poured it down the writer's neck.

The food and dishes, wishing to do their part, left the fiddle-rack, which was designed expressly to keep them on the table, and rose in a body. Everything was hurled across the cabin, and either plastered against the stateroom doors or thrown in confusion upon the berths in the rooms. Order was soon restored and we proceeded with our breakfast.

The steward was capable of constructing pudding and pies that were welcome to any hungry person. His bread and biscuits were never wasted; but he could not refrain from smoking his pipe at any time or in any place. One morning, while we were enjoying our breakfast, the mate hastily arose, and asked to be excused, starting for the deck.

The captain quickly possessed himself of the half biscuit that lay beside the mate's deserted plate. He carefully examined it, and by the unmistakable evidence of his eyes and his sense of smell he knew that the steward had been smoking when he mixed the dough for the biscuits. It was very fortunate that the Captain had not changed his slippers for his deck shoes. The slippers were much lighter and softer than the shoes, and did no more than ruffle the steward's dignity when they came in contact with his pants. The captain also warned him never to let himself be caught smoking in the pantry.

It was the custom on sailing ships for the officer who was on watch at night or early morning to call the captain at once when anything unusual occurred. The officer would make some noise directly above the captain's skylight, and the captain in turn would then ask what was wanted. At about four a.m. on September 18, 1882, Mr. Martins was on watch. He called out to the captain to come on deck, and explained that a large and beautiful comet[2] was to be seen just above the western horizon. That was a glorious sight which we watched that morning as it rose toward the zenith of the heavens.

The comet faded from our view only when the sun appeared in the east, and by its greater brilliance, eclipsed the new arrival. From that time on, and long after our arrival in San Francisco, the splendid comet was to be seen in the west. As it came unannounced to astronomers as well as to laymen, no name was given it until sometime after its appearance. It was called: "The Great September Comet of 1882."[3]

The *Glory of the Seas* headed north about 1,100 miles west of the coast of Chile. Eight days before, she crossed 50° south in the Pacific at long. 88° west, and fought stiff head winds all the way up to latitude 30° south. There she caught the northeast trades.[4] She was fighting these head winds when the incidents of the rolling ship and the flying "rolls" took place.

CHAPTER XVI

From the Line to San Francisco

Carl McLaughlin's voyage in the *Glory of the Seas* was now almost three-quarters over. Crossing the equator in the Pacific on October 11, 1882, they were 101 days from New York. The northeast trade winds still pushed the *Glory* in a northwesterly direction, and carried her up to latitude 11° north. Carl's narrative continues:

We were nearing the equator and in the latitude of the Galapagos, but not in sight of them, when the captain remarked: "We are now in turtle territory. Take the glasses and go forward and keep a sharp lookout. If you see anything that looks like a barrel, come aft and tell me where it lays. We will run down and investigate."

I obeyed orders. In a short space of time I was rewarded by seeing what I felt sure was an empty barrel bobbing up and down in the water on the long swells ahead, about three points off the starboard bow. After a long look through the glasses, the captain said, "It's a turtle, and a big one, too!" He gave the order to the man at the wheel to shape his course so as to bring the ship alongside of Mr. Turtle. The ship was slipping along at about five knots an hour, and was soon bumping the big bug, as the boatswain termed it.

Quickly grasping the grains, a twin-pointed spear, in both hands, the captain nimbly stepped out on the bumpkin, and poising the spear, made a dead center shot into the turtle's back, driving both barbs through the upper shell. The shot was so true, and the turtle so heavy, that when he upended, the strain became so great that the grains pulled out. All we got was the thrill and a few shreds of turtle flesh on the spear points. Carefully, the spear was hauled in and the line coiled about a belaying pin in readiness for another turtle, but none showed up. The captain's fame as a marksman must have spread abroad on the Pacific in advance of our coming, and we were soon out of the track of the turtles.

The *Glory* sped merrily on, and strange to relate, we saw no more vessels, either sail or steam, although the weather was clear and fine.

One morning, the captain remarked to me, "What's the matter? Can't you get your feet off the deck? Go aloft! There's no danger in weather like this. Hang on by the shrouds. You never see a sailor touch the ratlines. They are made to step on, and should one break when he is climbing, he can save himself if he has a good hold on the standing rigging. When you reach the top, go over by the futtock shrouds, not through the lubber hole."

I followed the captain's suggestion and obeyed his instructions. I subsequently passed many hours aloft, sometimes in the mizzen top, and other times, seated on the cross trees far above. Below me lay a beautiful ship. Her regular lines inclosed her long and well-proportioned deck. Her lofty masts and spars swayed now to port, then to starboard, as she gracefully leaned first to one side, and then to the other. This was as the alternate ocean swells approached or receded. Not a sail was to be seen; just an endless expanse of azure ocean below and one of sky above.

I frequently amused myself by loafing in the galley and listening to George Jackson, as he spun his long sea yarns, which I am now convinced were largely romance. Many times, as I sat upon the box which contained the wood for the galley range, a white-cap from the windward side came over the rail, and through the galley door. It wet us thoroughly, and I can almost believe that I can still hear George's hearty laugh and his pleasant voice, as he said, "What you-all trying to do, drown me? I sure believe you-all is a Jonah, and I's goin' to hand you over to the very first whale we meets!"

We were now offshore too far to catch sight of any of the many coasting steamers or vessels which ply up and down the Pacific. Nor did we see any of the liners. The captain and officers declared that this was unusual.

The custom on windjammers, as sailing vessels were referred to in those days, was to keep well away from the land; also, to make considerable distance to the northwest until they met the prevailing trade winds. Then to shape their course, so that they might run in on a fair wind. This we were trying to do while under about a six-knot breeze upon our starboard quarter. Unfortunately, a thick fog had settled upon us, and we had sighted no land.

Eight bells struck in the afternoon of November 6, 1882. The ship was noiselessly skimming through the water. The captain, with eyes and ears alert, had been anxiously pacing the quarter deck since the fog had fallen about us. He now raised his never-to-be-forgotten voice, and in words plainly heard by every person on board the ship, he shouted, "Breakers ahead! Hard down your helm! Hard down! Let go the spanker! Clew up the cro'jack! All hands on deck!" Turning to me, he shouted, "Help that man at the wheel!"

I ran to the lee side of the wheel and climbed the spokes, riding it down; thus doing my part in getting it over to port. The man at the wheel was a flat-chested American sailor by the name of Owens, who knew his business, and how to execute an order when received. The captain rushed and cast off the spanker halyards. The big sail came down on the run. Then, seeing that the watch on deck was busy with the cro'jack, he ran to the wheel, and grasping the windward spokes with Owens, he added his great strength toward holding the helm over.

Like something conscious of the great danger that was threatening, the splendid ship turned her head away from the angry seas that leaped and foamed directly in her path. She passed so close to the jagged rocks that had we wished to do so, we might have thrown a biscuit onto them.

The captain then turned to the bos'n who had charge of the watch and asked, "Who was on lookout?" The bos'n replied, "That man who saw the mermaids, sir." The captain said, "My God, man! I told you never to put that man in any place where there might be danger. I don't mind to find fault with you, but any man who has once shown that he is the least bit off is never safe to trust again. If I had not seen the breakers when I did, the chances are, we would be all hands lost.

The water here must be fifty fathoms deep, and the ship would have backed off and sunk. It was fortunate that it was still daylight."

The captain and officers decided that the rock was the North Rock of the Farallones, which lies almost due west of San Francisco, and about 28 miles out. At that time they were inhabited by sea-birds and a family of people who lived at the fog alarm station.

Bearing to the northwest, so that we might have plenty of sea room, and with a sane and wide-awake man on lookout, the *Glory* with her thankful crew and valuable cargo, awaited the morning. The bos'n, who had been on duty when we had nearly gone on the rocks the evening before, remarked to me: "Listen, boy! I've sailed with many a captain, but I never saw a finer sailor or a more kind-hearted man than your father. Why, I expected that he would knock my fool head off with a belaying pin. Instead, he only spoke decently to me as he would have spoken to a kid. I shall never forget him."

Morning broke magnificently, clear and cool on the 7th of November 1882. The coast, perhaps 40 miles distant, and of a dim blue shade, was to be plainly seen to the eastward. We were approaching the enchanting shores which we had waited so long and patiently to tread.

Our breeze was fair, and with everything spread, we were running ahead. The captain and first officer, each with his marine glass leveled on the water, were striving to pick up the pilot boat. When at last, one of them spied it a little off the port bow, the man at the wheel was given his orders to change course, and soon hove to and the pilot, wearing spruce blue clothes, was not long in coming aboard. Soon, he was up on the quarter deck grasping the captain by the hand who at once introduced him to the first and second officer.

Upon being informed of our narrow escape of the evening before, the pilot related that less than a month before, a large English ship[1] had run on the rocks at nearly the same spot. Then it had backed off and sunk in deep water. Thick fog in her case had hid the rocks from view, and the crew had barely escaped in the ship's boats. They had finally reached the fog alarm on the middle rock.

Now that the pilot was in charge and the tide at the flood, the captain decided that we could make it through the Gate without a tug, and the pilot agreed with him. Gracefully, with all her canvas set, the ship passed between Fort Point and Marin Shore. The pilot gave orders to clew up the courses in order to reduce her speed, and then the jib, was lowered. At the command, "Let go the anchor!" the big hook dropped from the cat head, and with an awful roar, and in a cloud of rust, the chain paid out from the starboard hawse hole. We were in port again, 128 days from New York. It was a long voyage for the ship and her commander.

Even before the anchor was let go, a boatman with a passenger in the stern sheets of his Whitehall boat had thrown his painter over our rail, and the mate had made it fast to a belaying pin. Hardly had the ship stopped her headway, when the passenger, an elderly gentleman wearing a tall hat, came up the Jacob's Ladder, and stepped aboard. He introduced himself with his business card as Mr. Adams of the firm of Adams, McNear & Co., wholesale grocers of San Francisco and Sacramento. His visit was for the purpose of welcoming his son, Fred Adams, who had shipped as one of the crew in New York. The father had come out to meet him as soon as the *Glory* arrived. Father and son who had not met for many months grasped hands at last in friendly greeting.

Our captain went ashore with the pilot, and after calling at the office of the ship's agents and leaving the papers, he returned to the ship before nightfall. When he came overside, his first remark was, "Well, Carl, what do you think has happened?" I replied, "I can't guess." He said, "Mr. John L. Sullivan of Boston has licked Tug Wilson of England, and Ben Butler [former Civil War General], after two trials, has been elected governor of Massachusetts; so, our country is still safe."

The crew was not at liberty to leave until the ship docked the next morning. At high water the following forenoon, we were towed into our berth. When properly made fast, the crew went over the side after being informed that they would receive their pay that afternoon at the Shipping Commissioner's office.

Arrangements were now made for unloading our cargo. A donkey engine was brought to the wharf, and the task soon began. The merchandise which came from the hold of that ship would have filled a large warehouse. I shall not attempt to enumerate the articles, as it was termed a general cargo.[2]

Williams, Dimond & Co. were cargo agents for the *Glory of the Seas* at San Francisco, and fifty consignees obtained portions of her cargo. A list appeared in the maritime columns of the *Alta* following her arrival, with consignees ranging from the Central Pacific Railroad (C.P.R.R.) to the San Francisco Furniture Factory. An even greater variety of items made up her general cargo this year than in 1879. For instance, the C.P.R.R. received 571 tons of coal and 1,746 steel rails. There were also eight cases of books, six cases of piano stools, 319 barrels of whiskey, and 80 boxes of almanacs, just to name some of the cargo on board.[3]

To remind the consignees that they had best quickly pick up their order of four and five months past, Williams, Dimond & Co. published a "consignee notice" in the newspapers, in which they officially notified consignees that once stevedores unloaded cargo on the adjoining Green Street Wharf, ". . . if not removed before 4 o'clock p.m. of each day will be stored at their risk and expense."[4]

The small ship consignee notice section in the papers clearly indicated how the American intercoastal "clipper" trade diminished in the thirteen years since the completion of the Transcontinental Railroad. Only four vessels unloaded cargo from New York, two of which were represented by Williams, Dimond & Co.: the *Glory of the Seas* and the ship *Conqueror*. The other two ships were the *Sovereign of the Seas*, situated at Vallejo Street Wharf, and the *Manuel Llanguno*, berthed at Green Street. John Rosenfeld, local agent for the two latter craft, handled the affairs of the "Dispatch Line" at San Francisco.

Of the Cape Horn arrivals during the first half of November 1882, only two vessels made what could be termed good passages. They were a British iron ship, the *Clan MacFarlane*, and the medium clipper bark *Cassandra Adams*, a wooden-hulled vessel built on the West Coast of the United States. Both vessels made 115-day passages from the British Isles. The 249-foot *Clan MacFarlane* beat the entire British fleet, while the *Cassandra Adams* beat the American fleet, including the *Glory*. The 196-foot *Adams*, built at Seabeck, Washington Territory, in 1876, was originally constructed for service along the Pacific Coast, but proved to be such an excellent sea boat that John Rosenfeld purchased her for Cape Horn service in 1881. Subsequently, she made one round voyage to

Glory *unloading coal at Howard Street Wharves, San Francisco, ca. 1895. Shows replacement of "built" lower fore and main masts with solid sticks. Courtesy of the author. Robert W. Weinstein Collection.*

Liverpool and return to San Francisco; and earlier in the year 1882 made a 105-day passage to the British port with grain. Although half the tonnage of the *Glory of the Seas*, her original owners oversparred her with a main yard ninety feet in length, one foot less than the *Glory*; however, since becoming a Cape Horner, Rosenfeld's captain on board the *Adams* elected to reduce the size of her spars proportionately, so that her main yard was now eighty feet. The *Cassandra Adams'* ability to sail, especially in light winds, had already made a fine reputation in shipping circles.

McLaughlin's 128-day passage, however, was the best of the November 1882 arrivals at San Francisco from the East Coast of the United States. Captain Wood's passage in the *Sovereign of the Seas* took 143 days, while Captain Barstow of the *Norris* arrived on the same day as the *Glory*, 146 days from Philadelphia.

The British iron ship *Ennerdale* and the German ship *Carl Friederich* (formerly the American ship *Red Cloud*) both arrived at San Francisco from Liverpool the day before the *Glory*, the *Ennerdale* in 123 days, and the *Carl Friederich* in 138 days. Carl McLaughlin briefly mentioned that a half-dozen vessels had been encountered by the *Glory* off Cape Horn. Both of these vessels sailed from Liverpool and had been in company.

Captain Gunson, master of the *Ennerdale*, indicated in his published voyage summary that the weather his vessel experienced west of San Francisco exasperated him: "... have been within 300 miles of port for past eight days, with light winds and calms and beautiful, clear weather."[5] Captain McLaughlin's brief comments were similar with the exception of his mention of fog: "... have been nine days with light, baffling winds and fogs."[6]

Carl McLaughlin's first and last Cape Horn voyage was an unqualified success. In addition, the time spent with his father helped bridge the fifteen years since the death of his mother. In four-and-one-half months, father and son established an adult relationship, recompensing them for the many years when their only contact was by letter.

CHAPTER XVII

Lay-up and Retirement

Moving to the West Coast was an eye-opening change for Carl McLaughlin. Accustomed to the extremes of climate in New England with its distinctive four seasons, the mild fall weather in the San Francisco Bay Area surprised him:

> The season was autumn. In San Francisco that does not mean frost at night or morning but splendid weather. The markets were crowded with all the fruits and grapes which grew so abundantly in the Golden State.
>
> It had never been my privilege to hunt wild ducks in my eastern home. At that time the marshes around San Francisco Bay were alive with many varieties of them. I had only to cross on the Alameda ferry to enjoy such shooting. It is now impossible to get anywhere in the state unless one is a member of some shooting club. Quail were abundant on the hillsides in the outlying counties, but as the English hunter complained about the rabbits in Australia, "The blooming things were about a foot too short to hit, don't you know."
>
> Shortly after arrival in port, our captain had a little dinner on board for the ship's agents and some friends. There was no famine at that banquet. The ship's steward and his wife, the stewardess, gave a demonstration of what could be done when materials could be obtained. No diner could say that anything was wrong. I can distinctly remember the wine that was served on the occasion. Along that line,

the two varieties that pleased me best were the California port and sherry that had been in *Glory*'s lazaret for at least a year, having rounded the Horn twice in new barrels. Wine men claim that this ages sweet wine as nothing else can do. At that time our captain brought forth the baby seal skins which John Smith of New Bedford and Diego Ramirez had insisted on leaving for payment for provisions furnished him and his marooned crew off Cape Horn. They were handed to Captain J.N. Knowles, the San Francisco agent for the owners of *Glory*.

We had been in San Francisco perhaps a month, when our captain, who always scanned the daily papers for marine news each morning remarked: "Now, listen to this!" Then, he read a report from Valparaiso to the effect that a ship coming west around the Horn had seen a signal of distress from the Diego Ramirez. They had taken off the crew of a sealing vessel which had been wrecked in Magellan Straits. The entire crew, with the exception of a little Portuguese boy [and the men on Diego Ramirez], had been killed by the savage Patagonians. The little boy hid, and in some way managed to attract attention of another vessel. We were thankful that we had been of service to John Smith and his companions until they were taken to some more hospitable place.

The lower mast on the ship had never been replaced since she was launched, which at this time was over 13 years. The mast, which was a built one (its sections or staves being bound together with heavy iron bands) had commenced to show decay in some of the sections.

It had been brought to the attention of [Captain Knowles][1] to the danger of [the mast being unable to withstand the rigors of another Cape Horn passage]. He had wired to [Puget Sound] for a suitable stick that was trued to fit which would replace the lower mast. One was [shipped] down the coast [from Port Blakely on the down-East bark *Otago*].[2] [While berthed alongside Green Street Wharf, *Glory*'s] rigging was stowed before removing the old mast. [The main topmast, combination topgallant, royal and skysail mast, and all yards on her main were all sent down on deck, and the new Douglas fir main mast, 94 feet in length and 40 inches in diameter], was stepped into place. Shipwrights squared the head of the new timber to fit into the ironwork which was to [receive the main top mast].[3]

While *Glory of the Seas'* lower main mast was being replaced, an incident occurred on December 9, 1882, in which the *Glory* and the undisputed queen of the West Coast-built sailing ship fleet were involved in a minor collision. As the *Cassandra Adams* was brought alongside the Vallejo Street Wharf by a tug, she fouled the rigging of the *Glory,* carrying away the latter vessel's mizzen royal mast. When the two subsequently untangled and the *Adams* was safely alongside, she had to have her own foremast replaced.[4]

Although the incident between the *Glory* and the *Cassandra Adams* did not constitute a disaster, tradition and law required that the managing owners of both vessels file form letters at a government Custom House reporting the incident. In a letter sent to the general superintendent of the Life-Saving Service at Washington, D.C., the collector of customs at the Boston Custom House assured the superintendent he had "the honor to state that the owners of said vessels inform me that there was no disaster in either instance."[5] The matter was therefore closed.

Along with the *Cassandra Adams* at the Vallejo Street Dock was the *Glory*'s smaller sister, the *Sovereign of the Seas.* The *Sovereign* was loading miscellaneous cargo — 1,540 bales of wool, 1,147 cases of canned salmon, and 12,300 pigs of lead — for John Rosenfeld's Dispatch Line for New York.[6] Unlike thirty years before when vessels almost always departed San Francisco in ballast, they now hauled a variety of cargo eastbound. The *Sovereign* was one of the few sailing vessels in the Cape Horn fleet making money heading East. Unlike the *Glory,* the *Sovereign*'s New York owners did not depend on the prevailing charter rates being offered in the 1882-1883 grain year.

In mid-December 1882, Knowles didn't consider grain rates high enough to justify chartering the *Glory of the Seas.* The German ship *Carl Friederich* received a rate of £1 13s 9d ($8.02) and the new British iron ship *Amphitrite,* making her first passage as a grain carrier, obtained £2 ($9.68). The £1 13s ($7.99) rate obtained for the *Manuel Llanguno* in December strongly indicated to Captain Knowles that he most likely would not get a higher rate for the *Glory of the Seas.*[7]

Just forward of the *Sovereign of the Seas* at Vallejo Street Wharf lay the *Cassandra Adams,* loading cargo for New York in the Dispatch Line. This bark, having the distinction of being one[8] of the only two first-class, West Coast-built vessels in the Cape Horn trade, both contrasted with and resembled the *Glory* and the *Sovereign.* Like the *Glory,* she displayed ornate trailboards. Although all three vessels had striking figureheads, the *Adams'* decorative work was far more conservative than Donald McKay's designs. The *Glory's* white lady was unclad, except for flowing Grecian robes between her breasts. McKay's sovereign looked like a king with the exception of long, flowing robes. By contrast, the *Adams'* matron wore an ankle-length dress with high neck and covered arms — a fully-dressed Victorian woman. In fact, the *Adams'* first owner refused to have her original figurehead — a likeness of his wife — installed on the vessel because he felt the carver immodestly dressed her. That first carving portrayed a knee-length dress with an open neck and showed bare arms. Although nearly the same length, the *Sovereign of the Seas* and the *Cassandra Adams* represented different designs, the former vessel being almost a third larger in tonnage.

The *Sovereign* was more lofty than the *Adams* because of her main skysail (the *Adams* had nothing higher than royals), but the *Cassandra Adams'* yards were proportionately longer. When it came to hull form, the medium-built *Adams* was a much faster ship than the full-bodied *Sovereign of the Seas.* The *Glory's* 104-day passage in 1876-1877 was one day faster than the *Adams'* fastest eastward Cape Horn voyage; the *Sovereign's* best run on this route was only 114 days.

While the *Glory of the Seas* and the *Cassandra Adams* underwent replacement of existing spars, the *Glory* at Green Street, and the *Adams* at Vallejo, the *Alta California* under the heading of "Shipping-Vessels Up" called attention to the impending New York voyage of the two vessels:

> This splendid vessel [*Sovereign of the Seas*] is well known, and will receive Quick Dispatch. Having large engagements, shippers will please make early application for balance of freight. To be followed by the A-1 Clipper bark, *Cassandra Adams,* Henry, Master.[9]

The *Adams* hadn't made much money hauling 1,501 tons of steam coal from the British Isles, but she definitely would do so hauling general cargo on the return trip to New York.

On December 18, 1882, the arrival of a Custom House tonnage inspector relieved the dockside monotony on board the *Glory of the Seas.* His function under the title "Measurer of Vessels," was to re-measure portions of the *Glory*'s deck cabins to establish her "net" tonnage; this complied with a recently adopted Bureau of Navigation law passed on August 8, 1882, which stated in part:

> That from the gross tonnage of every vessel of the United States, there shall be deducted the tonnage of the spaces or compartments occupied by or appropriated to the use of the crew of the vessel.[10]

This meant that the government employee personally interviewed Captain McLaughlin and reached with him an agreement of what constituted deductible crew space on the *Glory of the Seas.* Then the surveyor measured the space and calculated an average length, breadth and height for the area. The result benefited the ship's owners. Henceforth, a revised lower figure would be used in determining tonnage taxes. In fact, the tax prior to June 26, 1884 was "thirty cents per ton per annum."[11] The gross tonnage of the *Glory* was 2,102.57 (one gross ton equalling 100 cubic feet). Her new "net" tonnage would be 2,009.09 with the deletion of: (1) her fo'c'sle crew space and two small cabins from her forward house; (2) the small cabin abaft the main mast; and (3) space from her after house. The captain convinced the surveyor that half of the after house was his personal space (measuring 21.5 x 22.5 x 7.1 feet). The measurer of vessels likewise deleted the forward cabin as well as the Chappell's cabin, bringing a total of 93.48 registered tons, henceforth, to be deducted from her gross tonnage.[12]

On December 21, the *Sovereign of the Seas* sailed for New York, closing a chapter in the lives of the two vessels. This was the last time the two McKay-built ships crossed paths at San Francisco.[13]

In the following weeks, Captain Knowles had the *Glory*'s lower foremast replaced by a solid stick like her main mast. By the first week of January 1883 she was back in first-class condition, ready to face the rigors of Cape Horn.[14] However, she still had to contend with the existing grain rates. Rather than accept a less than profitable rate, Knowles decided to lay her up. On January 13, a tug hauled the *Glory of the Seas* off Green Street Wharf and towed her across the Bay to the east side of Goat Island to await better economic times.

Shortly thereafter, Captain McLaughlin left the *Glory* in the care of Chief Mate Martins while he and Carl went to Oleander to work on the vineyard property.

On February 15, 1883, the captain deeded twenty acres to Carl. On the same day he also deeded ten acres of land to Millie Ann Chappell, the ship's stewardess. From then on, Frank would go to sea alone while Millie developed their vineyard property. They agreed that she would stay ashore and build up the land, so that Frank could eventually come ashore permanently. In the following years the Chappells produced muscat grapes and peaches and eventually added a modest home and barn to their property.[15]

While the McLaughlins were at Fresno, the *Glory of the Seas*' mate decided to go into business for himself. Basil Lubbock, whose prolific maritime writings have become a standard for maritime historians, incorporated the incident into one of his works:

> Martin was a first-class officer, a wonderful navigator, and a linguist of some ability; he was also a swell dresser, with all the outward appearances of a gentleman; but after he had sold a hawser, a new mainsail, and several coils of Manila rope to a junk-man at San Francisco, the "old man" of the *Glory of the Seas* declared that, though Martin was beyond reproach as an officer, he was a bit too slippery for him, and he went on to remark, that if he had not returned from his ranch when he did, he would have found that Martin had sold the "whole blooming ship.[16]

By spring 1883, grain shipping on San Francisco Bay worsened. A gloomy newspaper reporter had the following to say;

The ships keep piling in Mission Bay, and there are now idle in that vicinity over 25 ships representing fully one million and a quarter dollars in value not earning a dollar; and back of Goat Island, there are six or eight first-class vessels in the same condition, which swells the amount tied up to fully one million and a half. Hard times is the word with them.[17]

By January 1, 1884, the number of disengaged deep-sea sailing vessels on San Francisco Bay swelled to one hundred. Forty-six of this number were American wooden squareriggers. Nineteen vessels were laid up in Mission Bay, and another ten lay at anchor in Richardson Bay off Sausalito.

The "Clam Fleet" of the late 1870s was renamed to encompass all the other ship lay-up areas on the Bay. The fleet was now identified as the "Mercantile Marine, Waiting Development" fleet.[18] Captain Emmons, master of the ship *Palestine*, had the dubious distinction of being named "Commodore," because of his vessel's having been laid up the longest.

As of January 1, 1884, the *Palestine* had been in port almost eighteen months, two months longer than the *Glory*. While the *Palestine* was lying at anchor in Mission Bay, four vessels lay at anchor on the east side of Goat Island: the *America*, the four-mast bark *Ocean King*, the *Carrolton*, and the *Glory of the Seas* — all under the management of Captain Knowles and unable to obtain a profit-making grain charter.

In the fall of 1884 Capt. McLaughlin made an important decision: to relinquish command of the *Glory of the Seas* and retire from the sea. He was almost sixty-one, in good health, and he looked forward to working his vineyard. Thus he brought down the curtain on a successful maritime career stretching back forty-seven years. During that time he rounded Cape Horn forty-two times and circumnavigated the world three times.[19] From the diminutive brig *Stephen G. Bass* to the magnificent *Glory of the Seas*, he brought much honor to himself and the American Merchant Marine.

Several months after leaving the *Glory,* the captain and Maggie suffered major financial setbacks, forcing them to file a "Declaration of Homestead" document on February 26, 1885, at the Fresno County Court House. He placed a value of $5,000 on their Oleander real estate holdings. The following September they borrowed $3,000 from Capt. Knowles on a three-year note secured by a mortgage on their property. After two years, however, they recouped their fortunes. Apparently the muscat grape crop was excellent in 1886, because Capt. McLaughlin paid off the entire loan on September 6, 1886. In addition, he purchased twenty acres for expansion of the vineyard in November 1886.[20]

Initially, the McLaughlins lived in a basement-type home, later termed the "subterranean" house by the family; but eventually, they built a two-story New England-style home on the Oleander property. The following years were successful for the captain and his wife, and he became prominent in the small town as a community leader.[21]

In May 1892, the McLaughlins made an extended visit to the East Coast, including Grand Manan Island. Carl McLaughlin, now a married man, was in a position where he and his wife Elizabeth could reside on the Oleander property and generally oversee operations. Daniel McLaughlin and Maggie visited Boston, Malden, and Eastport. Finally they arrived at Grand Manan, where the captain had many fond memories of childhood.[22]

The captain's visit to the East Coast became permanent when they purchased a two-story home at Seal Cove on Grand Manan and the captain and Maggie began enjoying a full retirement. One of Daniel McLaughlin's next projects was building a small yacht about forty feet long which he named the *Tramp.* In the following years he visited his birthplace at Lower Granville, and sailed to St. John and other ports on the Bay of Fundy. He started a yacht club and took a leadership role in the promotion of boat races on Grand Manan island.[23]

As the annual celebration of Dominion Day approached, July 1, 1894, McLaughlin felt that a fitting nautical celebration should accompany the local festivities. He offered to co-sponsor a

Captain McLaughlin's home at Grand Manan, N.B., ca. 1895. McLaughlin standing in front and his daughter Josephine McLaughlin Lane standing on front step.

Oil painting of Captain McLaughlin's yacht Tramp *by William E. Hans. Courtesy of
the artist and Merlyn McIntyre.*

special boat race of sailing vessels twenty-one feet and over. The following letter appeared in the *Eastport Sentinel* on June 6, 1894:

> Grand Manan, N.B., June 4, 1894
>
> EASTPORT SENTINEL,
>
> Dear Sir:
>
> The Queen's birthday having passed without any notice being taken — with the exception of raising a few flags and taking a few extra drinks. Now Dominion day is in sight which appears to swell the hearts of the good people of this island beyond all other days, they having on that day gained a victory over themselves.
>
> I would be pleased in helping them to get up a boat race so that some one of them may be happy in knowing he has the "crack" boat in a sailing match over any course that may be decided upon by a committee for the same. Boats to belong to the Island; say 21 feet or upwards with allowance for length of water line.
>
> If the owners of boats will combine with me, that the boats may be brought together and entered for the race, I will help swell the stakes so that the best boat, 2d and 3d will each take a suitable purse. In order that this may get before the owners of the boats, please insert in your next issue and oblige.
>
> Yours truly,
>
> Daniel McLaughlan

The *Sentinal* is silent as to whether his offer was accepted in time for Dominion Day. However, Captain McLaughlin's suggestion became a reality on July 1, 1895. From the *Sentinel*, July 10, 1895:

> Dominion Day was well observed on this Island. In fact, it looked like a young Fourth of July in American ports; flags were flying the whole length of the Island. At Grand Harbor the boat race was the principal feature and cause no small excitement along the shores of the south part . . . a distance of 15 miles. The boats of course were mostly fishing boats that were only provided with two sails; therefore those that had light sails had to dispense with them or not be allowed to enter . . . the Old Man of the Sea [Captain McLaughlin] was in it with his little *Tramp* and did good work and bid well to take the plum

had a small bolt that connected the rudderstock with the rudder not
worked out which rendered her unmanageable so it was hard to keep
her out of the wind . . .

There were foot races and ball playing and everything that could
help out the sports of the day . . . There was a fine supper and after the
church people left, the rank and file came in and danced till daylight.
And so ended the best day that many islanders ever spent.

It appeared that Daniel and Maggie McLaughlin were going to enjoy a lengthy retirement on Grand Manan. They subsequently leased the vineyard at Oleander for a five-year period commencing on December 30, 1895.[24]

Unexpectedly, Captain Daniel McLaughlin became ill and
died at Grand Manan on Monday, January 13, 1896, at the age of
seventy-two. Margaret McLaughlin lived until December 30, 1901,
when she died at the age of sixty-three.[25]

Daniel McLaughlin was not forgotten by the shipping community on the West Coast. After his death, the *San Francisco Daily
Commercial News and Shipping List* on January 29, 1896, stated:

Captain Daniel McGlaughlin, a native of Grand Manan, N.S., on
the Bay of Fundy, but always hailing from Eastport, Me., died at his
birth place on January 16th at the ripe age of 72 years. He was well
known here, having made his first voyage to California in 1851 in command of the clipper ship *Grey Feather*. Subsequently he was master of
the *Aetos*, and then commanded a steamer which was lost. He returned
to sailing vessels and was commander of the . . . *Swallow, Herald of the
Morning*, and *Glory of the Seas*, the latter vessel being still on the coast in
command of Captain Freeman. His record as a shipmaster was a clean
one and as master of some of the old time clipper ships he made record
passages.

The *Glory of the Seas* outlived the McLaughlins by many years.
Brought out of lay-up in early 1885 she actively sailed until 1910,
more than four decades after Donald McKay built her. In 1911,
the *Glory* was ingloriously stripped of her spars and converted to a
fish-processing towing barge. Ironically, she made far more money

in this capacity than she had since the turn of the century when the decay of the American merchant square-rig fleet began accelerating at an alarming rate.

In 1921, the *Glory*'s last owners became insolvent. The receiver for her main creditor sold her for scrap. On a gravel beach just south of Seattle, Washington, the once-proud medium clipper ship *Glory of the Seas*, the last merchant built by Donald McKay and the final command of clipper ship captain Daniel McLaughlin, was burned for her metal fittings on Sunday, May 13, 1923.

The *Sentinal* paid a fitting final tribute to Daniel McLaughlin:

> He was a man of sterling qualities, honest and upright in his dealings and very successful in his calling. He lies in the little rural church yard at a spot where one can view a large expanse of the ocean that he loved . . . He sleeps well."[26]

Tombstone of Captain Daniel McLaughlin and his wives Hannah and Margaret at Seal Cove, Grand Manan Island. Gale McLaughlin and Merlyn McIntyre standing alongside, left to right. Courtesy Merlyn McIntyre.

Appendix A
Ship Statistics

Name of Vessel	Flag	Type	Year Built	Hull Type	Reg. Tonnage	Registerd Dimensions Length	Breadth	Depth
Aetos	Am	Ship	1854	Wood	1,286	202.0	39.0	23.9
Alameda	Am	Ferry	1866	Wood	813	193	38	16.2
America	Am	Ship	1874	Wood	2,054	232.8	43.1	28
Aminta	Br	Ship	1862	Iron	1,132	214	35	23
Anasha	Am	Str	1862	Wood	39			
Arcadia	Br	Bark	1863	Wood	417	136.4	27.3	17.1
Arcturus	Am	Bark	1866	Wood	1,054	170	35	23
Baltic	Am	Bark 4mst	1850	Wood	2,552	280	45	31.6
Blengfell	Br	Ship	1876	Iron	1,210	232.4	35.2	21.1
Borrowdale	Br	Ship	1868	Iron	1,277	226.4	36.4	22
Brodick Castle	Br	Ship	1875	Iron	1,827	258.6	40.3	23.0
Brown Brothers	Am	Ship	1876	Wood	1,493	208.6	40.4	24
Cannanore	Br	Ship	1877	Iron	1,655	247	38.6	23.6
Carl Friedrich	Ge	Ship	1878	Wood	2,208	230.5	43.2	29.5
Carondelet	Am	Ship	1872	Wood	1,438	202.5	40.3	24
Cassandra	Am	Str	1863	Wood	1,221	207.0	35.5	17.3
Cassandra Adams	Am	Bark	1876	Wood	1,127	196.5	40.3	22.2
Centennial	Am	Ship	1875	Wood	1,287	190.4	38	24
Chandos	Am	Ship	1869	Wood	1,506	186.2	39.9	26
Charles Dennis	Am	Ship	1875	Wood	1,710	220	40	24.1
Chinsura	Br	Ship	1866	Iron	1,266	215.5	37.1	22.8
City of Rome	Br	Stmsp	1881	Iron	8,144	560.2	52.3	37.0
Clan Macfarlane	Br	Ship	1881	Iron	1,484	249.1	38.3	22.8
Clarissa B. Carver	Am	Ship	1876	Wood	1,144	187	37	24
Concordia	Am	Str	1862	Iron	1,681	248.8	33.4	20.9
Conqueror	Am	Ship	1874	Wood	1,621	215	41	24
Cornelius Grinnell	Am	Ship	1850	Wood	1,316	172	37	28

Name of Vessel	Flag	Type	Year Built	Hull Type	Reg. Tonnage	Registerd Dimensions		
						Length	Breadth	Depth
County of Dumfries	Br	Ship 4mst	1878	Iron	1,718	266.2	38.9	23.6
County of Inverness	Br	Ship 4mst	1877	Iron	1,716	266.6	38.9	23.6
County of Kinross	Br	Ship 4mst	1878	Iron	1,716	267	38.9	23.7
Cumberland	Ca	Ship	1876	Wood	1,555	220.7	41.6	24
Donald McKay	Br	Ship	1855	Wood	2,408	257.9	46.3	29.5
Eller Bank	Br	Ship	1876	Iron	1,171	232.4	35.2	21.1
Emilie Schroeder	Am	Sch	1870	Wood	85			
El Capitan	Am	Ferry	1868	Wood	933	244	40	15.9
Ennerdale	Br	Ship	1874	Iron	1,284	226.4	36.3	21.8
Eureka	Am	Ship	1876	Wood	2,101	230.9	42	26.5
Flying Cloud	Am	Ship	1851	Wood	1,139	219	40	21
Friedlander	Am	Ship	1872	Wood	1,638	219	39.8	26
Frolic	Am	Ship	1869	Wood	1,368	192.5	39.9	24.6
Glencairn	Br	Ship 4mst	1878	Iron	1,620	252.4	40	22.5
Glory Of The Seas	Am	Ship	1869	Wood	2,103	240.2	44.1	28.3
Governor Tilley	Br	Ship	1875	Wood	1,420	201.4	38.3	24.2
Granite State	Am	Ship	1877	Wood	1,684	228.9	41.4	24
Grasmere	Br	Ship	1874	Iron	1,304	226.0	36.1	22.1
Gray Feather	Am	Ship	1850	Wood	586	138.4	30.5	19
Grecian	Am	Ship	1876	Wood	1,677	215.8	40.5	26.9
Hagarstown	Am	Ship	1874	Wood	1,903	223.7	42.3	26.1
Harriet F. Hussey	Am	Bark	1868	Wood	685	141.2	31.6	20.7
Harvey Mills	Am	Ship	1876	Wood	2,187	231	43	29.7
Hecla	Am	Ship	1877	Wood	1,529	210.3	40.2	24.3
Hecla	Br	Bark	1875	Wood	901	174.6	35.5	20.2
Helen Morris	Am	Ship	1868	Wood	1,285	174.3	36.5	23.6
Herald of the Morning	Am	Ship	1853	Wood	1,109	203	38	23.6
H. S. Gregory	Am	Ship	1875	Wood	1,653	228.9	41.9	29.1
Inglewood	Br	Bark	1875	Iron	1,077	215	34.1	21.1
Invincible	Am	Ship	1873	Wood	1,460	202.4	40.3	24
Ivanhoe	Am	Ship	1865	Wood	1,611	202.3	39.3	27.6
Jenny Pitts	Am	Bark	1852	Wood	552	139	26	17
Joseph S. Spinney	Am	Ship	1874	Wood	1,988	230.9	42.6	27.5
Loretto Fish	Am	Ship	1869	Wood	1,840	218	42.2	29.3
Louisiana	Am	Ship	1873	Wood	1,436	202	40	24.2
Manuel Llanguno	Am	Ship	1879	Wood	1,733	221.3	41.5	25.5
Mariposa	Am	Ship	1874	Iron	1,058	221	34.3	20.7
Middlesex	Br	Bark	1861	Wood	1,191	223	36	23
Mitredale	Br	Ship	1875	Iron	1,231	225.8	36.2	21.7
Mogul	Am	Ship	1869	Wood	1,365	203	39	23.9
New World	Am	Ship	1846	Wood	1,417	187.7	40.6	27.6
Nereide	Br	Bkte	1858	Wood	432	122.5	27.8	17.1

Name of Vessel	Flag	Type	Year Built	Hull Type	Reg. Tonnage	Registerd Dimensions		
						Length	Breadth	Depth
Norris	Am	Ship	1874	Wood	1,155	181.6	35.5	23.4
Ocean King	Am	Bark 4mst	1874	Wood	2,516	250.5 x	42.3 x	30.1
Otago	Am	Bark	1864	Wood	895	169.7	33.3	22
Palestine	Am	Ship	1877	Wood	1,469	209.6	40	24
Palmyra	Am	Ship	1876	Wood	1,360	197.9	38.8	24.2
Paul Revere	Am	Ship	1876	Wood	1,735	221	41.2	24.6
Pizarro	Br	Ship	1875	Iron	1,439	233.0	36.3	22.8
St. Charles	Am	Ship	1866	Wood	1,166	188	38	23
St. Stephen	Am	Ship	1877	Wood	1,392	208.5	40.5	23.7
Samaria	Am	Ship	1876	Wood	1,509	217.6	39.1	24.1
Seaforth	Br	Ship	1862	Iron	1,189	218	34.9	23.6
Sea Serpent	Am	Ship	1850	Wood	975	194.6	39.3	20.8
Seminole	Am	Ship	1865	Wood	1,511	196.6	41.7	25
Stephen G. Bass	Am	Brig	1845	Wood	194	72.7	24	9.8
Simla	Br	Ship 4mst	1854	Iron	2,288	330.2	39.8	26.7
Sterling	Am	Ship	1873	Wood	1,732	208.4	42.7	26.1
Southern Cross	Am	Ship	1868	Wood	1,129	176.8	37.5	22.3
Sovereign Of The Seas	Am	Ship	1868	Wood	1,502	199.5	41	23.9
Springwood	Br	Bark	1862	Wood	990	180.1	34	22.5
Solano	Am	Ferry	1879	Wood	3,549	420.5	65	18.3
Spartan	Am	Ship	1874	Wood	1,449	207.6	40.4	24.3
Swallow	Am	Ship	1854	Wood	1,239	210	38.6	23.6
Sydney Dacres	Br	Ship	1864	Iron	1,386	213.5	36.0	23.5
The Douglas	Br	Ship	1869	Iron	1,428	225.2	37.9	23.6
Thomas Dana	Am	Ship	1873	Wood	1,445	203.5	39.5	24.2
Thrasher	Am	Ship	1876	Wood	1,512	211.9	39.7	24
Three Brothers	Am	Ship	1856	Wood	2,972	311	47	29.8
Titan	Am	Ship	1869	Wood	1,229	189.4	37.3	23.5
Triumphant	Am	Ship	1874	Wood	2,046	234.5	43.0	27.5
Trojan	Am	Ship	1875	Wood	1,608	211	40	24
Victoria Nyanza	Br	Ship	1863	Iron	1,022	200.2	32.5	22.5
Western Empire	Am	Ship	1852	Wood	1,399	195	41	28.6
Wildwood	Am	Ship	1871	Wood	1,099	198.4	40	20.8
William H. Marcy	Am	Ship	1875	Wood	1,607	214.8	41.3	24.2
Young America	Am	Ship	1853	Wood	1,429	239.6	43.2	26.9

Legend:

4mst—Four-mast	Am—American	Br—British
Ca—Canadian	Ge—German	Stmsp–Steamship
Str—Steamer		

NOTE: Registered tonnages for the above American flag vessels are extracted from Post-Civil War sources with the exception of the brig *Stephen G. Bass*, and therefore are calculated according to the British admeasurement rules. These were adopted by the

U. S. government on May 6, 1864. For instance, the original gross tonnage of the *Young America* was 1,962, and as readmeasured under the new law was 1,439. The gross tonnages for foreign flag vessels have been extracted from Post-Civil War shipping registers. All registered dimensions are in feet and decimals.

Appendix B
Line Drawings

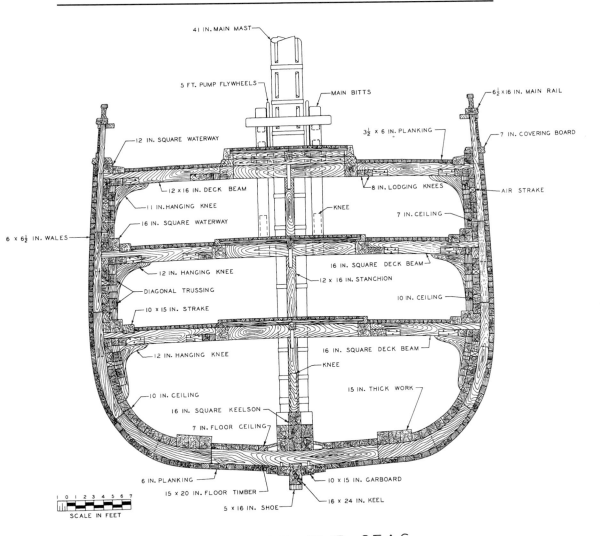

41 IN. MAIN MAST

5 FT. PUMP FLYWHEELS

MAIN BITTS

6½ x 16 IN. MAIN RAIL

12 IN. SQUARE WATERWAY

3½ x 6 IN. PLANKING

7 IN. COVERING BOARD

12 x 16 IN. DECK BEAM

8 IN. LODGING KNEES

AIR STRAKE

11 IN. HANGING KNEE

KNEE

7 IN. CEILING

16 IN. SQUARE WATERWAY

6 x 6½ IN. WALES

12 IN. HANGING KNEE

16 IN. SQUARE DECK BEAM

DIAGONAL TRUSSING

12 x 16 IN. STANCHION

10 x 15 IN. STRAKE

10 IN. CEILING

12 IN. HANGING KNEE

16 IN. SQUARE DECK BEAM

KNEE

10 IN. CEILING

15 IN. THICK WORK

16 IN. SQUARE KEELSON

7 IN. FLOOR CEILING

6 IN. PLANKING

10 x 15 IN. GARBOARD

15 x 20 IN. FLOOR TIMBER

16 x 24 IN. KEEL

5 x 16 IN. SHOE

0 1 2 3 4 5 6 7
SCALE IN FEET

GLORY OF THE SEAS

MIDSHIP SECTION

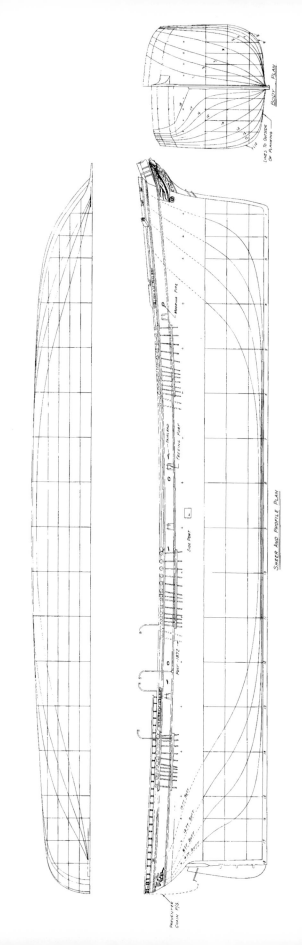

BODY PLAN

LINES TO OUTSIDE OF PLANKING

SHEER AND PROFILE PLAN

SIDE PORT

FREEING PORT

HAWSE PIPE

PLAN END

PLAN END

PREVENTER CHAIN PIPE

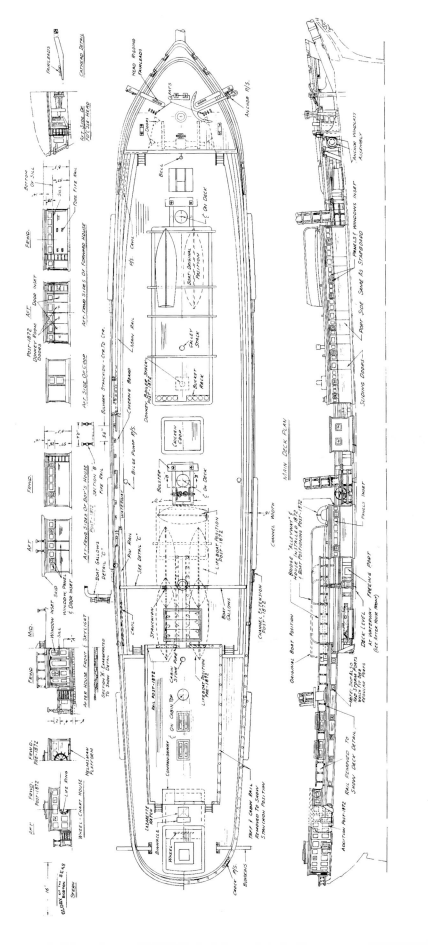

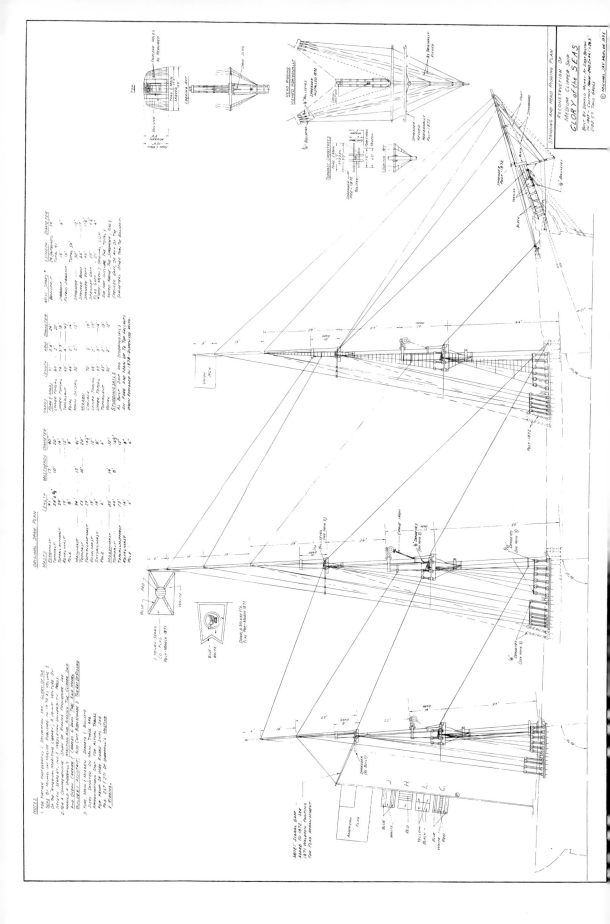

RECONSTRUCTION OF
STANDING AND HEAD RIGGING PLAN
OF
MEDIUM CLIPPER SHIP
GLORY of the SEAS

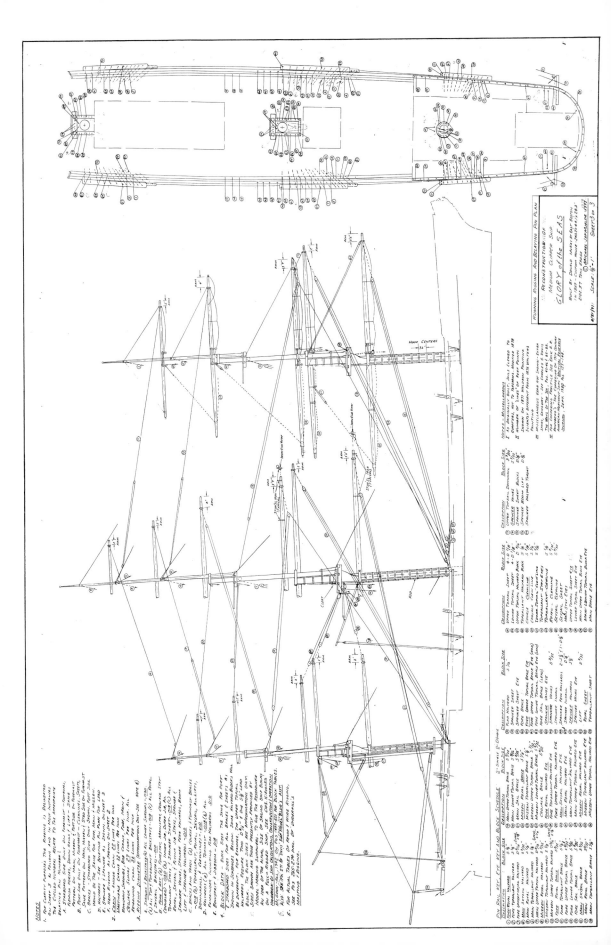

RUNNING RIGGING AND BELAYING PIN PLAN
MEDIUM CLIPPER SHIP
GLORY of the SEAS
SCALE 1/8" = 1'   SHEET 3 OF 3

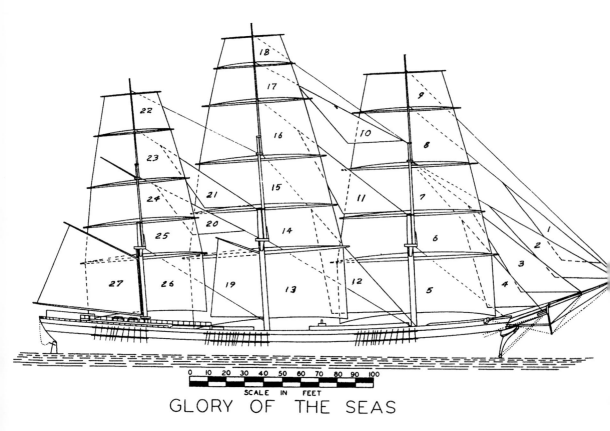

GLORY OF THE SEAS

Identification of sails on the Glory of the Seas, *as of 1876. Sail plan by the author, courtesy*
Mystic Seaport Museum.

1. Flying jib
2. Outer jib
3. Inner jib
4. Fore Staysail
5. Foresail or Fore-course
6. Fore Lower-topsail
7. — Upper-topsail
8. — Topgallant-sail
9. — Royal-sail
10. Main Topgallant-staysail
11. — Topmast-staysail
12. — Staysail
13. Mainsail or Main-course
14. Main Lower-topsail
15. — Upper-topsail
16. — Topgallant-sail
17. — Royal-sail
18. — Skysail
19. Main Spencer
20. Mizzen Topmast staysail
21. —— Topgallant staysail
22. —— Royal-sail
23. —— Topgallant-sail
24. —— Upper-topsail
25. —— Lower-topsail
26. Cross-jack or Crojack
27. Spanker

Notes

CHAPTER I - Sailing Day

[1] "Growth," *The World Book Encyclopedia*, 1989 ed., (Chicago: World Book, Inc., 1989) Vol. 8, pp. 428-429. In 1876 the average American male stood five feet, six inches. A Seaman's Protection Certificate issued 4th quarter, 1843, in District of Norfolk and Portsmouth provides the only accurate description of Captain Daniel McLaughlin besides authenticating his initial claim to American citizenship and lists him as age: 20, height: five feet, eight inches, complexion: ruddy, hair: brown, eyes: blue, and home: Eastport, Maine; National Archives, Civil Archives Branch, Washington, D.C.

[2] B.E. Lloyd, *Lights and Shades in San Francisco* (San Francisco, Calif.: A.L. Bancroft & Co., 1876), p. 398. This two-story structure had Custom House and Shipping Commissioner offices situated in the second floor and basement and the Post Office on the first floor. Locally, it was called the Federal Building, Custom House, or Post Office. According to Lloyd, this building, which fronted on Washington and Battery Streets, was "an old dilapidated [brick] structure much weatherbeaten and certainly no credit to Uncle Sam's taste." Customs was open for public business from nine a.m. to three p.m., Monday through Saturday.

[3] April 8, 1997, statement of Captain Francis E. "Biff" Bowker of The Sailor's Snug Harbor, Sea Level, N.C. "Captains and guests usually boarded a ship at anchor by the starboard gangway. When vessels at wharf, they boarded the side to wharf same as crew." Captain Adrian F. Raynaud of Seattle, Wash., confirmed this statement on April 8, 1987, by saying that boarding a vessel was "carried out in style." He said that it was tradition for captains to board and disembark a sailing ship from the starboard gangway. Crew always boarded on the port gangway when at anchor.

[4] *The Encyclopaedia Britannica*, Eleventh Edition. (New York: The Encylopedia Britannica Company, 1910-1911) Vol. 27 p. 598. "United Kingdom of Great Britain and Ireland, the official title since the 1st of January 1801 of the political unity of England and Wales, Scotland and Ireland."

[5] The term "clipper" in the California trade initially referred to fine-lined vessels like the *Flying Cloud, Challenge*, and those of similar lines, which

arrived during the initial years of the gold rush. In the 1870s this term commonly referred to full-rigged ships engaging in trade between East Coast ports like New York and Boston to San Francisco. It included some of the remaining clippers like the *Young America*, but the majority of the vessels engaging in this trade were down-Easters and ships fairly full in build. The term actually became a misnomer.

CHAPTER II - The Master

[1] *Register of Approved Shipmasters* (New York, N.Y.: American Shipmasters Association, March, 1864). McLaughlin's certificate number was number 2459 issued in 1863. Registration for shipmasters was enacted in 1871 by U.S. Statutes at Large, Sec. 4438-4440, but applied only to those "masters, chief mates, engineers and pilots of all steam-vessels."

[2] Records of Boston Marine Society, Boston, Mass.; and brochure, "The Boston Marine Society," Boston Marine Society.

[3] *Pen Pictures from the Garden of the World, Memorial and Biograhical History of the Counties of Fresno, Tulare and Kern, California* (Chicago, Ill.: The Lewis Publishing Company, 189_): and McLaughlin family records.

[4] L. Keith Ingersoll, "The Great Debate of 1877," *The Grand Manan Historian* (Grand Manan, New Brunswick: Grand Manan Historical Society, 1968), pp. 9-12, incl.

[5] "Great Debate," *op. cit.*, p. 9; L.K. Ingersoll, "The Saga of Captain Dan," *National Fisherman,* June 1965, p. 48.; Statement of Merlyn L. McIntryre, September 1, 1971, and August 2, 1988.

[6] *Patterson's Illustrated Nautical Encyclopedia* defines "hand" as: "To hand a sail is to furl it;" to "reef" a sail: "To contract a sail is to reef it . . . To shake out a reef is to open out the sail to the value of a breadth contained between the reef bands;" and "steer" means: "To guide a vessel on her course by the movement of the helm." This implies that an able-bodied seaman had the necessary qualifications and years of experience to carry out the orders of the mates in sailing a vessel. This included duties on deck such as steering the ship, hauling on lines, general ship maintenance, and also handling himself aloft in furling and setting sail in all kinds of weather.

[7] Richard Peters (editor), *The Public Statutes at Large of the United States of America,* Volume I (Boston, Mass.: Charles C. Little and James Brown, 1845), pp. 477-478, incl.

[8] Obituary, *Eastport Sentinel,* Jan. 29, 1896; "Great Debate," *op. cit.,* p. 9.

[9] Obituary, *op. cit.*

[10] Obituary; Shipping Articles for *Stephen G. Bass* dated October 11, 1848, and Register for this vessel dated October 10, 1848, issued at New York, Custom House Records, National Archives, Washington, D.C.

[11] The date of marriage is confirmed from Eastport city records; however, full authentication of the church wedding has not been confirmed due to the church records having been burned (per letter of Joyce E. Kinney, former

church secretary). The assumption of place of marriage is based on later newspaper records as well as p. 79 of Joyce E. Kinney, *The Vessels of Way Down East* (Eastport, Maine: Joyce E. Kinney, 1989).

[12] The list of people attending the wedding has not been preserved due to their being no extant copies of the *Eastport Sentinel* in 1848 (per letter of Joyce E. Kinney). It is logically assumed that both Bass and Huston would have attended the wedding.

[13] Kinney, *op. cit.*, p. 90.

[14] Carl Cutler, *Greyhounds of the Sea* (Annapolis, Maryland: United States Naval Institute, 1930), pp. 176-177, 302, 433; Frederick C. Matthews, *American Merchant Ships*, 1850-1900, Vol. I. (Salem, Mass.: Marine Research Society, 1930), p. 139. Although Cutler consistently spells the name of this vessel as "*Grey Feather*" in *Greyhounds of the Sea*, a Custom House document issued to her on January 10, 1851, at the New York Custom House (Record Group 36) spells it as *Gray Feather* as well as does the abstract log in Lieut. M.F. Maury's records, Record Group 27 and 36, National Archives, Washington, D.C.; also *Way Down East, op. cit.*, p. 90.

The appearance of *Gray Feather* has been preserved on two paintings, one of which was executed by an unknown American artist. The original of this painting was once the property of Captain McLaughlin and was donated to the M. H. de Young Museum (The Fine Arts Museums of San Francisco) on April 27, 1922, by John W. McLaughlin. It was eventually sold through Herschl and Adler, New York art dealers, in 1972.

The *Gray Feather* was a main skysail-yarder and, like most clippers of that period, spread single topsails. She, likewise, had a set of studdingsails as evidenced by booms as high as her topgallants on the McLaughlin painting. The *Gray Feather* had a modified beakhead with ornate trailboards terminating forward in an ornate billethead. Unlike the *Glory of the Seas*, she had bulwarks about three-and-one-half feet high and had a square stern. Furthermore, her lower masts were solid sticks, unlike later down-Easters with their "built" sections banded by iron hoops. The McLaughlin painting dates from the early 1850s.

Another painting of the *Gray Feather* was executed by Walter Francis, a former crew member of the *Glory of the Seas* and a West Coast artist. It appears in Frederick C. Matthews' *American Merchant Ships: 1850-1900* (Salem, Mass.: Marine Research Society, 1928), p. 144. This painting substantially agrees in detail with the one commissioned by the captain.

[15] McLaughlin family records.

[16] *San Francisco Daily Alta California*, May 31, 1851.

[17] Whipple, A.B.C., *The Challenge*. (New York: William Morrow and Company, Inc., 1987) pp. 108-114.

[18] Douglas Stein, "Paths Through the Sea: Matthew Fontaine Maury and his Wind and Current Charts," *The Log of Mystic Seaport*, Fall 1980, pp. 99-107, incl.

[19] Stein.

[20] "Abstract Log for Ship *Gray Feather*," January 14-May 29, 1851, and general "Directions" for filling out logs, 1850, National Archives, Weather Records, RG 27, Washington, D.C.

[21] Log.

[22] Log.

[23] Log.

[24] Log. McLaughlin's abstract logs indicate that he had a tendency to misspell certain words ending with an "e".

[25] Cutler, *op. cit.*, p. 176-177, 433. On p. 479 Cutler states that *Gray Feather* made a 138-day voyage; whereas, on pp. 176-177 he corrects this to 136. The *Daily Alta* for May 31, 1851, fails to mention the number of days encompassed by this passage.

[26] Cutler, *op. cit.*, p. 177; and William Weber Johnson, *The Forty-Niners* (New York, N.Y.: Time-Life Books, 1974), p. 189.

[27] *San Francisco Call*, January 29, 1896.

[28] *Alta*, May 31, 1851.

[29] *Pen Pictures, op. cit.*

[30] Shipping Articles for *Gray Feather*, June 20, 1851; National Archives, San Francisco Custom House District, RG 36, Washington, D.C.; Douglas L. Stein, *American Maritime Documents*, 1776-1860, (Mystic, Conn., Mystic Seaport Museum, Inc., 1992) p. 58. (A Crew List for the ship *Jos Walker* dated September 16, 1852, shows the monthly wage rate for seamen at New York as being $15 with advance wage fee of $15.) Shipping Articles for *Gray Feather* dated June 20, 1851, at San Francisco implied that McLaughlin's crew was shipped for a specific voyage by the statement: "now bound from the Port of San Francisco to Calcutta, and there to be discharged, or to continue the voyage at port wages out of Calcutta to a port of discharge in Europe." They also stated under the "wage" column, "run."

[31] "Abstract Log for Ship *Gray Feather*," 1854; National Archives, Weather Records, RG 27, Washington, D.C. Also see James Horsburgh, *The India Directory*, 6th Edition (London, England, William H. Allen & Co.,1852) p. 618, which states in part "When abreast of False Point in 14 or 15 fathoms with False Point bearing WNW the course NE 10 leagues to clear the bank off Point Palmiras." This is another instance where Daniel McLaughlin dropped an "e" in False Point in his abstract log.

[32] McLaughlin family records.

[33] McLaughlin family papers. The name of this vessel is sometimes mistakenly spelled "Actos" in shipping registers. However, Register No. 112, issued at Eastport (Passamaquody), Maine, on July 11, 1855, spells it as "*Aetos*" (National Archives, Washington, D.C.) She later became the British ship *Lancastrian* of Liverpool. The *Aetos* had an eagle figurehead and a round stern. Although shipping registers commonly list this vessel as having been built in 1855, her first Custom House document (Custom House Register No. 233) was issued at Eastport on December 22, 1854. Register No. 112 lists Daniel McLaughlin as being master of the *Aetos* but does not show him as owning an

interest in the ship; Kinney, *op. cit.*, p. 82. The appearance of *Aetos* has been preserved by an oil painting of her by the English artist W.K. McMinn (1818-1898) which was originally the property of Captain McLaughlin. It was donated to M. H. de Young Museum (The Fine Arts Museums of San Francisco) on April 27, 1922, by John W. McLaughlin. The *Aetos* spread three skysails, had single topsails, and the McMinn painting shows studdingsail booms as high as topgallants. Unlike the *Gray Feather*, she had "built" lower masts which were painted white. The artist apparently catered to the McLaughlin family by depicting the captain, his wife Hannah, son John, and daughter Helena on the after-house top which dates the painting about 1858.

[34] Papers.

[35] Papers.; and Custom House Register No. 233 endorsement; National Archives, *op. cit.* The sword, a painting of the *Gray Feather*, and a painting of the *Aetos* were donated to the M. H. de Young Memorial Museum at San Francisco in 1922 by John W. McLaughlin. According to letters from the museum dated July 14 and August 25, 1992, "the sword has not been located in ages," the painting of the *Gray Feather* was traded for another work, and the *Aetos* painting is in storage.

[36] Obituary, *op. cit.*

[37] McLaughlin family records and Daniel Carleton (Carl) McLaughlin death certificate dated November 29, 1926, Records of Fresno County, Calif.

CHAPTER III - Civil War and Post War

[1] The general appearance of the *Western Empire* has been preserved in a large detailed model of her which is now owned by Captain McLaughlin's great-great granddaughter, Mrs. Deborah Burnham of Hingham, Mass. According to family tradition, this model was of the *Glory of the Seas*, (but it looks nothing like her). It has single top'sl yards which attribute fits a vessel built in the 1850s and, likewise, fits the description of the *Western Empire* which appears on Custom House Register 220, issued at New York on June 13, 1864, as a vessel with a billethead, square stern with a "round tuck" (stern like the yacht *America*) and three decks (National Archives, Record Group 41, Washington, D.C.). The first document, Register No. 189, issued at New York on March 17, 1863, is the first extant official record documenting McLaughlin as holding a 1/16 interest in the ship; whereas, Register No. 299, issued at New York on August 6, 1864, lists John Dougherty as being master, indicating that McLaughlin was apparently no longer in command of the *Western Empire*.

The actual date that Daniel McLaughlin acquired his interest in the *Western Empire* has not been officially preserved due to a number of fires at the Boston Custom House which destroyed bills of sale and abstracts of title for the Civil War period.

On August 26, 1959, Lovisa G. Weeks, widow of Carlton Brooks Weeks (son of Helena McLaughlin Weeks), wrote a letter in which she stated that "this ship [model] was made by my husband's grandfather, Captain Daniel

MacLachlan . . . The only time it has been out of possession of the family was when the Captain retired to California and loaned it to the Malden, Massachusetts, Public Library where it was on exhibition in their Reading Room. The Library later presented it to my husband and we have had it ever since."

[2] *Pen Pictures, op. cit.*

[3] *Pen Pictures, op. cit.*; Bruce Caton, *Never Call Retreat,* Vol. III (Garden City, N.Y.: Doubleday & Co., Inc., 1965), pp. 76, 205-206, 324-326, incl.

[4] *Pen Pictures, op. cit.*

[5] Enrollment No. 235 issued at New Orleans Custom House on January 24, 1867, for the steamer *Cassandra,* National Archives, Washington, D.C.; Erik Heyl, *Early American Steamers,* Vol. III (Buffalo, N.Y.: Erik Heyl, 1964), p. 53; John Leavitt, "Cradle of Ships," (Mystic, Conn.: Mystic Seaport Museum), p. 191.

[6] Enrollment No. 235 (*op. cit.*) lists McLaughlin as owning a 1/16 interest in the *Cassandra.*

[7] *Boston Daily Advertiser,* October 18 and 23, 1865.

[8] Heyl, *op. cit.*; Leavitt, *op. cit.*

[9] A strong, cold dry SW wind of the Argentine Pampas, generally advancing with a well-marked and very black cold front.

[10] *San Francisco Commercial Herald and Market Review,* August 19, 1867; Octavius T. Howe and Frederick C. Matthews, *American Clipper Ships,* 1833-1858 (New York, N.Y.: Argosy Antiquarian Ltd., 1967), pp. 643, 645.

[11] McLaughlin, *op. cit.* Hannah McLaughlin unexpectedly caught pneumonia while washing braided rugs down at a creek at Malden.

[12] McLaughlin family records.

[13] McLaughlin; *Commercial Herald, op. cit.,* August 19, 1867; *Clipper Ships, op. cit.,* p. 643-645 incl.

[14] McLaughlin, *op. cit.*

[15] *Boston Daily Advertiser,* February 23, 1869. The *Advertiser* on January 12, 1870, reported another "race" in which Captain McLaughlin and the *Swallow* were involved. Under the title "Quick and Close Sailing" the following appeared: "A remarkable ocean race over a course of 19,000 miles has just terminated by the arrival of both vessels at Liverpool. The ships *David Crockett,* Capt. John A. Briggs, and the *Swallow,* Capt. McLoughlin sld from San Francisco in company on Sept. 8, 1869, and the *David Crockett* arrived at Liverpool December 31, beating the *Swallow* which arrived next day [by] 30 hours in a passage of 112 days."

[16] Howe and Matthews, *op. cit.,* p. 260, 263. Registers and enrollments issued to the *Swallow* and the *Herald of the Morning* during the period 1867-1875 do not indicate that McLaughlin had any ownership interest in these vessels; letters of February 17, 1988, and March 8, 1988, National Archives, Washington, D.C.

[17] *San Francisco Daily Alta California,* October 1, 1873. The *Sunrise* incident constantly appeared in the San Francisco papers until the report on sentencing of the guilty officers appeared in the November 29 issue.

[18] *Alta, op. cit.*, October 10, 1873.

[19] *Alta.*

[20] *Alta, op. cit.*, November 7, 1873.

[21] Duplicate Shipping Articles for the *Herald of the Morning* dated January 7, 1875, and issued at San Francisco Custom House, National Archives, Washington, D.C.

[22] *New York Maritime Register*, April 9, 1879. An editorial stated in part: "Every day adds to the number of charges made against officers for brutality and against sailors for insubordination . . . yet brutality is not the rule on American ships."

[23] Crew list for the *Herald of the Morning* dated November 6, 1873, San Francisco Custom House Records, RG 36, National Archives, Washington, D.C. Note: the shipping articles have not been preserved which would show who actually sailed on the voyage. Both Peterson and Kelly's names appear on the crew list.

[24] *Alta, op. cit.*, October 19, 1873.

[25] *Alta, op. cit.*, Nov. 7, 1873.

[26] *Alta.*

[27] *San Francisco Chronicle*, Nov. 8, 1873.

[28] *Chronicle.*

[29] *San Francisco Daily Evening Bulletin*, November 7, 1873.

[30] *Chronicle*, op.cit., Nov. 7, 1873.

[31] *Chronicle.*

[32] *Chronicle, op. cit.*, Nov. 8, 1873.

[33] *Chronicle, op. cit.*, Nov. 9, 1873.

[34] *Chronicle.*

[35] *San Francisco Examiner*, Nov. 8, 1873.

[36] Howe and Matthews, *op. cit.*, p. 263.

[37] *Register, op. cit.*, August 25, 1875. The *Daily Advertiser* of August 30, 1875, lists the British steamer *China* which departed Liverpool on August 17 and arriving at Boston on August 28 as having ninety-eight cabin passengers and 202 steerage aboard. The list for cabin passengers contains the names "Capt. and Mrs. McLachlan."

[38] *Malden Mirror*, October 9, 1875.

[39] *Alta, op. cit.*, August 10 and September 11, 1876.

[40] Michael Jay Mjelde, *Glory of the Seas* (Mystic, Conn.: Marine Historical Association, Inc./Wesleyan University Press, 1970), p. 30. Author's Note: For purposes of consistency, efforts have been made herein to use registered length, breadth and depth from contemporary shipping registers which are sometimes at variance with Custom House registers.

All references to tonnage herein refer to "gross" tonnage (with the exception of the *Stephen G. Bass*) which measures the internal capacity of a vessel which procedure is commonly called "admeasurement." The unit of measure is "gross ton" which equals 100 cubic feet. Displacement of a vessel cannot be related to gross tonnage.

The navigation laws of the United States dated May 6, 1864, specified that the register length of a sailing vessel should be "from the fore part of the outer planking on the side of the stem to the . . . after part of the rudder-post . . . measured on the top of the tonnage deck, shall be accounted the vessel's length. [the *Glory*'s second deck was her tonnage deck.] The breadth of the broadest part on the outside of the vessel shall be accounted the vessel's breadth of beam." Depth of hold was "under side of the tonnage deck plank, amidships, to the ceiling of the hold." The "height" was measured "from the top of the tonnage-deck plank to the underside of the upper-deck plank." Shipping registers commonly added height and depth of hold together to come up with depth of hold as defined by insurance companies.

Net tonnage on sailing ships following the 1882 U.S. law on admeasurement excluded such items as fo'c's'le capacity, after cabin sleeping areas, dining saloon or forward cabin of after house, ship's boy's house (forward of mizzen hatch) and cabin for petty officers in forward house.

[41] Mjelde, *op. cit.*, p. 89

[42] Samuel Eliot Morison, *Maritime History of Massachusetts*, 1783-1860 (Boston, Mass.: Houghton Mifflin Company, 1921), p. 342. ". . . *Glory of the Seas* for [McKay's] last and in some respects his best creation."

[43] *Alta, op. cit.*, September 29, 1876.

CHAPTER IV - Glory of the Seas at San Francisco

[1] Lloyd, *op. cit.*, p. 78-80, incl.
[2] *Alta, op. cit.*, August 24, 1876.
[3] *Alta, op. cit.*, August 27, 1876.
[4] *Alta, op. cit.*, August 24, 1876.
[5] *Alta, op. cit.*, September 2, 1876.
[6] Mjelde, *op. cit.*, p. 94; also *Alta, op. cit.*, September 21, 1876.
[7] Mjelde, *op. cit.*, p. 94
[8] *Alta, op. cit.*, September 19, 1876.
[9] *Alta, op. cit.*, October 14, 1876.
[10] *Alta, op. cit.*, August 31, 1876.
[11] *Alta, op. cit.*, September 28, 1876.
[12] Mjelde, *op. cit.*, p. 258; manila hemp definition: René de Kerchove, *International Maritime Dictionary*, 2nd Edition (New York: Van Nostrand Reinhold Co., 1961) p. 488 as follows: "MANILA HEMP. A fibrous material obtained from the leaves of a textile plant name Abaea. Musa textilis. Also called Manila. It is native to the Philippine Islands. The raw material is shipped from Manila under supervision of the United states government inspectors who grade the different qualities. . . . Manila hemp is very resistant to wet and not affected by salt water. In the cheaper grades of ropes it is often mixed with other textiles such as sisal, Mauritius, or sunn hemps or jute to improve the color and lessen the cost. It is unequaled for large ropes but too stiff for small cords and twines. . . . MANILA ROPE. Manila rope is usually made up of three

strands up to 3-in. circumference, and above that size of four strands with a core. It is preferred to Italian or Russian hemp for hawsers and running gear because it is lighter, more flexible,and does not require tarring for preservation. Manila rope is stronger than tarred hemp. It is sometimes called Manila hemp."

[13] *Commercial Herald, op. cit.* December 13, 1877, advertised "wire rope for ship's standing rigging . . . manufactured to order."

[14] David R. MacGregor, *Sailing Ships,* 1850-1875 (Annapolis, Maryland: Naval Institute Press, 1984), pp. 113-114; Arthur H. Clark, *The Clipper Ship Era* (Riverside, Conn.: 7 C's Press, Inc., 1970), pp. 322-323.

[15] John G. B. Hutchins, *The American Maritime Industries and Public Policy,* 1789-1914 (Cambridge, Mass.: Harvard University Press, 1941), pp. 417-418, 423-430.

[16] *Maritime Register, op. cit.,* January 15, 1879. A general insurance life expectancy of forty months for copper sheathing was adhered to on first class wooden hulled vessels. This is borne out by Francis B. Dixon, *The Law of Shipping and Merchants and Shipmasters' Guide.* (New York, NY: Henry Spear, 1859), p. 524, as follows:

> "The following is the condition of one of the principal companies in New York, *viz.*:
> "A deduction of one-fortieth from the expense of repairing or replacing the metal sheathing, or any part thereof, after first deducting the value of the old metal and nails shall be made for every month since the vessel was last sheathed, until the expiration of forty months, after which time the cost of remetaling or repairing the same, shall be wholly borne by the assured.Æ And the following by one of the principal companies in New Orleans, *viz.*:
> ". . . and if the copper shall have been on forty months or more, the cost of recoppering shall be wholly excluded."

[17] Hutchins, *op. cit.,* pp. 371-373 and 417-418.

[18] Andrew J. Nesdall, "Down Easters, Trade and Commerce," Treatise delivered at Bath Marine Museum, Bath, Maine, 1974, p. 6-7.

[19] Hutchins, *op. cit.,* pp. 377-379.

[20] George H. Harlan, *San Francisco Bay Ferryboats* (Berkeley, CA: Howell-North Books, 1967), pp. 108-113.

[21] *Herald of the Morning* articles, *op. cit.*

[22] Crew List for the *Glory of the Seas* dated April 27, 1876, at Liverpool, National Archives, Washington, D.C.

[23] Crew List for the *Glory of the Seas* dated October 24, 1876, at San Francisco, National Archives, Washington, D.C.

[24] Shipping Articles for the *Glory of the Seas* dated February 5, 1872, at San Francisco, National Archives, Washington, D.C. In 1887 Captain Knowles paid Captain Herriman, master of the ship *America,* $175 per month — *Statement of General Average and Partial Loss in the Case of Ship* America.

[25] *Alta, op. cit.,* October 25, 1876.

[26] *Contra Costa Gazette,* September 16, 1876.

[27] *Gazette, op. cit.,* October 21, 1876.

[28] Hutchins, *op. cit.,* p. 418; Basil Lubbock, *The Down Easters, American Deep-water Sailing Ships, 1869-1929* (Glasgow, Scotland: Brown, Son & Ferguson, Ltd., 1929), p. 3.

CHAPTER V - Dead Horse and Blood Money

[1] *Alta, op. cit.,* September 1, 1876.

[2] Mjelde, *op. cit.,* p. 108.

[3] *Alta, op. cit.,* September 28, 1876. Only two photographic images of the *Glory of the Seas* have been discovered for the period 1876-1884. Copies of these images are in the Fireman's Fund Collection, National Maritime Museum Library (J. Porter Shaw Library), Fort Mason, San Francisco. One image (circa 1877) shows the ship in ballast lying at anchor out in San Francisco Bay. White boot top (anti-fouling copper paint) shows distinctly in this view. It predates a dockside view (dated 1880) of the *Glory* by reason of the ship still being rigged with her stun'sl booms and original Manila hemp standing rigging; whereas, the dockside image shows the ship rigged with wire standing rigging, no stun'sl rig, and boot topping.

[4] *Alta, op. cit.,* September 16, 1875.

[5] Duplicate Shipping Articles for the *Glory of the Seas* dated October 19, 1876, at San Francisco, National Archives, Washington, D.C. Although the Shipping Articles list the advance as $60, the "desertion" form filed at Liverpool shows the amount as being $66.52.

The Shipping Articles show the person who was actually paid the advance. Some of these persons were notorious boardinghouse masters immortalized by such writers as Stan Hugill, Richard Dillon, and William M. Camp: Alex Jackson, Joseph Franklin, Shanghai Henry Brown, C.E. Peterson, P. McMahon, Tommy Chandler, and E.C. Lewis.

[6] Articles; Crew List for the *Glory of the Seas* dated October 24, 1876, at San Francisco, National Archives, Washington, D.C.

[7] Herbert Asbury, *The Barbary coast, An Informal History of the San Francisco Underworld* (Garden City, NY: Garden City Publishiing Co., Inc, 1933) pp. 207-212, incl.

[8] Shipping Articles, *op. cit.*; Henry G. Langley, *The San Francisco Directory* (San Francisco, CA: Henry G. Langley, 1873) provides source of sailor's hotels.

[9] Shipping Articles, Oct. 19, 1876, *op. cit.*

[10] Elmo Paul Hohlman, *History of American Merchant Seamen* (Hamdon, Conn.: Shoe String Press, 1956), pp. 20-24, incl.

[11] Shipping Articles, Oct. 19, 1876, *op. cit.*

[12] Shipping Articles.

[13] Hohlman, *op. cit.,* pp. 20-24, incl.

[14] Hohlman; Also Admeasurement for the *Glory of the Seas* dated December 18, 1882, San Francisco Custom House records, National Archives, San Bruno, Calif.; Frederick Pease Harlow, *The Making of a Sailor, or, Sea Life Aboard a Yankee Squarerigger*, Salem, Mass. Marine Research Society, 1928, P. 99-100.

[15] Crew List, Oct. 24, 1876, *op. cit.*

[16] Crew List.

[17] Reference reports from Margaret Evans, Archive Assistant, Merseyside Maritime Museum, Liverpool, England, dated April 28, 1994, and June 29, 1994. Ship descriptions from collection of Captain Jack Beard, D.S.C. (1888-1965) who "compiled a record of particulars of all that one would want to know about all sailing ships" from brief biography.

CHAPTER VI - A Record Passage

[1] Rear Admiral Boyle T. Somerville, C.M.G., "The World Sailing Ship Routes," (British Admiralty, 1950) chart accompanying *Ocean Passages*; also Commander H.L. Jenkins, *Ocean Passages for the World, Third Edition*, 1973, British Admiralty.

[2] Basil Lubbock and Frederick C. Matthews both list this passage as being 103 days; however, the *New York Maritime Register* lists the arrival as being February 5, 1877, although an earlier issue of the *Register* lists her arrival as being February 4. The February 6, 1877, issue of the *Liverpool Journal of Commerce and Shipping Telegraph* also lists the *Glory* as arriving on February 5.

[3] *Maritime Register, op. cit.*, February and March issues.

[4] Brian Walker and Ann Hinchliffe, *In Our Liverpool Home* (Belfast, Ireland: Blackstaff Press, 1978), pp. 34-45; Michael Stammers, *Sail on the Mersey* (Birkenhead, England: Countyvise, Ltd., 1984), pp. 24-25. Apparently, the port authorities at this time required sailing ships to rig in their jibbooms and stow their anchors on the fo'c's'le-heads before they were allowed to dock, according to Captain Isaac Norris Hibberd, *Sixteen Times Round Cape Horn* (Mystic, Conn.: Mystic Seaport Museum 1980), p. 15.

[5] Certificate of Desertion dated March 29, 1877, for the *Glory of the Seas*, Custom House Records, San Francisco District, National Archives, Washington, D.C.

[6] Stan Hugill, *Sailortown* (New York, N.Y.: E.P. Dutton & Co., Inc., 1967), pp. 104-106, incl.

[7] Hohlman, *op. cit.*; James C. Healey, Ph.D., *Fo'c's'le and Gloryhole* (New York, N.Y.: Merchant Marine Publishers Assoc., 1936), pp. viii & 3-10, incl.

[8] *Glory* Desertion Certificate, *op. cit.*

[9] H.F. Farmer. *The Log of a Shellback* (London: H.F. & G. Witherby, 1925) pp. 2-3.

[10] *San Francisco Daily Evening Bulletin*, August 29, 1877.

[11]   Certificate of Shipment of Seamen for the *Glory of the Seas* dated March 29, 1877, Custom House Records, San Francisco District, Washington, D.C.

[12] *Alta, op. cit.,* March 12, 1877.

[13] *Boston Daily Advertiser,* January 2, 1871.

[14] *Alta, op. cit.,* July 17, 1877.

[15] *Alta, op. cit.,* July 24, 1877.

[16] Lubbock, *Down Easters, op. cit.,* pp. 263-265 incl.

[17] *Bulletin, op. cit.,* August 23, 1877.

[18] Whipple, *op. cit.,* p. 99.

[19] *Alta, op. cit.,* September 4, 1877.

[20] *Commercial Herald, op. cit.,* September 6, 1877.

[21] Captain J.N. Knowles Account Books, April 1871-January 1873, California Historical Society.

[22]   Return Crew List dated September 1877 for the *Glory of the Seas,* Custom House Records, San Francisco District, Washington, D.C.

CHAPTER VII - The Second Round Voyage

[1] John Haskell Kemble, *San Francisco Bay, A Pictorial Maritime History* (Cambridge, Maryland: Cornell Maritime Press, 1957), p. 38.

[2] *Commercial Herald, op. cit.,* January 18, 1877.

[3] Lubbock, *Down Easters, op. cit.,* p. 3.

[4] *Commercial Herald, op. cit.,* January 18, 1877.

[5] *Alta, op. cit.,* Novermber 13, 1877.

[6] *Commercial Herald, op. cit.,* November 15, 1877. The actual bill of entry at Liverpool was considerably at variance with what appeared in the *Commercial Herald.* The following was extracted from the *Liverpool Bills of Entry,* Liverpool City Record Office: *Glory of the Seas,* November 12 from San Francisco.

D.M. McLaughlin: 33 men.

R. Rodgers & Co.

84 sks ore	R. Rodgers & Co.
627 sks copper ore	Gruning and Co.
350 cs fruit	Pelling, Stanley & Co.
8 bls cotton	Balfour, Williamson and Co.
1 cs horns	A. Flower.
38,872 sks wheat	R. Rodgers & Co.
136 cs pearl shells	E. Sarasson.
75 bls orchella weed	O. Bartining.
547 " " "	O. Sobbe and Co.
500 cs meat	Pelling, Stanley & Co.
1,482 sks borax	H. Kendall and Son.
2,500 cs salmon	R. Rodgers & Co.
1 cs silver plate	Eastern Agency Co.
669 sks agri. seed	[To] Order

7,623 cs salmon	"
2,170 cs m'dize [sic]	"
412 sks ore	"
1,000 cs corned beef	"
8 cs corsets	"

Contemporary sources provide different dollar figures. The *Alta* on Nov. 11, 1877, stated that she had a cargo valued at $268,000 (about $2,400,000 in 1990 dollars).

According to the Nov. 11, 1877 issue of the *Commercial Herald*, the consignee was Amman, Gaspari & Co. "Importers, Commission & Shipping Merchants: who advertised "liberal advances made on ores, furs, produce, and other approved merchandise shipped to our Liverpool House." (Gaspari, Ammon & Co. of Liverpool, England).

[7] Crew List for the *Glory of the Seas* dated November 10, 1877, at San Francisco, Custom House Records, National Archives, Washington, D.C.

[8] Crew List.

[9] *Maritime Register, op. cit.*, February-April 1878 issues.

[10] *Liverpool Journal, op. cit.*, March 5, 1878; Maritime Register, March 20, 1878.

[11] *The Port of Liverpool* (Washington, D.C.: Government Printing Office, 1929), page 77.

[12] Research paper dated October 16, 1990, from A.E. Jarvis, Manager of Port Survey, Merseyside Maritime Museum, Liverpool, England.

[13] Jarvis.

[14] *Alta, op. cit.*, September 30, 1878.

[15] *Glory* Crew Papers for Voyage Commencing November 10, 1877, Custom House Records, San Francisco District, National Archives, Washington, D.C.

[16] Crew Papers.

[17] *Alta, op. cit.*, September 30, 1878.

[18] *Alta.*

[19] Basil Lubbock, *The Last of the Windjammers, Vol. I* (Glasgow, Scotland: Brown, Son & Ferguson, Ltd., 1927), p. 148.

[20] Captain Jack Beard, *op. cit.*, October 25, 1995. Letters and watercolor sketch from William G. Hartman, Birmingham, England, dated November 25, 1964, and January 28, 1965.

[21] Beard.

[22] *Alta, op. cit.*, September 30, 1878.

[23] *Commercial Herald, op. cit.*, February 1, 1877. Yellow metal is a yellow colored alloy of 60% copper and 40% zinc used in coppering wooden hulled ships' bottoms to prevent marine growth.

[24] Register No. 68 for bark *Jenny Pitts* dated February 20, 1877, Puget Sound Custom House Records, National Archives, Seattle, Wash.

[25] *Alta, op. cit.*, November 12, 1878.

[26] *Alta, op. cit.*, December 4, 1878.

[27] *Alta, op. cit.*, December 18, 1878.

CHAPTER VIII - The Clam Fleet

[1] *Commercial Herald, op. cit.*, January 9, 1879.

[2] *Alta, op. cit.*, January 5, 1879.

[3] Letter from Andrew Nesdall, Waban, Mass., dated July 1, 1972.

[4] *Alta, op. cit.*, January 15, 1879.

[5] *Alta, op. cit.*, February 1, 1879. Many sailing ships of this period used a capstan windlass which was a more "modern" innovation in comparison to the log windlass on the *Glory of the Seas*. Originally, in 1869 the *Glory* was supposed to have a capstan windlass installed (See *Glory of the Seas, op. cit.*, p. 257) but instead was fitted with a log windlass activated by brake handles. The Samuel Walters painting of the *Glory* (*Glory of the Seas, op. cit.*, dust jacket) as well as the Waldron painting (Ibid, p. 32) both show fittings for brake handles.

[6] *Alta.*

[7] *San Francisco Chronicle*, February 20, 1879; *Alta, op. cit.*, February 20, 1879; and *San Francisco Morning Call*, February 20-21, 1879.

[8] *Chronicle, Alta, Call.*

[9] *Chronicle, Alta, Call.*

[10] *Chronicle, Alta, Call.*

[11] *Chronicle, Alta, Call.*

[12] *Chronicle, op. cit.*, February 28, 1879.

[13] *Commercial Herald, op. cit.*, January 15, 1880.

[14] *Commercial Herald, op. cit.*, April 10, 1879; *Alta, op. cit.*, March 26, 1879.

[15] Frederick C. Matthews, *American Merchant Ships*, 1850-1900, Vol. 2 (Salem, Mass.: Marine Research Society, 1931), p. 208.

[16] Crew List for the *Glory of the Seas* dated April 7, 1879, at San Francisco, Custom House Records, National Archives, Washington, D.C.

[17] *Alta, op. cit.*, September 19, 1875.

[18] *Alta, op. cit.*, March 18, 1879; and *Call, op. cit.*, March 18, 1879.

[19] *Glory* Crew List-April 7, 1879, *op. cit.* It was unusual for a man rated as a quartermaster to be listed as such on a crew list of an American Cape Horner. According to *Patterson's Illustrated Nautical Encyclopedia*, p. 200, a quartermaster was a "petty officer who steers the vessel, attends the gangway in port, keeps the wheelhouse in order, and cleans the bright work belonging to the steering gear, etc." which seems to describe duties on a large steamship where the work on deck was more specialized. Sailing ships, however, rarely had men with these specific duties to the exclusion of working on deck and going aloft. It was common for all A.B.s to take their turn at the wheel. It is possible that, since there was such a shortage of sailors at San Francisco in March and April 1879, McLaughlin had to ship senior "quarter-masters" A.B.s because many of his so-called able-bodied seamen were substandard.

[20] *Glory, op. cit.*, pp., 96-97; Charles G. Davis, *The Ways of the Sea.* (New York, N.Y.: Rudder Publishing Co., 1930), p. 64; Harlow, *op. cit.*, pp. 103-106, incl.

CHAPTER IX - Queenstown, Le Havre, and New York

[1] Matthews, Vol. I, *op. cit.*, p. 281.

[2] *Maritime Register, op. cit.*, October 1, 1879.

[3] *New York Herald,* October 13, 1879.

[4] *New York Herald.*

[5] *Alta, op. cit.*, April 8, 1880. The value of the *Glory*'s cargo from New York was only $19,000 — per annual report, *Commercial Herald,* January 13, 1881. The value of her cargo on her first passage from New York in 1870 was $31,019. Sears Company chartered the *Glory* in 1879 at eight dollars dead weight (2,000 lbs) instead of by measurement (40 cu. ft.). Dead weight charters were more profitable for the ship, according to Captain I.N. Hibbard, *Sixteen Times Around Cape Horn, op. cit.*, p. 15. Captain Hibbard was a contemporary of Captain McLaughlin and specified in his reminiscences that dead weight was not long tons but 2,000 lbs. Rates fluctuated through the years especially after the completion of the Transcontinental Railroad. In 1870 dead weight rates ranged from six to ten dollars per ton.

[6] Hugill, *op. cit.*, pp. 159-163, incl.

[7] John Bunker, *Harbor and Haven, An Illustrated History of the Port of New York*, Woodland Hills, Calif.: (Windsor Publications, Inc., 1979) p. 144. Note: Contemporary illustrations of New York do not appear to show any cockbilling of lower yards. This is unlike San Francisco during this period. Also see John Haskell Kemble, *San Francisco Bay*, op.cit., pp.19-21. These illustrations show yards being cockbilled for cargo-discharging purposes.

[8] *Bulletin, op. cit.*, December 10, 1879.

[9] McLaughlin, *op. cit.*; letter from Josephine Ball dated September 3, 1984, states: [Her mother Jennie Alfaretta, daughter of Josephine McLaughlin Lane] "never knew her real grandmother, but she dearly loved her step-grandmother [Maggie]. They visited her a number of times when mother was little. She even started school on [Grand Manan] at age 5."

[10] *New York Shipping and Commercial List,* November 22, 1879.

[11] *Glory* Crew List, October 13, 1876, *op. cit.*

[12] Crew List for *Sovereign of the Seas* at New York dated May 31, 1883, Custom House Records, National Archives, Washington, D.C.

[13] Crew List for *New World* at New York, dated August 7, 1879, Custom House Records, National Archives, Washington, D.C. This represented a reduction of six personnel from Crew List of December 5, 1870, when she was still carrying passengers.

[14] *Commercial List, op. cit.*, November 18, 1879.

[15] *Bulletin, op. cit.*, October 18, 1879.

CHAPTER X - The Cape Horn Road

[1] William W. Bates, *American Navigation, The Political History of its Rise and Ruin and the Proper Means for its encouragement.* (Boston & New York: Houghton, Mifflin & Co., 1902) See pp. 204-205 of text.

[2] *Glory* Crew List, December 6, 1879, *op. cit.*

[3] *Alta, op. cit.,* April 6, 1880. Also *Chronicle, op. cit.* April 18, 1880.

[4] Matthews, Vol. I, *op. cit.,* p. 281.

[5] *Alta, op. cit.,* April 4 & 6, 1880.

[6] *Down Easters, op. cit.,* p. 265.

[7] Joseph Malcolm Perry, *Cruising In Many Seas* (Springfield, Mass.: Privately printed, 1930), pp. 72-73; Asbury, *op. cit.,* pp. 200-207. Perry's statement shows that the crew of the *Southern Cross* left the ship once sails were furled and "fastened to the towboat." This indicates that the directive issued by the Shipping Commissioner's office at San Francisco in 1879 was not adhered to always. Although runners were supposedly prohibited from coming on board ships upon arrival in the Bay, they still did it when given opportuity by the ship's officers. A statement made by Carl McLaughlin regarding the crew of the *Glory of the Seas* leaving the ship once a tug berthed her at Green Street Wharf shows that Daniel McLaughlin kept boardinghouse runners from taking men off his ship until he discharged them.

[8] *Alta, op. cit.,* April 8, 1880.

[9] *Alta.*

[10] The images of the *Glory of the Seas* and the *Southern Cross* may possibly be the work of Ernest W. Newth as disclosed by John Maounis and Daniel L. Keller, *Four Maritime Photograph Collections,* (San Francisco, Calif.: National Maritime Museum, 1982), p. 26.

[11] *Commercial Herald, op. cit.,* January 13, 1881.

[12] *Historical Atlas Map of Solano County* (San Francisco, Calif.: Thompson and West, 1878) and *Historical Atlas of Solano County* (San Francisco, Calif.: Thompson and West, 1877), John F. Kennedy Library, Vallejo, Calif.

[13] *Commercial Herald, op. cit.,* June 3, 1880.

[14] *Commercial Herald, op. cit.,* April 8, 1880.

[15] Matthews, Vol. I, *op. cit.,* p. 324.

[16] *Commercial Herald, op. cit.,* May 19 and May 30, 1880.

[17] Crew List for the *Glory of the Seas* at San Francisco dated May 29, 1880, Custom House records, National Archives, Washington, D.C.

[18] Crew List; San Francisco Custom House records contain two references to the *Glory of the Seas* (1870 & 1880) as bound for Cork, not Queenstown. However in actuality ships lay at anchor at Queenstown as indicated by a specific photograph and caption – Basil Greenhill & Denis Stanham, *Seafaring Under Sail, the Life of the Merchant Seaman* (Cambridge: Patrick Stephens, 1981) p. 129

[19] Mjelde, *op. cit.,* p. 107.

CHAPTER XI - A Close Call

[1] Mjelde, *op. cit.*, pp. 107-108, Richard C. McKay, *Some Famous Ships and Their Builder* (Donald McKay, New York & London: G.P. Ptunam's Sons, 1928) p. 325. In Carl McLaughlin's "Around in the *Glory*" he refers to her draft as being twenty-six feet. Contemporary shipping registers list her loaded draft as twenty-four feet.

[2] *New York Maritime Register, op. cit.*, October 13, 1880

[3] *New York Maritime Register, op. cit.*, October 27, 1880; *Dublin Evening Mail*, October 7, 1880.

[4] *Register, Mail.*

[5] Reference report prepared by Dr. Philip Smyly, committee member of the Maritime Institute of Ireland dated September 20, 1990, and by Gerald Daly, Archivist for the Dublin Port and Docks Board.

[6] *Lloyd's List*, October 8, 1880.

[7] Captain Adrian F. Raynaud, "Discharging a Cargo in Dublin, Ireland" from the bark *Edward Sewall* in 1914. This represents a first person account of unloading a grain-laden sailing vessel at Dublin. It is assumed that few, if any, changes took place from 1880.

[8] Raynaud.

[9] Dublin Port and Docks Board records.

[10] Abstract of Wreck Report No. 1662, dated October 4, 1880, Record Group 26, National Archives, Washington, D.C.

[11] *Record of American and Foreign Shipping* (New York, N.Y.: American Shipmasters Association, 1879), pp. xvi-xviii.

[12] *Glory* Crew List, May 29, 1880, *op. cit.*

[13] *Alta, op. cit.*, May 6, 1881.

[14] A Certificate of Desertion of Seamen report dated December 1, 1880, at Dublin listed all men who deserted at Dublin. Joseph's name was not included. However, McLaughlin's Return Crew List from Cardiff dated May 5, 1881, does not include Joseph's name other than mentioning in general that eleven other persons except for fourteen men listed had deserted. Apparently, William Joseph jumped ship at Cardiff. It is possible that he may have been discharged there and the record has not been preserved.

[15] Mjelde, *op. cit.*, pp. 108-109. Note: As of March 9, 1988, this model, which was on display at the Oakland Museum in 1963, is no longer there, and members of the curatorial staff have no idea of its present whereabouts. It appears that the Joseph family lent the model, and no accession record was ever retained by the museum staff.

[16] *Alta, op. cit.*, May 6, 1881.

[17] *Alta.*

[18] Lubbock, *Windjammers, op. cit.*, p. 242.

[19] Lubbock, *Windjammers, op. cit.*, p. 503.

[20] Mjelde, *op. cit.*, p. 110.

[21] Daniel Carlton McLaughlin, "Around in the *Glory*" circa 1920. According to the late Elizabeth Frances McLaughlin Savory (Mrs. Clarke Savory), her father attempted unsuccessfully to publish his "Around in the *Glory*" story in the early 1920s. At that time, publishers told Carl it was too "contemporary." On September 25, 1988, the late Clarke Savory, Attorney at Law, wrote a release to the author allowing him to use this account on the condition "that my wife and I will be credited as the source of the material, and that it was through my wife's efforts that the story was preserved." According to Mr. and Mrs. Savory, her father's original journal was not preserved.

[22] *Alta, op. cit.*, May 27, 1881.

[23] Mjelde, *op. cit.*, p. 110.

[24] Mae F. Purcell, *History of Contra Costa County*, (Berkeley, Calif.: The Gillick Press, 1940), p. 415.

[25] Mjelde, *op. cit.*, p. 109.

CHAPTER XII - Disaster Averted

[1] Crew List for the *Glory of the Seas* at San Francisco dated July 9, 1881, Custom House records, National Archives, Washington, D.C.

[2] *Alta, op. cit.*, July 9-11, 1881. Full cargoes for the two vessels were as follows:

Glory of the Seas 67,438 ctls grain 7,000 bd. ft. lbr $94,560 30 gal. wine
Hagerstown 60,025 ctls " $ 81,534 25,000 bd. ft.

[3] *Maritime Register, op. cit.*, July 20, 1881.

[4] *Glory* Crew List, July 9, 1881, *op. cit.*; Lloyd, *op. cit.*, p. 99-101; and Frank T. Bullen, *The Men of the Merchant Service* (Stanfordville, N.Y.: Earl M. Coleman, 1979), pp. 149-158, incl.

[5] Lloyd, *op. cit.*, pp. 99-101; Fo'c's'le, *op. cit.*, p. 24.

[6] Lloyd.

[7] *Glory* Crew List, July 9, 1881, *op. cit.*; Gribble's maritime career started in September 1868 by his joining the British Navy as a sixteen-year-old seaman apprentice. He soon excelled at his new trade and ultimately became captain of the main top on his first vessel, HMS *Dasher*. In 1870, the British Navy assigned John Gribble to the ill-fated iron-clad battleship HMS *Captain*. The *Captain* was one of Britain's first attempts to build a low freeboard, ocean-going vessel with the turret features of John Ericsson's steam-powered *Monitor*, but conventionally powered by sail as well. Unfortunately, the British Admiralty blundered seriously in the design of the *Captain* so that she was extremely unstable. During a training cruise on September 7, 1870, the *Captain* overturned in a severe squall and sank in the Bay of Biscay with the loss of 472 men. Only eighteen men, including Gribble, survived the disaster.

HMS *Captain* and HMS *Monarch* were the first sea-going "battleships" built on the principle of main armament being on the centerline of the vessel. With four twelve-inch guns, the 320-foot *Captain* was a formidable gun platform. Both vessels were square-rigged on all three masts although the 330-foot *Monarch* had one screw; whereas, *Captain* had two and also had four feet less beam.

Unfortunately, *Captain* was oversparred and drew two more feet than her original design called for, leaving a freeboard of only 6.5 feet. When caught in a squall she quickly overturned and sank in a matter of seconds. According to Admiral G.A. Ballard, 472 (not 508, according to Gribble) officers and men (*The Black Battlefleet*, Annapolis, Maryland: Naval Institute Press, 1980, pp. 99-113, incl.) were lost, becoming the largest British naval peacetime disaster during the reign of Queen Victoria. Gribble became very disillusioned with the British Navy in the aftermath of the loss of *Captain*, feeling that the survivors were actually mistreated by the service. He left the Navy in the mid-1870s – unwillingly, however, following a twenty-four-hour shore leave from the British gunboat HMS *Dart* at Rio de Janeiro. Crimps drugged and shanghaied Gribble aboard a German sailing vessel bound for Hamburg, and thereafter, he sailed on merchant craft. His first American vessel was the 685-ton bark *Harriet F. Hussey* of Richmond, Maine. In his autobiography, Gribble's comments give some idea of his fond memories of this particular craft; also of how a sailor equated a good-feeding ship with an outstanding vessel: "I think [the *Harriet F. Hussey*] was the best ship I ever sailed in. We were fed as well as any hotel that I have ever been in, and although I was told when I joined her that she was 'red hot' [possibly her officers were viewed as brutal], I never saw one cause to complain. We were paid off at Havre de Grace in France." Apparently, Gribble felt that the food, although adequate on the *Glory of the Seas* and meeting the "Scale of Provision" allotted under maritime law, did not compare with the Hussey.

[8] John Gribble, *Autobiography of John Gribble*, unpublished, ca. 1926.

[9] It was not uncommon for deep water sailors to use an alias when signing articles. This is one of the reasons why it is difficult to match up names. The late Samuel Campbell (1880-1983), who sailed on the *Glory* in 1900 (and who had sailed on both British and American ships including the *Palmyra* and *Kenilworth*), told the author that he used the alias "Samuel Jackson." This was borne out by shipping articles on file with the National Archives.; *Glory* crew list, July 9, 1881, *op. cit.*

[10] *Maritime Register, op. cit.*, September 14 and December 7, 1881. Abstract of Wreck Report, No. 1073, dated February 25, 1882, Record Group 26, National Archives, Washington, D.C.; *Pen Pictures, op. cit.*; Comments of Captain Harold D. Huycke, retired master mariner and marine surveyor, dated March 10, 1997: "Shifting cargo pretty clearly indicates one of two things, or more likely, both: poor stowage by the longshoremen in San Francisco which allowed unfilled spaces in the 'tween decks, into which sacked grain tumbled when the ship rolled; or, the ship was loaded to her maximum allowable marks (whatever they were) before all of the lower hold and 'tween deck spaces were filled. If this latter condition was the case, then the mate should have taken it upon himself to make bloody well sure that the exposed cargo was shored off

or tommed off against any kind of shifting and that the empty spaces were well used with shoring timbers. My guess is, the longshoremen 'blew out the spaces' [void space blocked off with a wall of cargo to give the appearance of being full] and the mate on watch didn't catch it. Many, many ships were lost in those years and recently too, by 'blown spaces' whether it be with lumber, coal, grain, fertilizers, or bulk cargoes, to say nothing of general cargoes, when a ship sails with unfilled spaces. The hazards are obvious. But one never knows what happened in the case of the *Glory of the Seas*. Missing ships don't tell."

[11] Gribble, *op. cit.*

[12] Gribble.

[13] *Pen Pictures, op. cit.*

[14] Gribble, *op. cit.*

[15] Hugill, *op. cit.*, pp. 246-251, incl.

[16] Gribble, *op. cit.*; Capt. C.R.W. Beavis, (Editor: M.S. Cline), *Passage from Sail to Steam* (Bellevue, Wash.: Documentary Book Publishing Corp., 1986), p. 77.

[17] *Alta, op. cit.*, November 1, 1881; and *Maritime Register, op. cit.*, November 23, 1881.

[18] *Alta, Maritime Register.*

[19] Hugill, *op. cit.*, pp. 246-251, incl.

[20] *Maritime Register, op. cit.*, December 7 and 28, 1881, and January 18, 1882; David Trumbull Child (1875-1960), Admiralty Attorney, "General Average — Particular Average and Damage to Cargo," privately printed, Mrs. Elizabeth Engle.

[21] Wreck Report, *op. cit.*; Child, *op. cit.*

[22] Mjelde, *op. cit.*, p. 113; Gribble, *op. cit.*

[23] Statement of Captain Adrian F. Raynaud, Marine Surveyor: "The cost of repairs, discharging and reloading appears to total $26,600 [including "Estimated Loss or Damage to Cargo" of $20,000; Wreck Report No. 1073, *op. cit.*]. This isn't too much for all the work involved, but I think the hull repairs and caulking must have exceeded $6,600. Heaving a ship down requires a great deal of work, and recaulking must have been a lengthy job, especially if the copper sheathing had to be removed and replaced. Then, there are the gratuities that are inevitable in these affairs. No doubt, the sails had to be replaced or repaired, boat replaced, etc." – June 12, 1989; *Alta, op. cit.*, January 13, 1882, corrected the estimated loss figure from $20,000 to $25,000. The "Along the Wharves" reporter sarcastically stated, "Valparaiso is a dear port."

[24] Gribble, *op. cit.*

[25] Gribble.

[26] Gribble.

CHAPTER XIII - Winter, North Atlantic

[1] *Maritime Register, op. cit.*, April 12, 1882.

[2] *Herald, op. cit.*, May 5, 1882.

[3] *Herald, op. cit.,* May 9, 1882.

[4] *Maritime Register, op. cit.,* May 31, 1882.

[5] *Commercial List, op. cit.,* May 10, 1882.

[6] According to the March 11, 1882, issue of the *Commercial List,* the *Glory* was chartered for general cargo "private terms, quotable $9.50 per [2,000 lb.] ton, dead weight capacity." Her builder initially advertised the *Glory of the Seas* as a 4,000-ton capacity vessel which appears to be unverifiable. As a grain carrier for four consecutive voyages (excluding 1877-1878) the *Glory* hauled about 3,400 short tons of cargo. Based on these figures, the final New York-San Francisco voyage of the *Glory of the Seas* grossed about $32,300 which shows that the few vessels still engaged in the "clipper" intercoastal trade could still make money, and in some years sailing ships were making higher profits in general trade from New York or Boston than as grain carriers. It was more expensive to haul certain commodities from the East Coast via train; so the clipper trade, although limited to fewer vessels, was still flourishing in the year 1882.

[7] *Commercial List, op. cit.,* June 21, 1882.

CHAPTER XIV - A Memorable Voyage

[1] Crew List for the *Glory of the Seas* at New York dated June 30, 1882, Custom House records, National Archives, Washington, DC.

[2] The *City of Rome* at 560.2 x 52.3 x 37.0, 8,144 gross tons was smaller than the *Great Eastern,* also afloat at the time, at 679.6 x 82.8 x 48.2, 18,915 gross tons.

[3] It may have appeared to be "rosewood" to Carl; however, the after cabin framing was southern pine covered with mahogany veneer. The paneling was a combination of walnut and birds-eye maple. All doorknobs were glass and hardware was brass. Note: The author has in his possession one of the locker doors from the after cabin of the *Glory of the Seas.*

[4] Carl fails to mention Margaret McLaughlin throughout the original text. It appears that she elected to not make this voyage with her husband. This might have been due to an estrangement between Margaret and Carl. No mention of the relationship of Carl and Maggie McLaughlin appears to have survived in the McLaughlin family papers. No reference to them appears on any official Custom House papers preserved by the National Archives, Washington, D.C.

[5] Author's comment: It is not distinctly clear from Carl's account whether the mates boarded in cabins on each side of the forward cabin (which was customary) or in the house forward of the mizzen hatch which Captain Knowles used as a ship boy's cabin.

Regarding the term "forward cabin," this term was commonly used on the West Coast of the United States but apparently not so in some circles on the East Coast. However, the newspaper description of the *Glory of the Seas*

(Mjelde, *op. cit.*, p. 257) refers to "the forward cabin or dining saloon" as being the same room.

At least one contemporary writer (Bullen, Frank T., *Log of a Sea-Waif*, pp. 250-251) uses the term "saloon" to describe the dining cabin or forward cabin and refer to "saloon table."

(Data for notes 6, 7, & 8 below were extracted from June 30, 1882, Crew List:)

(Crew Member	Position	Age	Born	Height	Hair Color)
[6] George Williams (aka Jackson)	cook	33	New York	5'9"	Black
[7] Charles Donahue (aka Donahoo)	seaman	31	Louisiana	5'6"	Brown
[8] James Smith	seaman	40	New York	5'9"	Brown

[9] Carl McLaughlin, *op. cit.*

CHAPTER XV - Cape Horn Weather

[1] *Alta, op. cit.*, November 8, 1882.

[2] *The Encyclopedia Americana*, 1956 edition, (New York: Americana Corporation, 1956) Vol. 7, p. 358 calls the 1882 Comet "the finest of the [19th] century."

[3] Carl McLaughlin, *op. cit.*

[4] *Alta, op. cit.*, November 8, 1882.

CHAPTER XVI - From the Line to San Francisco

[1] The British bark (ex-steamer) *Bremen* (321 x 39.4 x 19.8 feet) of 2,398 tons went ashore on the northwesterly side of South Farallon Island just after midnight, October 16, 1882, in thick fog. In the inquiry as reported in the October 21st issue of the *Alta*, Captain Dougall, the *Bremen*'s master, stated "that all went well on the voyage previous to the night of the 15th instant; about 8 o'clock a light was sighted; stood in toward it; the fog came on about 11 o'clock and hid the light; at 15 minutes past one o'clock a light was seen overhead [Farallon Light] and two minutes after the ship struck; had expected to hear a whistle . . . [Captain Dougall] had given instructions to the lookout to be more vigilant than usual; always had two lookouts, one on the forecastle, the other on the gangway."

How easily the *Glory of the Seas* could have run ashore as the circumstances were similar. In the October 18th issue of the *Alta*, a brief mention was made about the *Bremen*: "The tug *Rescue* returned at eight P.M. from the wreck of the *Bremen*. Found her hard and fast on the rocks, full of water up to the main deck, and lying very easy in smooth water and well sheltered from the sea; the chances good for wrecking the vessel, but not much probability of getting her off."

[2] Carl McLaughlin, *op. cit.*

[3] *Alta, op. cit.*, November 8, 1882.

[4] *Alta, op. cit.*, November 13, 1882.

[5] *Alta, op. cit.*, November 8, 1882.

[6] *Alta, op. cit.*, November 7, 1882.

CHAPTER XVII - Lay-up and Retirement

[1] The extensive editorial comments in this paragraph are due to part of the original manuscript page being missing. The author has added material so that the paragraph conforms to what happened.

[2] A telegraph message dated December 7, 1882, from J.N. Knowles to Renton Holmes & Co., proprietors of the Port Blakely Mill on Bainbridge Island in then Washington Territory stated: "Has *Otago* sailed and has the forty-inch mast for *Glory of the Seas?*" Port Blakely Mill Co. Collection, University of Washington Library, Seattle, WA; *Alta, op. cit.*, December 10, 1882, and January 7, 1883.

[3] Carl McLaughlin, *op. cit.*

[4] *Alta, op. cit.*, December 10, 1882.

[5] Letter regarding collision of the *Glory of the Seas* and the *Cassandra Adams* dated July 27, 1883, Record Group 36, National Archives, Washington, D.C. This letter mistakenly refers to "the ship *Glory of the Seas* and the bark *Hayden Brown*," but was meant to reference the *Cassandra Adams.*

[6] *Alta, op. cit.*, December 21, 1882.

[7] *Alta, op. cit.*, December 10, 1882.

[8] The other West Coast-built vessel was the bark (ex-ship) *Wildwood*, which was built at Port Madison, Washington Territory, in 1871. It was purchased by J. Henry Sears *et al*, managers of the *Glory* in 1879, and was en route from San Francisco to New York at the time of the *Glory/Adams* collision.

[9] *Alta, op. cit.*, December 16, 1882.

[10] *Alta, op. cit.*, August 18, 1882.

[11] The U.S. government modified the tonnage law on June 26, 1884 so that reductions were made "to remove certain burdens of the American merchant marine and encourage the American foreign carrying trade." For example, all vessels, henceforth both American (registered) and foreign-flag (trading with Canada) were levied a tax of three cents per ton "not to exceed the aggregate fifteen cents per ton," and vessels entering an American port from England were levied "a duty of six cents per ton, not to exceed thirty cents per ton per annum." *The Navigaion Laws of the United States*, 1886, *op. cit.*, p.27; *Custom Regulations under the Customs and Navigation Laws of the United States* (Washington: Government Printing Office, 1884), pp. 126-131.

[12] Admeasurement for *Glory of the Seas* dated December 18, 1882, Custom House records, National Archives, San Bruno, Calif.

[13] Nearly seven years later, a seemingly common occurrence took place at Nanaimo, British Columbia. It was an event, literally, of "ships that pass in

the night." The shipping column of the February 9, 1889, issue of the *Nanaimo Free Press* reported: "The ship *Glory of the Seas* has completed her cargo of 3,300 tons of V.C. Co.'s coal and awaits the arrival of a tug to tow her to sea." The shipping entry immediately following read: "The German barque *Elvira* arrived last night to load coal at the V.C. Co.'s shutes [sic]." That evening both vessels lay at anchor in the harbor. The bark *Elvira* was the former ship *Sovereign of the Seas* — the *Glory*'s smaller sister.

[14] F.C. Matthews, "*Glory of the Seas*," *Pacific Marine Review*, May 1922, p. 278.

[15] Reference report prepared by Chicago Title Insurance Company dated January 6, 1989, on the Chappell property.

[16] Lubbock, *Down-Easters, op. cit.*, p. 35.

[17] Mjelde, p. 115.

[18] Matthews, Vol. 1, *op. cit.*, p. 329.

[19] *Pen Pictures, op. cit.*

[20] Title Insurance and Trust Company (Fresno Branch) report, February 3, 1965.

[21] Mjelde, *op. cit.*, p. 115.

[22] McLaughlin papers, *op. cit.*

[23] McLaughlin papers, *op. cit.*; McLaughlin obituary, *op. cit.*

[24] Title Insurance, *op. cit.*

[25] McLaughlin papers and obituary.

[26] *Sentinel, op.cit.* January 29, 1896.

Illustration Notes

Bookjacket. The oil painting *"Glory of the Seas* on the North Atlantic" was painted by Thomas Wells in 1992 and was commissioned by D. Gene Kennedy, President and CEO of Land Title Company of Kitsap County for presentation to the author to commemorate 20 years of service to the company. Color transparency by David Leniton, Silverdale, Washington.

In a letter to the author dated June 3, 1997, Wells said regarding his painting: "The vessel is in fairly heavy seas. Royals and main skysail furled. She is running before the Westerlies, perhaps mid-Atlantic, with grain cargo for England."

p.4. This painting of the *Glory* is attributed to Samuel Walters (1811-1882) by the Knowles' family but is not signed. For many years it hung in the offices of the San Francisco Marine Exchange and in 1964 the late Josiah N. Knowles III donated it to the San Francisco Maritime Museum (now the San Francisco Maritime NHP). In spite of the lack of a definite signature, experts such as the late Marion V. Brewington felt that it was an authentic Walters' painting. It is 33 x 53 inches and is prominently displayed in the John Lyman Room of the San Francisco Maritime NHP library at Fort Mason. It is a highly detailed painting of the *Glory of the Seas*. Walters depicted her off Liverpool and even detailed the paneling on the deck cabins besides showing crew members carrying out their various duties on deck

p.14. In prefacing his comments regarding figures on pages 14, 83, 92 and 126 in a letter dated December 2, 1995, Captain Adrian F. Raynaud stated the following: "My opinions and thoughts are based upon the years of experience around and on vessels of all kinds and styles and some of them were of ancient age. I've tried to remember them as closely to the originals as I can."

Captain Raynaud's description of the painting of the *Gray Feather*: "The vessel is under full sail on all three masts and is rigged with three large head sails or jibs. [She] carries a full course or fore sail, a large topsail and three small topgallants. The company flag is at mast head. The ship's name is carried on the pennant–*Gray Feather*. A gaff-headed spanker is aft with a gaff top and the American flag is flown from the peak. The vessel is carrying full sail, but is evidently well loaded as she stands up right in a good breeze. A small two-masted schooner is forward of the vessel flying an American flag."

p.18. Caption on the back of this image. "Vallejo Street Wharf. San Francisco, ca. [1871]. Looking from Telegraph Hill to Vallejo Street Wharf. (first from left) and Broadway Wharf (second from left) *Julia* (built 1870; paddle riverboat) (left) and *Capital* (built 1866; paddle river) (right). Cunningham Warehouse, left (roof with four peaks). Stack of *Paul Pry* (built 1859; paddle riverboat) visible between Broadway and Vallejo Street Wharves."

p.30. This NOAA (C & GS) chart of the West Coast of the United States is corrected to 1874. On the north end of San Francisco Bay it intersects with San Pablo Bay and runs southerly about 40 miles. San Pablo Bay intersects with Carquinez Strait and Mare Island Strait to reach Martinez and Port Costa to the east of San Pablo Bay.

p.42. The primary source materials for this map as well as figures on pages 117 and 146 are the hydographic and topographic records of the National Oceanic and Atmospheric Administration, formerly the U.S. Coast & Geodetic Survey. The author had access to these records over a period of years and prepared maps of the San Francisco waterfront to complement the photographs of the period. One survey, "The Hydrography of San Francisco Bay, Cal. Near San Francisco" in Register No. 1214a, conducted in 1871-1873 and dated 1874, shows the wharves prior to establishment of a pierhead line by the California State Harbor Commissioners. Map No. 4 of "State Harbor Com Ms, 1877, Southern Part," appearing in Olmsted, *op. cit.*, shows details of the wharves and the proposed pierhead line as of 1877. These maps along with the plans of *Glory of the Seas* were processed on CD-Rom for this publication courtesy of Alpha Information Management Services, Seattle, Wash.

p.46. Figurehead of the ship *Glory of the Seas*. Note that the right arm has been broken off and that the decorative work on the ship's stem has not been replaced. This calls attention to the fact that the economic picture for older American full-riggers in 1900 dictated owners not spending money on frills that did not affect the efficiency of a ship's operation

p.56. Deck view of the *Glory of the Seas* facing aft at Howard Street Wharf. Henry Cottrell, the photographer, stood on the port side of the ship's fo'c'slehead to take this image. The ship is being unloaded of her coal cargo. She is in the British Columbia/California coal trade and is under the command of Capt. Joshua Freeman (from 1884-1901). The man standing next to the hawsers is Capt. Josiah N. Knowles.

The lower fore and main masts are solid stick replacements of her original built masts. The jagged vertical line in the foremast is a thick bead of putty which has been inlaid on the mast to fill a wide weather check.

Note that the after house front is "grained," to simulate natural wood, not painted white, and that the corners of the deck houses are also grained.

The photographer, Henry Cottrell, was a mining engineer. The late Robert W. Weinstein identified the other two men (besides Captain Knowles) as Cottrell's brother, Floyd, and son Marion. This image as well as that on page 63 and page 193 were originally exposed on glass plates and were taken on the same day.

p.58. Deck view of the *Glory of the Seas* facing forward at Howard Street Wharf. Henry Cottrell, the photographer, is standing on the port side of the quarterdeck. The ship has been in port only a short time and is being unloaded. This explains the disarray on deck. No repainting will be done until all her cargo is out and the ship thoroughly cleaned of coal dust.

p.63. This image of the *Brodick Castle* shows her rigged to royals. Capt. Beard's descriptions of ships at the Mersyside Maritime Museum mentions this vessel as crossing a main skysail

p.68. The *Glory of the Seas* off the Welsh coast. Oil painting by Charles J. Waldron (1836-1891), Liverpool artist. Note that this painting shows the ship still rigged with studdingsail booms on fore and main masts to topgallants. Waldron painted the *Glory of the Seas* at least twice for two of her captains. He customarily painted ships on a 30 x 48-inch canvas (3 x 5-feet, including frame) and received payments of about $150 for his work in the early 1870s.

This painting of the *Glory of the Seas* was painted by Waldron after modifications had been carried out by Capt. Knowles. It shows several distinct changes in the deck furniture. The wheel house was extended forward to cover the wheel and a donkey boiler was added as indicated by the stack and wooden housing.

Charles Waldron's first painting of the *Glory of the Seas* appears on page 33 of Mjelde, *op.cit.* It shows her as she originally appeared under J. Henry Sears & Company management in 1871 under command of Capt. Elisha F. Sears.

p.75. Mark H. Myers described his painting of the *Glory* in a letter to the author dated March 3, 1997, as follows: "This was painted in August 1980 for the Second National ASMA show in [New York City] ... I'm pretty sure that I painted the *Glory* as a response which your book aroused in me. The picture stems from the entry in Knowles' journal covering her departure from Liverpool at the beginning of July, 1873 (page 58 of your book). There's enough there on wind, weather, and time of day to set the scene, as it were, so I decided to paint her making sail after casting off the *Retriever*'s towline. You are looking to the south, into the light, although the sun is masked by the clumps of heavy grey cloud that go hand in hand with SW'ly weather around here. Knowing no better, I put the ship on the port tack initially so as to give her an offing out into St. George's Channel. I don't think that I was trying to make any particular statement about the ship in that picture beyond attempting to show her faithfully, engaged in her everyday work. She was a powerful, handsome vessel so I expect that I was trying to get this across as well."

p.78. The *Glory of the Seas* at anchor. She has been recently unloaded after a long sea voyage. Shortly her hull will be completely repainted, including the wide, white stripe immediately above her copper sheathing. Note that studdingsail booms are rigged underneath her foreyard, not above the yard which was common with some British vessels.

p.83. The author asked Captain Raynaud whether the unnamed artist of the painting of the *Young America* depicted her as being near San Francisco.

His reply was as follows: "I doubt very much if this is off the Farallons [Islands] as it is hardly likely that the vessel would have been put under sail to this extent if she were just leaving San Francisco or would have carried that much sail if she were arriving there."

p.92. Captain Raynaud's general description of the water color of the British ship *Borrowdale*. "[She is] under full sail and running before the wind and on a moderate sea. The head sails or jibs are all set. Vessel [is] on port tack."

p.96. The British four-mast ship *County of Kinross*. She has just arrived at San Francisco and bears the stain marks of a ship many months at sea.

p.105. The steam tug *Rescue* of 172 tons (built in 1875) and powered by a 300 nominal horsepower steam engine. The bowsprit of the ship *Young America* is at the right of this image. Note that another Griffiths tug is berthed on the north face of the Vallejo Street Wharf. These tugs are berthed on the south extension (the "Y") of the wharf depicted on the Tabor image on page 135 as well as the 1881 drawing on page 146 of the waterfront prepared by the author.

p115. Image of lower Manhattan taken in 1876 by Joshua H. Beales. Beales hoisted his camera to the top of the 276-foot Brooklyn Tower of the unfinished Brooklyn Bridge. He took five images and spliced them together to form a seven-foot panorama of New York. This is image No. 1. From the right the covered pier of Mallory & Company is situated at Pier 20. Immediately next (south) is Fletcher Street Wharf (Pier 19) where ships chartered by Sutton & Company for the California "clipper" trade berthed. Note that two full-riggers lay next to the north face of this wharf. Next to it is the covered pier for the Morgan's Line of steamers. In the center of the image are the Wall Street ferry slips and south to Pier 9 the half dozen-plus wharves berthed sailing ships, some of which engaged in the California trade. Also vessels like the *New World* still engaged in trade to the British Isles loaded and unloaded cargo in this area.

p.117. This chart is based on NOAA Survey Register No. 2323 entitled "Hudson and East Rivers" as of 1887 and essentially shows the lower Manhattan waterfront of 1885.

p.119. The Ship *Sovereign of the Seas*, second ship of this name built by Donald McKay. Note that studdingsail booms are rigged underneath her foreyard.

p.126. Carl G. Evers painted the *Glory of the Seas* following the publication of the author's book Mjelde, *op.cit.*, and depicted her in two highly detailed watercolors. (The second print is entitled "South Street, New York, 1879). Permission to use "Conquerors of Cape Horn" was provided through the assistance of Robert J. Barry, Attorney at Law, of Southbury, Conn., Mr. Evers' attorney-in fact. This print is being published by permission of Mr. Evers, and the transparency has been provided through the courtesy of Richard Kirsten, Kirsten Gallery, Seattle, Washington.

Captain Raynaud wrote the following in describing the painting: "The *Glory of the Seas* is headed for a harbor on the port tack with the *Young America* close astern of her. Both vessels are shortening down to be prepared for the completion of the voyages and to ease the strain on the upper sails. The vessels are in rough weather and both pictured in a turbulent sea and sky.

"The standing rigging supporting the masts is in good order and the reefing bands across the sails and the buntlines are clearly shown by the curves in the sails, maintaining a heavy strain on them."

Thomas W. Wells, a longtime personal friend of Mr. Evers stated the following in a letter to the author dated June 3, 1997:

"Carl is one of my mentors and, of course, the best in marine painting. We do all make mistakes, no matter how good we are. For example, I forgot to put reef points on my lower course in my painting of *Glory*. In Carl's painting I think the two vessels are dangerously close. In heavy weather like that the ships do not maneuver that easily.

"I think that the seams of the sails are too pronounced for that distance away. You keep your bunt lines slack so they do not chaff the sail but his are too taut. You see those who have not sailed do not know that. The painting, of course, is excellent.

"Now about Carl. I met him through correspondence some 35 years ago. I wrote to him to compliment him on a painting he did in *Oceans* magazine and, of course, mentioned a few details that were wrong. For a man who never sailed square rig he is a very accurate researcher.

"Wanda [Tom's wife] and I visited his home in Heritage Village some years ago. We always corresponded until he became ill and could no longer write.

"One interesting thing when he came to U.S.A. in 1947, he took a studio apartment next door to Gordon Grant."

p.135. San Francisco waterfront. Part of a six-part panorama of the San Francisco waterfront taken by I. W. Tabor. This image shows part of the completed Seawall. The outer limits of the wharves have been redefined and extension of the existing wharves are being constructed to conform to the new pierhead line. The first wharf jutting out into the Bay from the left is at Union Street. The next wharf is at Green Street and third from the left is Vallejo Street. Several units of Millin Griffiths' tug fleet are berthed at the Vallejo Street Wharf where the old wharf forms a "Y."

p.141. This is a detail from a chart of Dublin Bay dated 1874 provided to the author courtesy of the Hydrographer of the [British] Navy, Hydrographic Department, Taunton, Somerset, England.

p.146. This chart is based on NOAA Survey Register No. 1625 entitled "San Francisco, Coast & Geodetic Survey, San Francisco Bay & Approaches," surveyed in 1881-1882. It corresponds with Image No. 6 of the Tabor Panorama.

p.154. This pencil drawing of John Gribble was drawn by the author's daughter and is based on a small newspaper photo of Gribble pasted in his autobiography. It depicts him as a Royal Navy sailor and was probably taken in the early 1870s.

p.175. This is a reconstruction of the after house of the *Glory of the Seas* that is based on several sources: Duncan McLean described the two basic divisions of this house in his published description of the ship (See Mjelde, op.cit., p. 257). The size of the captain's quarters are confirmed by the 1882 Custom House admeasurement of the ship at San Francisco.

In 1963 the author interviewed the late Mrs. Marguerite Twigg, granddaughter of Captain Freeman. Mrs. Twigg assisted the author over a period of three years to detail the various rooms and arrangement in the after house. Being the only sailing ship she ever sailed on, (from 1890 to 1895) an indelible impression was made on her young mind. One possible modification that could be made is to increase the size of the berth in the "daybreak" cabin to conform to a statement made by Carl McLaughlin in his "Around in the *Glory*" account that his berth was "wide." The question is: what was a wide berth to Carl who was only five feet, two inches? Also, in Carl's original account he places the bathroom forward of the "daybreak" cabin.

In the original illustration of the after house appearing on page 70 of *Glory of the Seas, op.cit.*, the master's cabin berth was incorrectly placed athwartships. Captain Adrian F. Raynaud brought to the author's attention that this would "never" be the case in a master's cabin because of the discomfort he would suffer on a rolling ship. It was changed accordingly for *Clipper Ship Captain*.

The only area where athwartship bunks were commonly installed on large American sailing ships of this period was in the fo'c'sle customarily located in the forward house. The late Samuel Campbell (1880-1983) informed the author that he occupied one of the athwartship bunks when he sailed on the *Glory of the Seas* in 1900 on a voyage from San Francisco to Union Bay, B.C., and return. Campbell confirmed the fact that the master's bunk would never be placed athwartships.

p.193. *Glory of the Seas* unloading coal at Howard Street Wharf. Henry Cottrell took this image on the same day he took figures 19 and 20. This image shows that the rigging of the ship has been modified so that the sails no longer clew up to the quarters but clew up to the yard arms. Note the portable coal chute on the adjoining wharf.

p.208. Merlyn McIntyre is great-grandson to Capt. McLaughlin. James McLaughlin, brother to Capt. McLaughlin was the great-grandfather of Gale McLaughlin.

p.213. This drawing is provided through the courtesy of the Mystic Seaport Museum.

Bibliography

I. Official Documents of the United States

Bureau of Marine Inspection and Navigation. Record Group 41, National Archives and Records Administration, Washington, D.C., San Bruno, Calif., and Seattle, Wash.

Custom House Records. Record Group 36, National Archives and Records Administration, Washington, D.C., San Bruno, Calif, and Seattle, Wash.

Customs Regulations of the United States Prescribed for the Instruction and Guidance of Officers of Customs, 1900.

Customs Regulations under the Customs and Navigation Laws of the United States, 1884.

Weather Bureau Records. Record Group 27, National Archives and Records Administration, Washington, D.C.

Hall, Henry. *Report on the Shipbuilding Industry of the United States*, 1882.

Holdcamper, Forrest R. *List of American Flag Merchant Vessels: Port of New York, 1789-1867*, 2 Vols., 1968.

The Navigation Laws of the United States. Bureau of Navigation, 1886.

U.S. Coast Pilot, Atlantic Coast, Section B, Cape Cod to Sandy Hook. 1918.

U.S. Coast Pilot, Pacific Coast, California, Oregon and Washington. 2nd Edition, 1909.

Sailing Directions for South America. Vol. II, (Southern Part), 1941.

The Port of Liverpool, 1929.

U.S. Statutes at Large.

U.S. Department of Commerce *Annual List of Merchant Vessels of the United States*. Separate vols. 1872-1884 incl.

II. British Admiralty Hydrographic Office Publications.

British Islands Pilot. Vol. I. 1915.
British Islands Pilot. Vol. II. 1917.
Irish Coast Pilot. 1941.
Jenkins, Comm, H.L., O.B.E., D.S.C., Royal Navy. *Ocean Passages for the World*. 3rd Edition. 1973.
Somerville, Rear Admiral Boyle T., C.M.G. *The World Sailing Routes*. 1950

III. Shipping Registers.

American Lloyd's Universal Standard Record of Shipping and Record of American and Foreign Shipping. Mystic, Conn: G. W. Blunt White Library, and San Francisco, Calif.: National Maritime Museum.
Lloyd's Register of British and Foreign Shipping. San Francisco, Calif.: National Maritime Museum.
Register of Approved Shipmasters. March 1864, Penobscot Marine Museum.

IV. Maritime History, Sailing Ships

Ballard, Admiral G.A. *The Black Battlefleet*. Annapolis, Maryland: Naval Institute Press, 1980.
Beavis, Captain L.R.W. (ed. M.S. Cline). *Passage from Sail to Steam*. Bellevue, Wash.: Documentary Book Publication Corp., 1986.
Bullen, Frank T. *Log of a Sea Waif*. New York: D. Appleton and Company, 1899.
Clark, Arthur H. *The Clipper Ship Era*. Riverside, Conn.: 7 C's Press, 1970.
Cogill, Burgess. *When God was an Atheist Sailor, Memories of a Childhood at Sea, 1902-1910*. New York: W.W. Norton & Co., 1990, 1985.

Cutler, Carl C. *Greyhounds of the Sea.* Annapolis, Maryland: United States Naval Institute, 1930.

Davidson, A.S. *Samuel Walters – Marine Artist: Fifty Years of Sea, Sail & Steam.* Coventry: Jones-Sands Publishing, 1992.

Davis, Charles H. *The Ways of the Sea.* New York, N.Y.: Rudder Publishing Co., 1930.

Dillon, Richard H. *Shanghaiing Days.* Toronto, Canada: Longmans, Green & Co., 1961.

Duncan, Fred B. *Deepwater Family.* New York: Pantheon Books, 1969.

Fairburn, William Armstrong. *Merchant Sail.* 6 Vols., Center Lovell, Maine: Fairburn Marine Educational Foundation, Inc., 1944-1955.

Farmer, H.F. *The Log of a Shellback.* London: H.F. & G. Witherby, 1925.

Greenbill, Basil and Stonham, Denis. *Seafaring Under Sail: The Life of the Merchant Seaman.* Cambridge: Patrick Stephens, 1981.

Harland, John (author) and Mark H. Myers (illustrator). *Seamanship in the Age of Sail.* Annapolis, Maryland: Naval Institute Press, 1985.

Harlow, Frederick Pease. *The Making of a Sailor, or Sea Life Aboard a Yankee Square-rigger.* Salem, Mass.: Marine Research Society, 1928.

Howe, Octavius T. and Matthews, Frederick C. *American Clipper Ships, 1833-1858.* 2 Vols., Salem, Mass.: Marine Research Society, 1926-1927.

Lubbock, Basil. *The Down Easters, American Deep-Water Sailing Ships, 1869-1929.* Glasgow, Scotland: Brown, Son and Ferguson, Ltd., 1929.

Lubbock, Basil. *The Last of the Windjammers.* Vol. I, Glasgow, Scotland: Brown, Son and Ferguson, Ltd., 1927.

MacGregor, David R. *Merchant Sailing Ships, 1850-1875.* Annapolis, Maryland: Naval Institute Press, 1984.

McKay, Richard C. *Some Famous Sailing Ships and Their Builder, Donald McKay.* New York and London: G.P. Putnam's Son, 1928.

Matthews, Frederick C. *American Merchant Ships, 1850-1900.* 2 Vols., Salem, Mass.: Marine Research Society, 1930-1931.

Mjelde, Michael Jay. *Glory of the Seas.* Mystic, Conn.: Mystic Seaport Museum, (formerly Marine Historical Association, Inc.,)/Wesleyan University Press, 1970.

Perry, Joseph Malcolm. *Cruising in Many Seas.* Springfield, Mass: privately printed, 1930.

Sears, J. Henry. *Brewster Shipmasters.* Yarmouthport, Mass: C.W. Swift, 1906.

Whipple, A.B.C. *The Challenge.* New York: William Morrow and Company, Inc., 1987.

Williams, Herold. *One Whaling Family.* Boston: Houghton Mifflin Company, 1964.

V. Shipping and Maritime Economics.

Bates, William W. *American Navigation, The Political History of its Rise and Ruin and the Proper Means for its Encouragement.* Boston and New York: Houghton, Mifflin and Company, 1902.

Bullen, Frank T. *The Men of the Merchant Service.* Standfordville, N.Y.: Earl M. Coleman, 1979.

Bunker, John. *Harbor and Haven, An Illustrated History of the Port of New York.* Woodland Hills, Calif.: Windsor Publications, Inc., 1979.

Dixon, Francis B. *The Law of Shipping and Merchants and Shipmasters Guide.* New York, N.Y.: Henry Spear, 1859.

Harlan, George H. *San Francisco Bay Ferryboats.* Berkeley, Calif: Howell-North Books, 1967.

Healy, James C., PhD. *Fo'c's'le and Glory-Hole.* New York, N.Y.: Merchant Marine Publishers Association, 1936.

Heyl, Erik. *Early American Steamers.* Vol. III, Buffalo, N.Y.: Erik Heyl, 1964.

Hohlman, Elmo Paul. *History of American Merchant Seamen.* Hamdon, Conn.: Shoe String Press, 1956.

Horsburgh, James. *The India Directory.* 6th Edition, London, England, William H. Allen & Co.,1852.

Hugill, Stan. *Sailortown.* New York, N.Y.: E.P. Dutton & Co., 1967.

Hutchins, John B. *American Maritime Industries and Public Policy, 1789-1914.* Cambridge, Mass.: Harvard University Press, 1941.

Johnson, Harry, and Lightfoot, Frederick S. *Maritime New York in Nineteenth-Century Photographs.* New York, N.Y.: Dover Publications, Inc., 1980.

Kemble, John Haskell. *San Francisco Bay, A Pictorial Maritime History.* Cambridge, Maryland: Cornell Maritime Press, 1957.

Leavitt, John Faunce. *Cradle of Ships: Chronological List of Vessels Built in the Stonington-Groton Area.* Mystic, Conn.: Mystic Seaport Museum (no date).

Maounis, John, and Keller, Daniel L. *Four Maritime Photograph Collections.* San Francisco, Calif.: National Maritime Museum, 1982.

Morison, Samuel Eliot. *Maritime History of Massachusetts, 1783-1860.* Boston, Mass.: Houghton Mifflin Company, 1921.

Nerney, Michael T. *A History of Williams, Dimond & Co. Since 1862.* San Francisco, Calif.: Williams, Dimond & Co., 1988.

Patterson, Howard. *Patterson's Illustrated Nautical Encyclopedia.* Cleveland, Ohio: The Marine Review Publishing Co., 1901.

Stammers, Michael. *Sail on the Mersey,* Birkenhead, England: Countryvise Limited, 1984.

Stein, Douglas L. *American Maritime Documents, 1776-1860.* Mystic, Conn., Mystic Seaport Museum, Inc., 1992.

VI. Local Histories.

Asbury, Herbert. *The Barbary Coast, An Informal History of the San Francisco Underworld.* Garden City, N.Y.: Garden City Publishing Co., Inc., 1933.

Camp, William Martin. *San Francisco: Port of Gold.* Garden City, N.Y.: Doubleday & Co., 1948.

Caton, Bruce. *Never Call Retreat.* Vol. III, Garden City, N.Y.: Doubleday & Co., 1965.

Historical Atlas of Solano County. San Francisco, Calif.: Thompson & West, 1877.

Historical Atlas Map of Solano County. San Francisco, Calif.: Thompson & West, 1878.

Hittell, John S. *A History of the City of San Francisco.* San Francisco, Calif.: A.L. Bancroft & Co., 1878.

Johnson, William Weber. *The Forty-Niners.* New York, N.Y.: Time-Life, 1974.

Kinney, Joyce E. *The Vessels of Way Down East.* Bangor, Maine: Joyce E. Kinney, 1989.

Langley, Henry G. *The San Francisco Directory.* San Francisco, Calif.: Henry G. Langley, 1873.

Lloyd, B.E. *Lights and Shades in San Francisco.* San Francisco, Calif.: A.L. Bancroft & Co., 1876.

Olmsted, Roger and Nancy and Allen Pastrom. *San Francisco Waterfront Report on Historical Cultural Resources.* San Francisco: San Francisco Wastewater Manager Program, 1977.

Purcell, Mae F. *History of Contra Costa County.* Berkeley, Calif.: Gillick Press, 1940.

Walker, Brian, and Hinchliffe, Ann. *In Our Liverpool Home.* Belfast, Ireland, Blackstaff Press, 1978.

VII. Special Publications, Private Manuscripts, and Periodicals.

Brown, C. Donald. "Eastport: A Maritime History." *The American Neptune.* Salem, Mass.: The American Neptune, Inc., April 1968.

Canright, Stephen. "100 Years of San Francisco Tugboating: 1860-1969." *Sea Letter,* Fall/Winter 1989.

Gribble, John. *Autobiography of John Gribble* (c. 1926). Michael Jay Mjelde.

Hall, Henry. *Private Notebooks.* Penobscot Marine Museum.

Hibbard, Isaac Norris. *Sixteen Times Round Cape Horn.* Mystic Seaport, 1980.

Ingersoll, L. Keith. "The Great Debate of 1877." *The Grand Manan Historian.* Grand Manan, New Brunswick: Grand Manan Historical Society, 1968.

Ingersoll, L. Keith. "The Saga of Captain Dan." *National Fisherman,* June, 1965.

Kerchove, de, René. *International Maritime Dictionary.* 2nd Edition, New York: Van Nostrand Reinhold Co., 1961.

Lyman, John. "Register Tonnage & Its Measurement (Parts I & II)." *The American Neptune,* Salem, Mass.: The American Neptune, Inc., July and October 1945.

McLaughlin, Daniel Carlton. "Around in the Glory." Fresno, Calif.: c. 1920. Mary Ann Snedeker.

Matthews, Frederick C. Miscellaneous articles on *Glory of the Seas, Pacific Marine Review,* February and May 1923.

Pen Pictures From the Garden of the World, Memorial and Biographical History of the Counties of Fresno, Tulare and Kern, Chicago, Ill.: The Lewis Publishing Co., 189_.

Smith, Melbourne. "The U.S. Brig *Niagara,* Part 4: Spars, Standing Rigging." *Seaways,* March/April 1992.

Stein, Douglas. "Paths Through the Sea: Matthew Fontaine Maury and his Wind and Current Charts." *The Log of Mystic Seaport,* Fall 1980.

Statement of General Average and Partial Loss in the Case of Ship America. Michael Jay Mjelde.

VIII. Newspapers.

Boston Daily Advertiser.
Contra Costa Gazette.
Dublin Evening Mail.
Eastport Sentinel.
Liverpool Journal of Commerce and Shipping Telegraph.
Lloyd's List.
Malden Mirror.
New York Herald.
_____ *Maritime Register.*
_____ *Shipping and Commercial List.*
San Francisco Chronicle.
_____ *Commercial Herald and Market Review.*
_____ *Daily Alta California.*
_____ *Daily Evening Bulletin.*
_____ *Morning Call.*

IX. Interviews and Special Correspondence.

Ball, Mr. and Mrs. E.S. Bakersfield, Calif. (McLaughlin family records).

Bowker, Captain Francis E."Biff." Sea Level, N.C. (maritime traditions).

Burnham, Mrs. Deborah. Hingham, Mass. (McLaughlin ship model).

Chicago Title Insurance Company, Fresno, Calif. (Chappell property records).

Child, David Trumbull (1875-1960), Admiralty Attorney, Seattle, Wash.. "General Average–Particular Average and Damage to Cargo," (Treatise on insurance relating to cargo shippers and shipowners, written in 1946), Mrs. Elizabeth Engle, Edmonds, WA.

Crothers, William L. Eikens Park, PA (American Shipmasters Association records).

Daly, Gerald. Dublin, Ireland (port information).

Dean, Nicholas. Edgecomb, Maine (copper sheathing).

G. W. Blunt White Library. Mystic Seaport Museum, Mystic, Conn. (contemporary ship data).

Evans, Margaret, Merseyside Maritime Museum, Liverpool, England (Information from statistical ship files of Captain Jack Beard, D.S.C. (1888-1965)).

Hartman, William G., Birmingham, England (data on ship *Borrowdale*).

Huycke, Captain Harold D., Edmonds, Wash. (cargo data).

Jarvis, A.E. Merseyside Marine Museum (grain storage and unloading procedures at Liverpool).

John F. Kennedy Library, Vallejo, Calif. (grain elevator data).

Kinney, Joyce E. Eastport, Maine (McLaughlin family information).

McIntyre, Mr. and Mrs. Merlyn. Hemet, CA (McLaughlin family records).

Malden Public Library, Malden, Mass. (map and data on Malden).

Merseyside County Museums, Liverpool, England (Liverpool Bill of Lading).

Morgan, Charles S. Concord, Mass. (contemporary sailing ship history).

Myers, Mark H. Surrey, England. (Description of his watercolor painting of "*Glory of the Seas*, off Holyhead.")

National Maritime Museum Library, San Francisco, Calif. (contemporary ship data).

Nesdall, Andrew. Waban, Mass. (nautical terminology and "Grain Trade" treatise).

Price, Andrew. Seattle, Wash. (Port Blakely Mill Co. information).

Raynaud, Captain Adrian F., master mariner and marine surveyor. Seattle, Wash. (contemporary sailing ship history including analysis of repair at Valparaiso and ship-unloading procedure at Dublin, Ireland. Also, description of ships under sail, and maritime traditions).

Savory, Mr. and Mrs. Clarke. Fresno, Calif. (McLaughlin family records and "Around in the *Glory*").

Smyly, Dr. Philip. Dublin, Ireland (data on Dublin).

Snedeker, Mrs. Mary Ann. ("Around in the *Glory*").

Spaulding, Philip F., Naval Architect. Seattle, Wash. (naval architecture terminology pertaining to ship *Western Empire*).

Westmancoat, Mrs. H.T. London, England (Dublin and Liverpool newspapers).

Index